A MAN CALLED KEV

Writer: Garth Ennis
Artist: Carlos Ezquerra
Colors: David Baron

Letters: Phil Balsman and Travis Lanham (#4)
Covers: Glenn Fabry and David Baron
Special thanks: Tony Luke & Alan Passalaqua

This one's for anyone who's ever had a pint at The Blarney Stone,
on 32nd street, in the shadow of the Empire State Building

And Martin, and all the other barmen

And my mate Stev

-Garth Ennis

...LED KEV published by WildStorm Productions. 888 Prospect
...#240, La Jolla, CA 92037. Compilation © 2007 WildStorm
..., an imprint of DC Comics. All Rights Reserved. WildStorm
...go, all characters, the distinctive likenesses thereof and all
...ments are trademarks of DC Comics. Originally published in
... magazine form as A MAN CALLED KEV #1-5 © 2006, 2007
WildStorm Productions, an imprint of DC Comics.

..., characters, and incidents mentioned in this magazine are
... fictional. Printed on recyclable paper. WildStorm does not
... accept unsolicited submissions of ideas, stories or artwork.
Printed in Canada.

DC Comics, a Warner Bros. Entertainment Company.

ISBN: 1-4012-1324-3
ISBN-13: 978-1-4012-1324-4

AG MAN

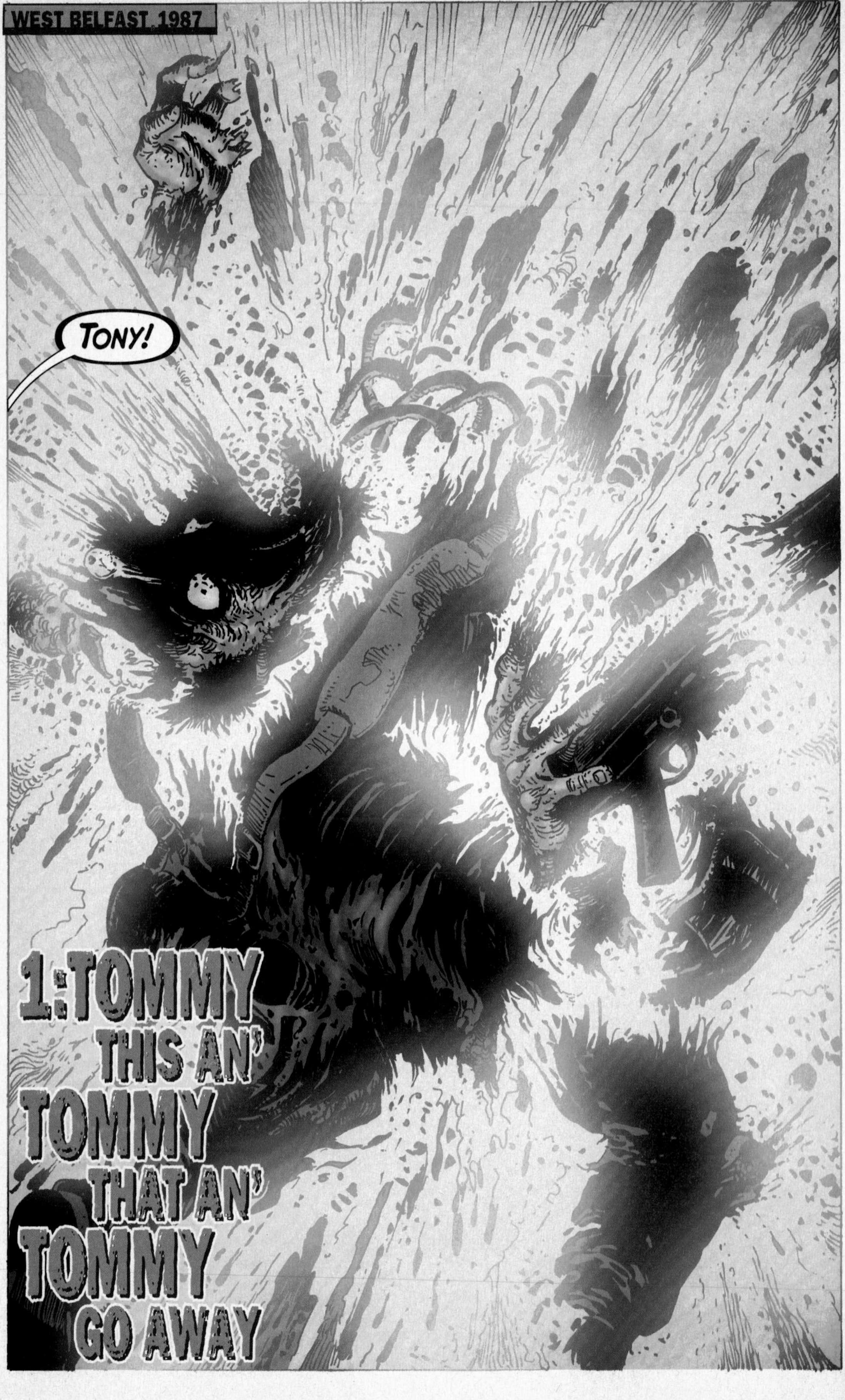
WEST BELFAST, 1987
TONY!
1: TOMMY THIS AN' TOMMY THAT AN' TOMMY GO AWAY

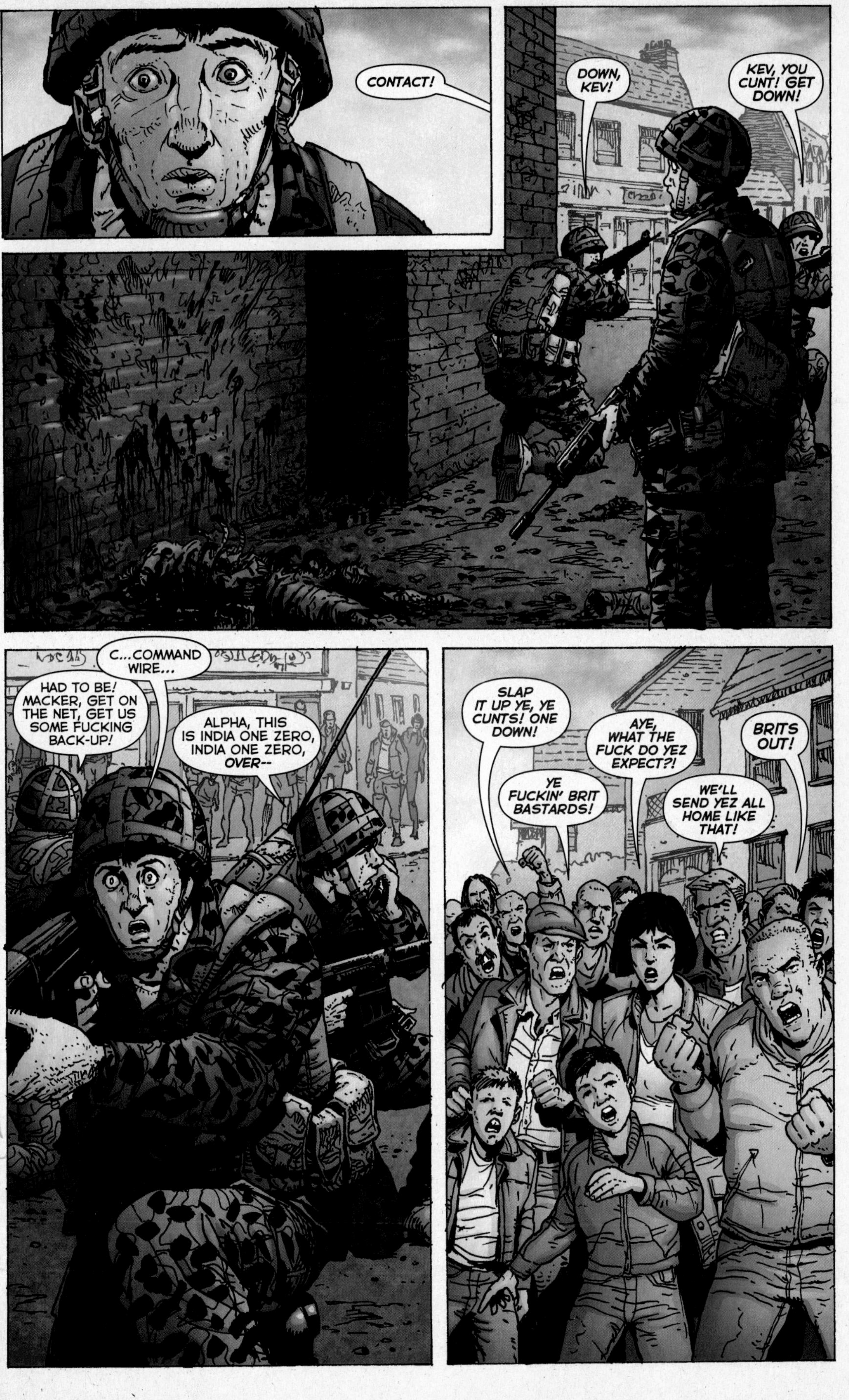
CONTACT!
DOWN, KEV!
KEV, YOU CUNT! GET DOWN!
C...COMMAND WIRE...
HAD TO BE! MACKER, GET ON THE NET, GET US SOME FUCKING BACK-UP!
ALPHA, THIS IS INDIA ONE ZERO, INDIA ONE ZERO, OVER--
SLAP IT UP YE, YE CUNTS! ONE DOWN!
YE FUCKIN' BRIT BASTARDS!
AYE, WHAT THE FUCK DO YEZ EXPECT?!
WE'LL SEND YEZ ALL HOME LIKE THAT!
BRITS OUT!

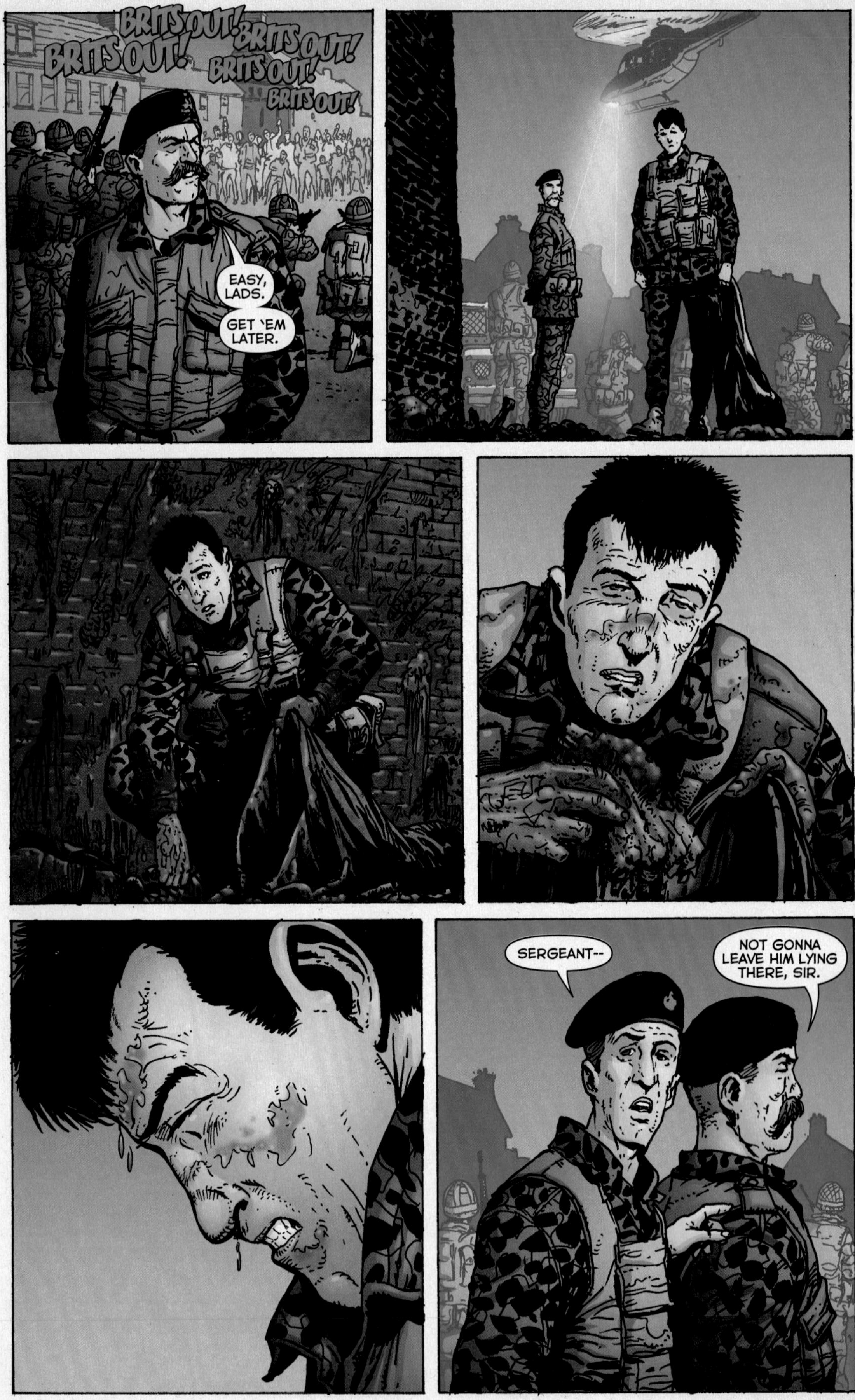
BRITS OUT!
BRITS OUT!
BRITS OUT!
BRITS OUT!
BRITS OUT!
EASY, LADS.
GET 'EM LATER.
SERGEANT--
NOT GONNA LEAVE HIM LYING THERE, SIR.

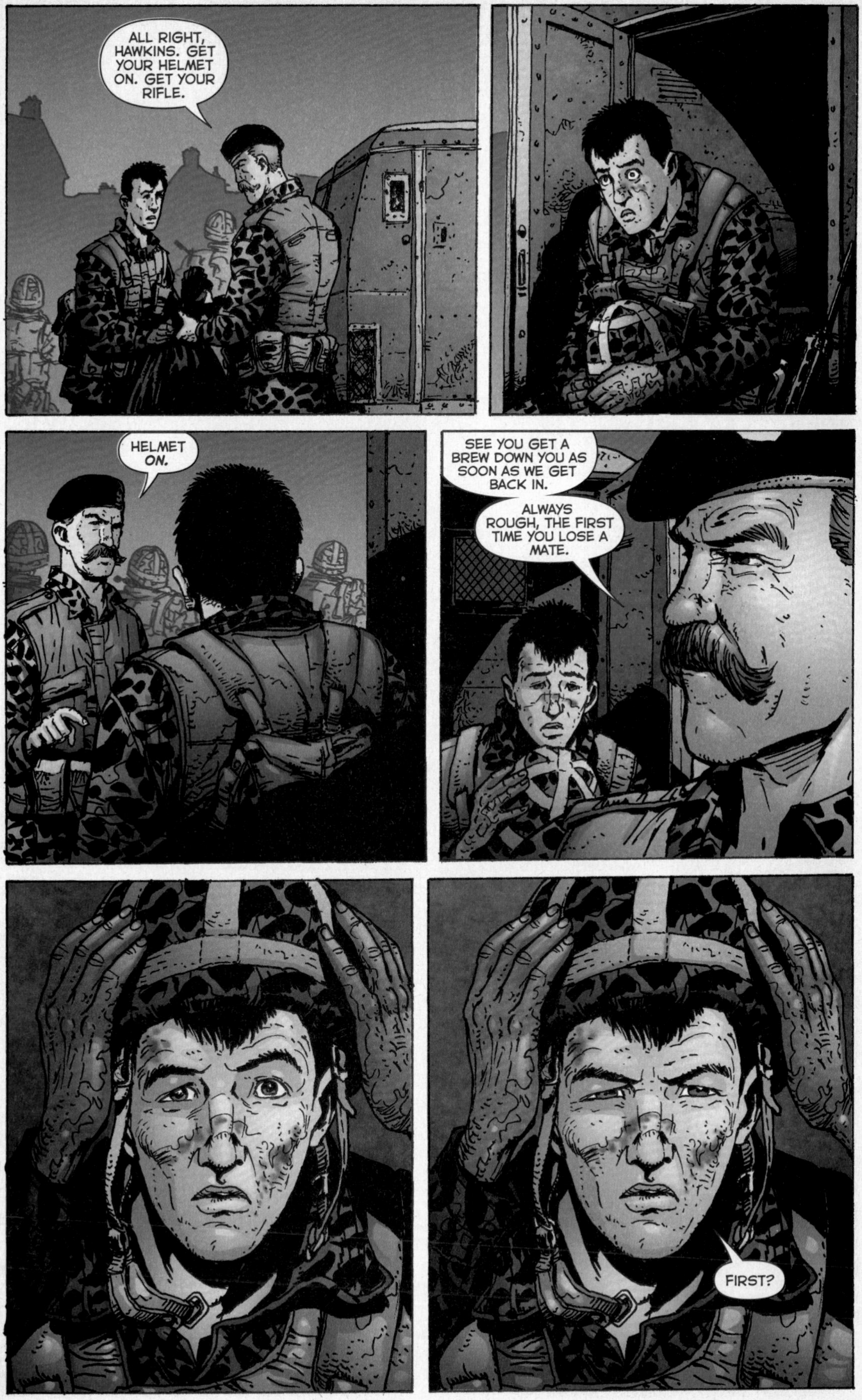
ALL RIGHT, HAWKINS. GET YOUR HELMET ON. GET YOUR RIFLE.
HELMET *ON.*
SEE YOU GET A BREW DOWN YOU AS SOON AS WE GET BACK IN.
ALWAYS ROUGH, THE FIRST TIME YOU LOSE A MATE.
FIRST?

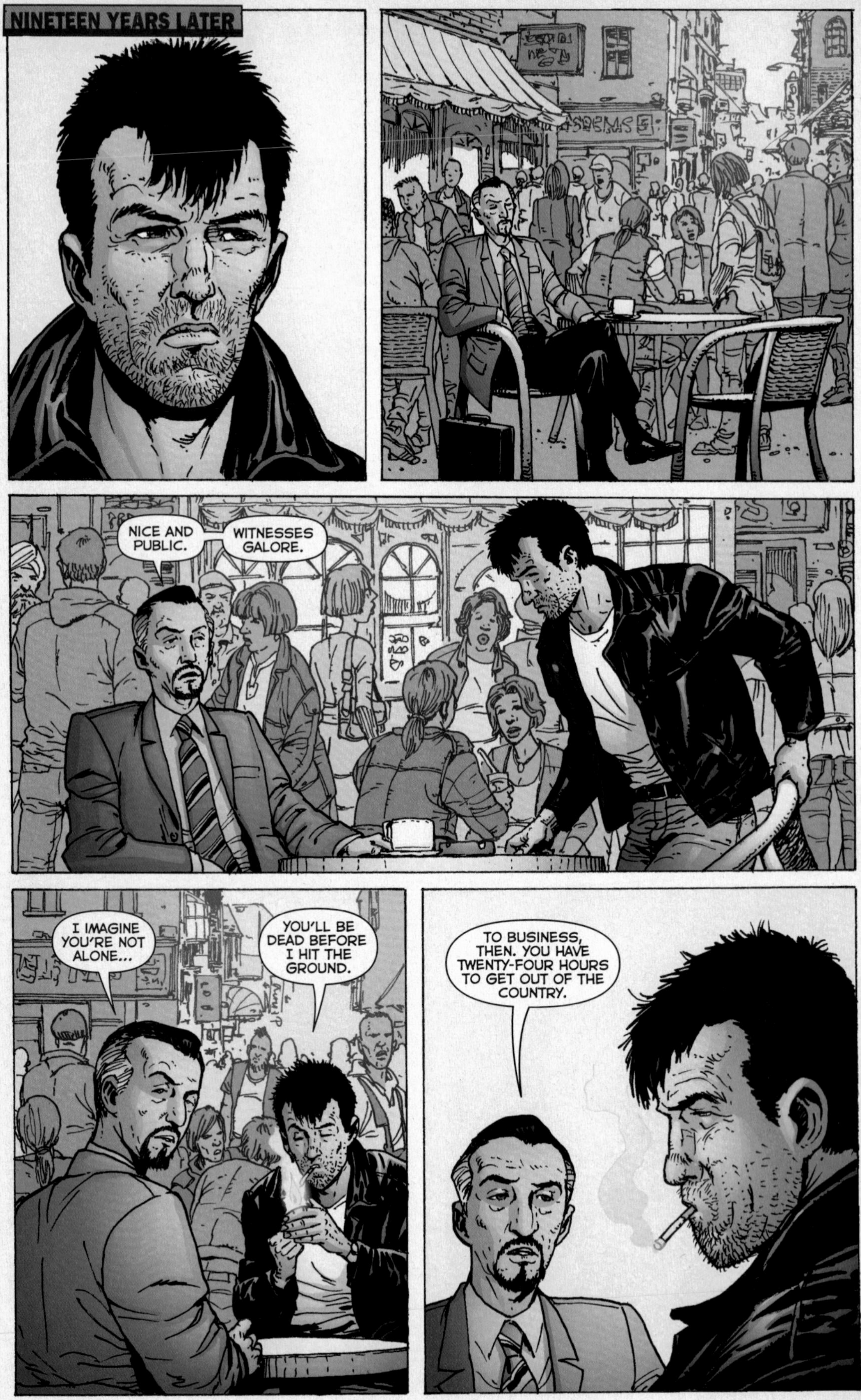
NINETEEN YEARS LATER
NICE AND PUBLIC.
WITNESSES GALORE.
I IMAGINE YOU'RE NOT ALONE...
YOU'LL BE DEAD BEFORE I HIT THE GROUND.
TO BUSINESS, THEN. YOU HAVE TWENTY-FOUR HOURS TO GET OUT OF THE COUNTRY.

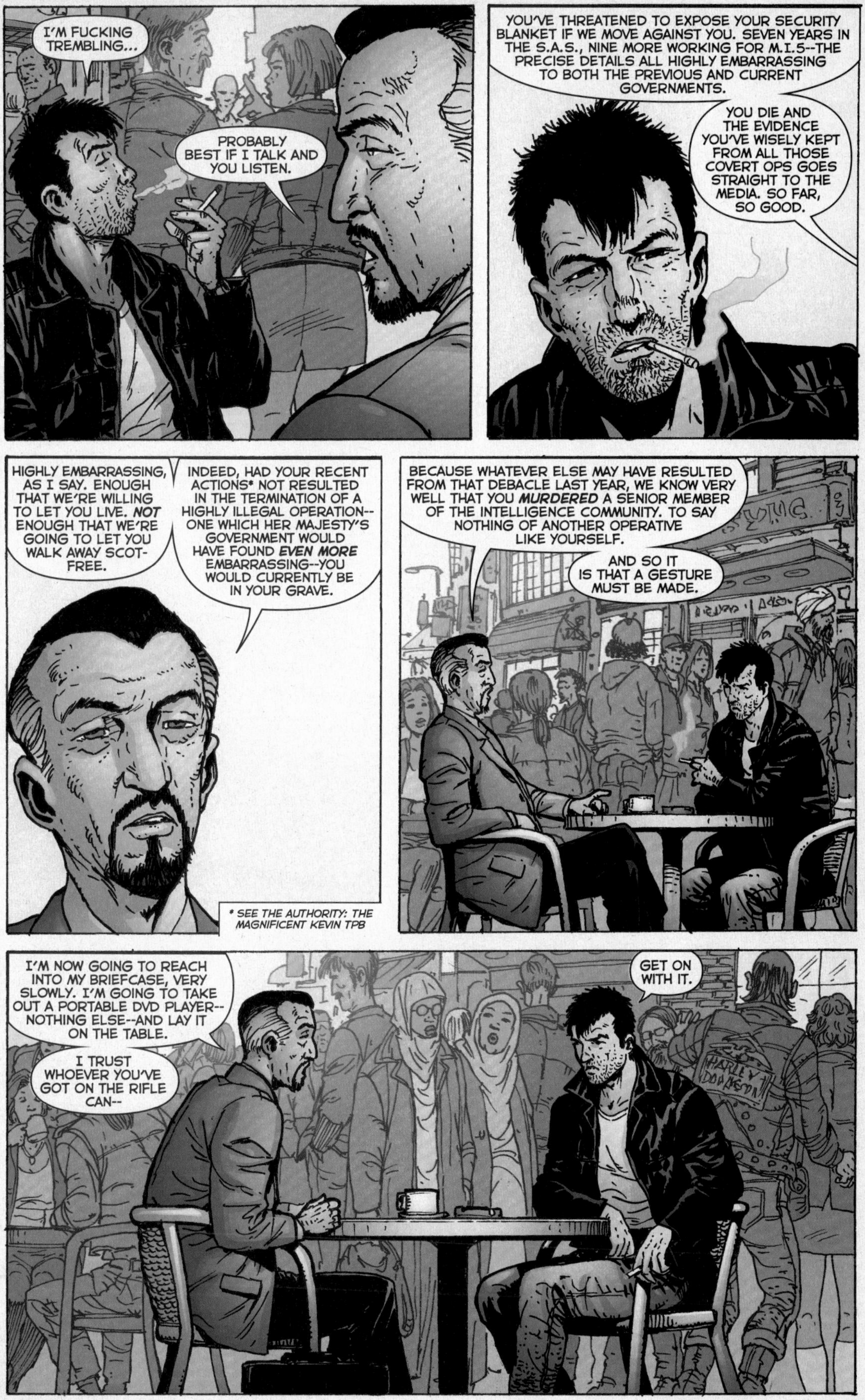
I'M FUCKING TREMBLING...
PROBABLY BEST IF I TALK AND YOU LISTEN.
YOU'VE THREATENED TO EXPOSE YOUR SECURITY BLANKET IF WE MOVE AGAINST YOU. SEVEN YEARS IN THE S.A.S., NINE MORE WORKING FOR M.I.5--THE PRECISE DETAILS ALL HIGHLY EMBARRASSING TO BOTH THE PREVIOUS AND CURRENT GOVERNMENTS.
YOU DIE AND THE EVIDENCE YOU'VE WISELY KEPT FROM ALL THOSE COVERT OPS GOES STRAIGHT TO THE MEDIA. SO FAR, SO GOOD.
HIGHLY EMBARRASSING, AS I SAY. ENOUGH THAT WE'RE WILLING TO LET YOU LIVE. NOT ENOUGH THAT WE'RE GOING TO LET YOU WALK AWAY SCOT-FREE.
INDEED, HAD YOUR RECENT ACTIONS* NOT RESULTED IN THE TERMINATION OF A HIGHLY ILLEGAL OPERATION--ONE WHICH HER MAJESTY'S GOVERNMENT WOULD HAVE FOUND EVEN MORE EMBARRASSING--YOU WOULD CURRENTLY BE IN YOUR GRAVE.
* SEE THE AUTHORITY: THE MAGNIFICENT KEVIN TPB
BECAUSE WHATEVER ELSE MAY HAVE RESULTED FROM THAT DEBACLE LAST YEAR, WE KNOW VERY WELL THAT YOU MURDERED A SENIOR MEMBER OF THE INTELLIGENCE COMMUNITY. TO SAY NOTHING OF ANOTHER OPERATIVE LIKE YOURSELF.
AND SO IT IS THAT A GESTURE MUST BE MADE.
I'M NOW GOING TO REACH INTO MY BRIEFCASE, VERY SLOWLY. I'M GOING TO TAKE OUT A PORTABLE DVD PLAYER--NOTHING ELSE--AND LAY IT ON THE TABLE.
I TRUST WHOEVER YOU'VE GOT ON THE RIFLE CAN--
GET ON WITH IT.

IN NINETEEN EIGHTY-SEVEN YOUR INFANTRY UNIT WAS STATIONED IN WHAT WAS THEN WEST GERMANY, PART OF THE BRITISH ARMY ON THE RHINE.

YOU WERE STRAPPED FOR CASH.

SO YOU DID A BIT OF MOON-LIGHTING.

ARSCHFICKE!

ARSCHFICKE! JA! JA! GOTT IN HIMMEL!

ARSCHFICKE!

HOW THE FUCK DID YOU GET *THAT*?!

QUITE BY ACCIDENT. A FRIEND OF MINE IS A KEEN MASTURBATOR.

DONNER UND BLITZEN! *JA!* ARSCHF--✲

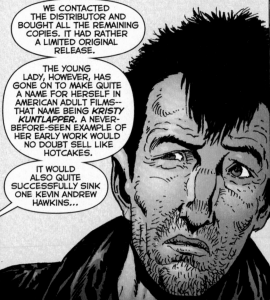

WE CONTACTED THE DISTRIBUTOR AND BOUGHT ALL THE REMAINING COPIES. IT HAD RATHER A LIMITED ORIGINAL RELEASE.

THE YOUNG LADY, HOWEVER, HAS GONE ON TO MAKE QUITE A NAME FOR HERSELF IN AMERICAN ADULT FILMS-- THAT NAME BEING *KRISTY KUNTLAPPER.* A NEVER-BEFORE-SEEN EXAMPLE OF HER EARLY WORK WOULD NO DOUBT SELL LIKE HOTCAKES.

IT WOULD ALSO QUITE SUCCESSFULLY SINK ONE KEVIN ANDREW HAWKINS...

YOU WILL LEAVE THE U.K. BY THIS TIME TOMORROW, OR WE WILL SEND THIS LITTLE GEM TO EVERY ADULT FILM OUTFIT IN LOS ANGELES. WE WILL ALSO ALERT EVERYONE ON THE CIRCUIT TO YOUR NEW-FOUND FAME.

AT THAT POINT, ANYONE STILL WANTING TO EMPLOY A *PORN STAR* AS A BODYGUARD OR SECURITY CONSULTANT WILL BE MORE THAN WELCOME TO YOU. BUT SOMETHING TELLS ME THERE WON'T BE MANY TAKERS.

GET OUT. GO WHEREVER YOU WANT--DO WHATEVER YOU WANT--BUT NOT HERE.

GET OUT OF THE COUNTRY AND DON'T EVER TRY TO COME BACK.

CHRIST-ALL-BLOODY-MIGHTY.

MEET THE NEW BOSS, EVEN BIGGER CUNT THAN THE OLD BOSS.

I'M NOT YOUR EMPLOYER.

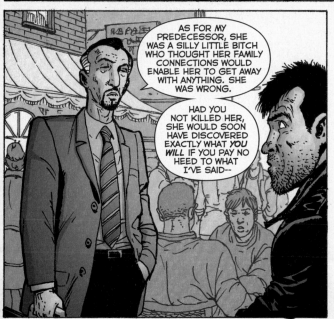

AS FOR MY PREDECESSOR, SHE WAS A SILLY LITTLE BITCH WHO THOUGHT HER FAMILY CONNECTIONS WOULD ENABLE HER TO GET AWAY WITH ANYTHING. SHE WAS WRONG.

HAD YOU NOT KILLED HER, SHE WOULD SOON HAVE DISCOVERED EXACTLY WHAT *YOU WILL* IF YOU PAY NO HEED TO WHAT I'VE SAID--

WHICH IS THAT I AM THE BIGGEST CUNT OF ALL.

GOODBYE.

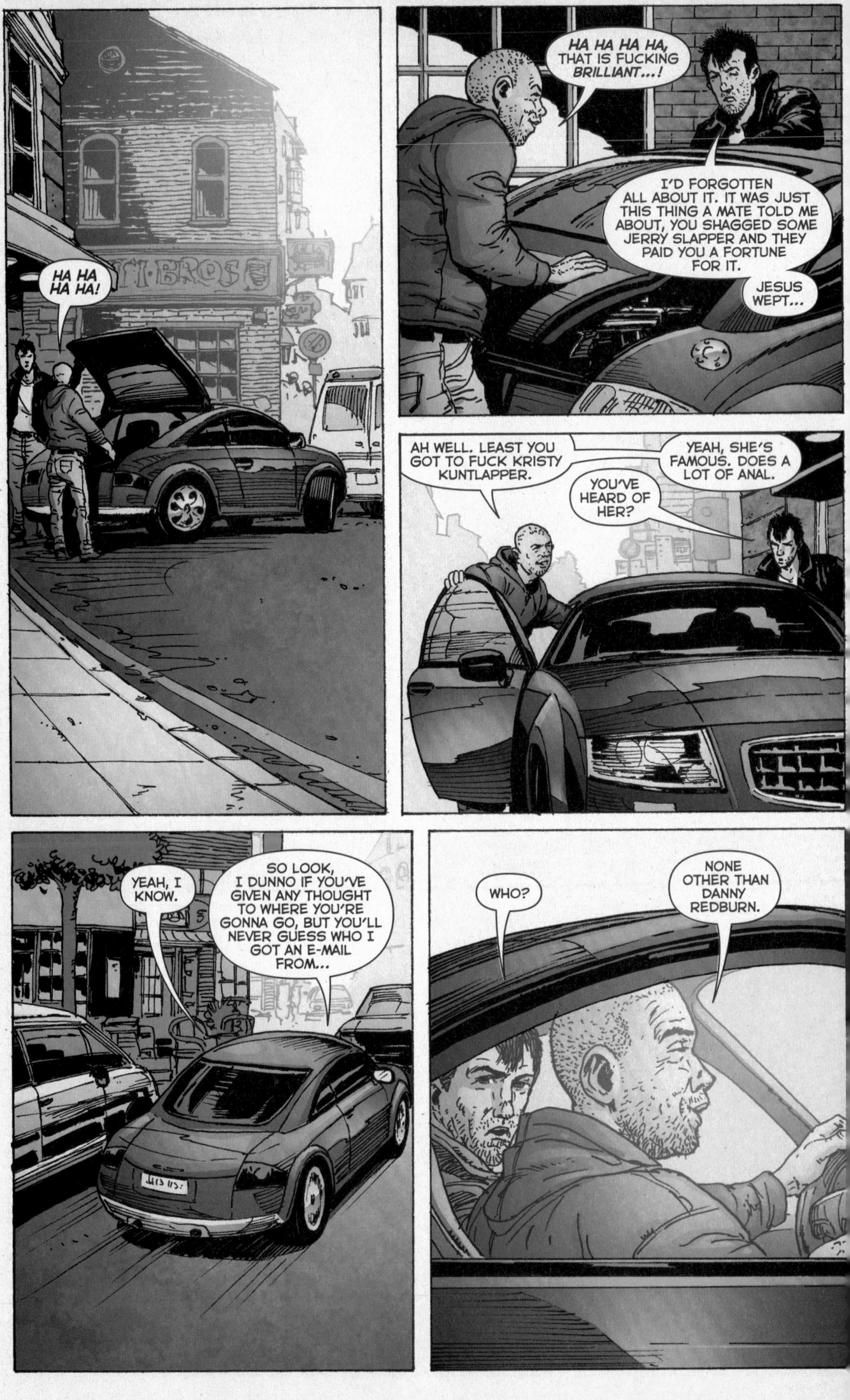
HA HA HA HA!
HA HA HA HA, THAT IS FUCKING BRILLIANT...!
I'D FORGOTTEN ALL ABOUT IT. IT WAS JUST THIS THING A MATE TOLD ME ABOUT, YOU SHAGGED SOME JERRY SLAPPER AND THEY PAID YOU A FORTUNE FOR IT.
JESUS WEPT...
AH WELL. LEAST YOU GOT TO FUCK KRISTY KUNTLAPPER.
YEAH, SHE'S FAMOUS. DOES A LOT OF ANAL.
YOU'VE HEARD OF HER?
YEAH, I KNOW.
SO LOOK, I DUNNO IF YOU'VE GIVEN ANY THOUGHT TO WHERE YOU'RE GONNA GO, BUT YOU'LL NEVER GUESS WHO I GOT AN E-MAIL FROM...
WHO?
NONE OTHER THAN DANNY REDBURN.

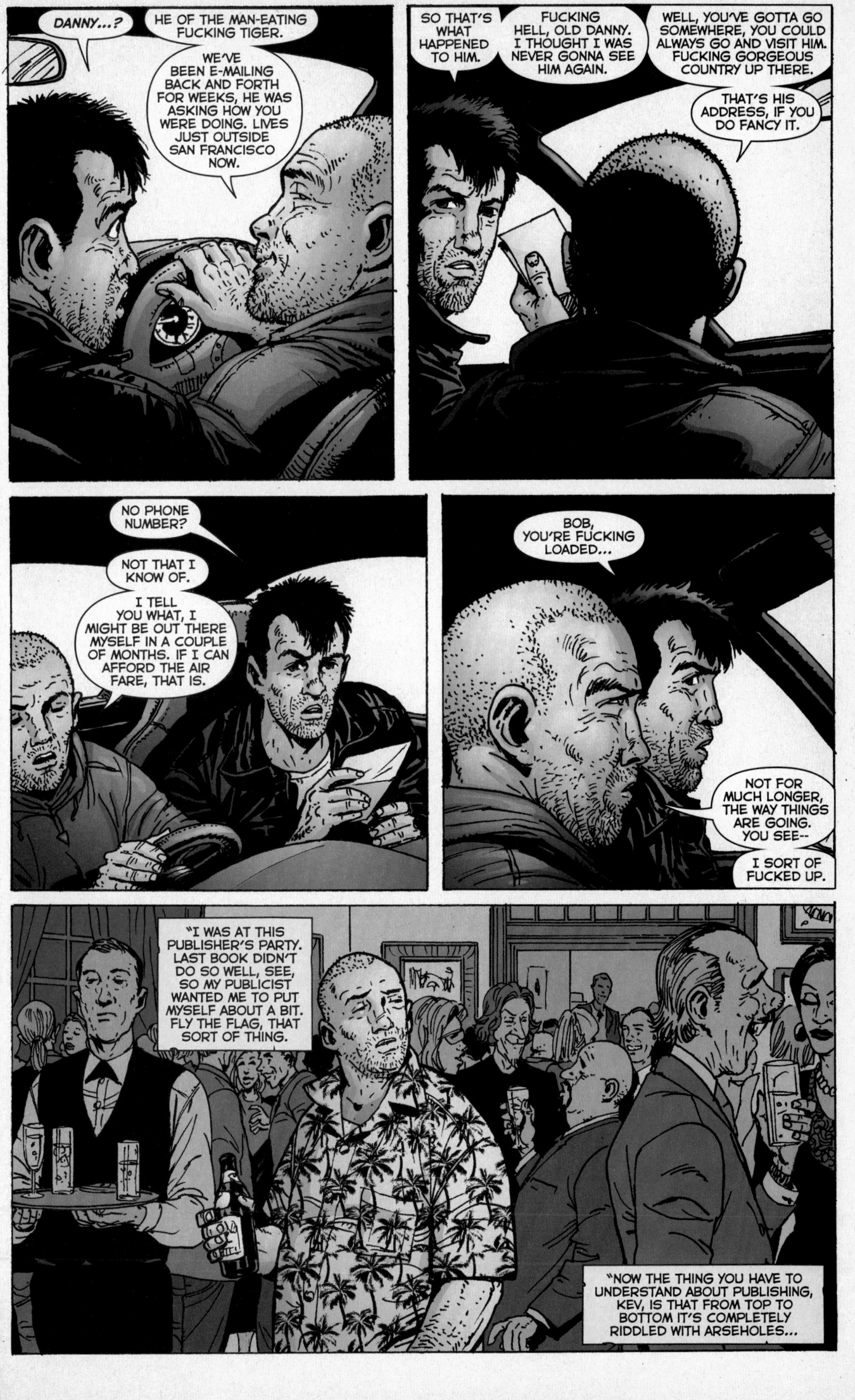
DANNY...?
HE OF THE MAN-EATING FUCKING TIGER.
WE'VE BEEN E-MAILING BACK AND FORTH FOR WEEKS, HE WAS ASKING HOW YOU WERE DOING. LIVES JUST OUTSIDE SAN FRANCISCO NOW.
SO THAT'S WHAT HAPPENED TO HIM.
FUCKING HELL, OLD DANNY. I THOUGHT I WAS NEVER GONNA SEE HIM AGAIN.
WELL, YOU'VE GOTTA GO SOMEWHERE, YOU COULD ALWAYS GO AND VISIT HIM. FUCKING GORGEOUS COUNTRY UP THERE.
THAT'S HIS ADDRESS, IF YOU DO FANCY IT.
NO PHONE NUMBER?
NOT THAT I KNOW OF.
I TELL YOU WHAT, I MIGHT BE OUT THERE MYSELF IN A COUPLE OF MONTHS. IF I CAN AFFORD THE AIR FARE, THAT IS.
BOB, YOU'RE FUCKING LOADED...
NOT FOR MUCH LONGER, THE WAY THINGS ARE GOING. YOU SEE--
I SORT OF FUCKED UP.
"I WAS AT THIS PUBLISHER'S PARTY. LAST BOOK DIDN'T DO SO WELL, SEE, SO MY PUBLICIST WANTED ME TO PUT MYSELF ABOUT A BIT. FLY THE FLAG, THAT SORT OF THING.
"NOW THE THING YOU HAVE TO UNDERSTAND ABOUT PUBLISHING, KEV, IS THAT FROM TOP TO BOTTOM IT'S COMPLETELY RIDDLED WITH ARSEHOLES...

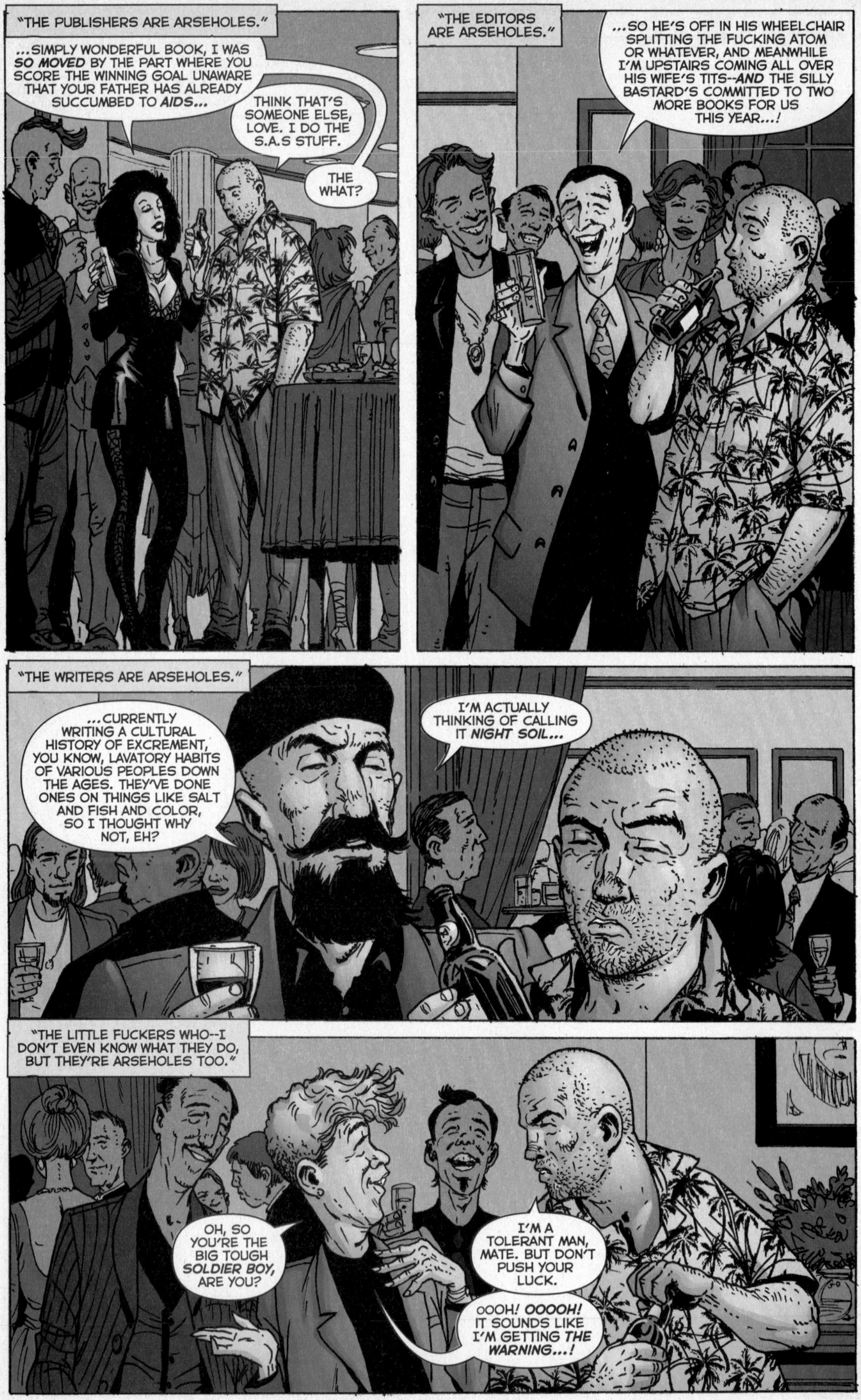
"THE PUBLISHERS ARE ARSEHOLES."
...SIMPLY WONDERFUL BOOK, I WAS SO MOVED BY THE PART WHERE YOU SCORE THE WINNING GOAL UNAWARE THAT YOUR FATHER HAS ALREADY SUCCUMBED TO AIDS...
THINK THAT'S SOMEONE ELSE, LOVE. I DO THE S.A.S STUFF.
THE WHAT?
"THE EDITORS ARE ARSEHOLES."
...SO HE'S OFF IN HIS WHEELCHAIR SPLITTING THE FUCKING ATOM OR WHATEVER, AND MEANWHILE I'M UPSTAIRS COMING ALL OVER HIS WIFE'S TITS--AND THE SILLY BASTARD'S COMMITTED TO TWO MORE BOOKS FOR US THIS YEAR...!
"THE WRITERS ARE ARSEHOLES."
...CURRENTLY WRITING A CULTURAL HISTORY OF EXCREMENT, YOU KNOW, LAVATORY HABITS OF VARIOUS PEOPLES DOWN THE AGES. THEY'VE DONE ONES ON THINGS LIKE SALT AND FISH AND COLOR, SO I THOUGHT WHY NOT, EH?
I'M ACTUALLY THINKING OF CALLING IT NIGHT SOIL...
"THE LITTLE FUCKERS WHO--I DON'T EVEN KNOW WHAT THEY DO, BUT THEY'RE ARSEHOLES TOO."
OH, SO YOU'RE THE BIG TOUGH SOLDIER BOY, ARE YOU?
I'M A TOLERANT MAN, MATE. BUT DON'T PUSH YOUR LUCK.
OOOH! OOOOH! IT SOUNDS LIKE I'M GETTING THE WARNING...!

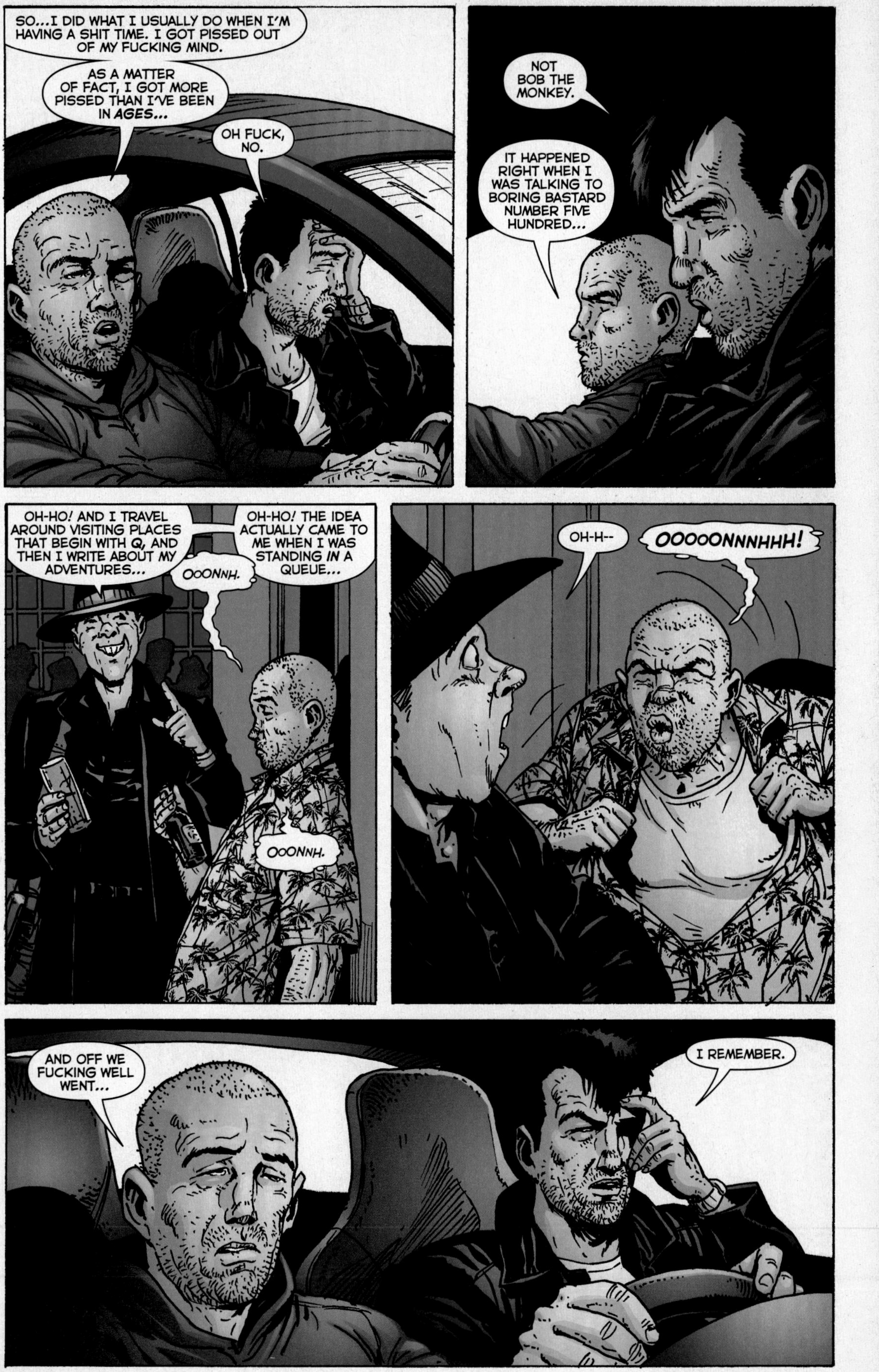
SO...I DID WHAT I USUALLY DO WHEN I'M HAVING A SHIT TIME. I GOT PISSED OUT OF MY FUCKING MIND.
AS A MATTER OF FACT, I GOT MORE PISSED THAN I'VE BEEN IN AGES...
OH FUCK, NO.
NOT BOB THE MONKEY.
IT HAPPENED RIGHT WHEN I WAS TALKING TO BORING BASTARD NUMBER FIVE HUNDRED...
OH-HO! AND I TRAVEL AROUND VISITING PLACES THAT BEGIN WITH Q, AND THEN I WRITE ABOUT MY ADVENTURES...
OOONNH.
OH-HO! THE IDEA ACTUALLY CAME TO ME WHEN I WAS STANDING IN A QUEUE...
OOONNH.
OH-H--
OOOOONNNHHH!
AND OFF WE FUCKING WELL WENT...
I REMEMBER.

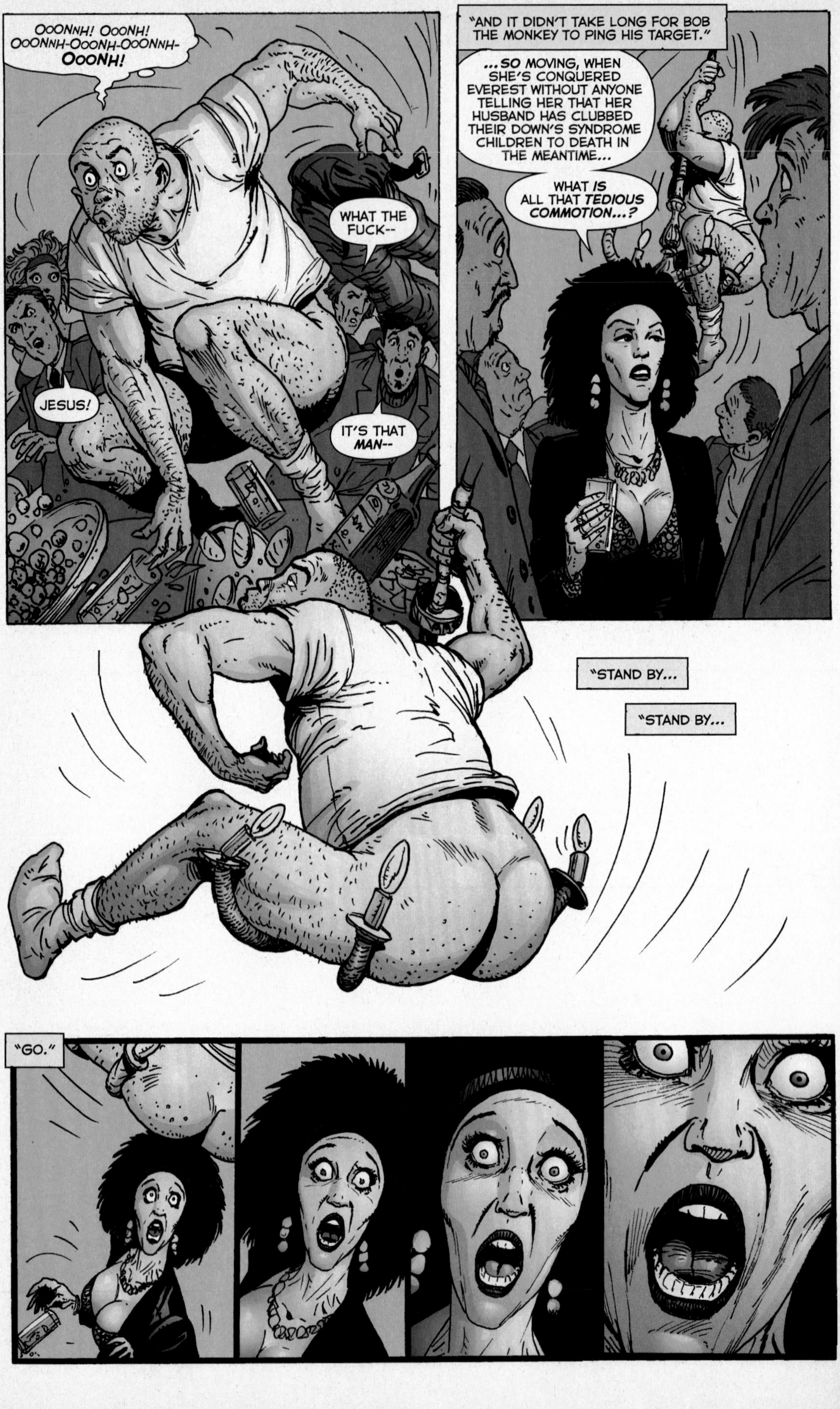
OOONNH! OOONH! OOONNH-OOONH-OOONNH-OOONH!
WHAT THE FUCK--
JESUS!
IT'S THAT MAN--
"AND IT DIDN'T TAKE LONG FOR BOB THE MONKEY TO PING HIS TARGET."
...SO MOVING, WHEN SHE'S CONQUERED EVEREST WITHOUT ANYONE TELLING HER THAT HER HUSBAND HAS CLUBBED THEIR DOWN'S SYNDROME CHILDREN TO DEATH IN THE MEANTIME...
WHAT IS ALL THAT TEDIOUS COMMOTION...?
"STAND BY...
"STAND BY...
"GO."

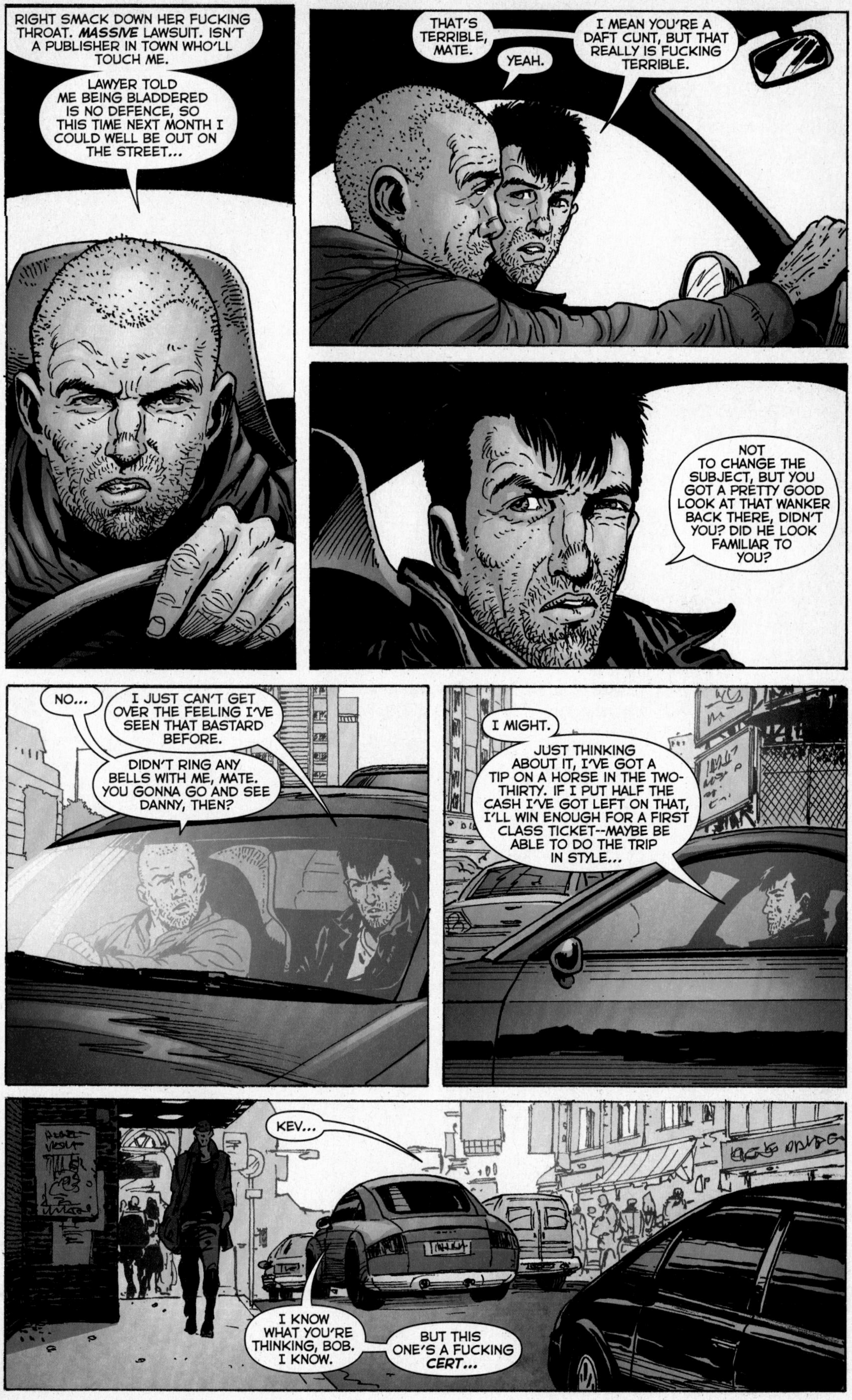
RIGHT SMACK DOWN HER FUCKING THROAT. *MASSIVE* LAWSUIT. ISN'T A PUBLISHER IN TOWN WHO'LL TOUCH ME.
LAWYER TOLD ME BEING BLADDERED IS NO DEFENCE, SO THIS TIME NEXT MONTH I COULD WELL BE OUT ON THE STREET...
THAT'S TERRIBLE, MATE.
YEAH.
I MEAN YOU'RE A DAFT CUNT, BUT THAT REALLY IS FUCKING TERRIBLE.
NOT TO CHANGE THE SUBJECT, BUT YOU GOT A PRETTY GOOD LOOK AT THAT WANKER BACK THERE, DIDN'T YOU? DID HE LOOK FAMILIAR TO YOU?
NO...
I JUST CAN'T GET OVER THE FEELING I'VE SEEN THAT BASTARD BEFORE.
DIDN'T RING ANY BELLS WITH ME, MATE. YOU GONNA GO AND SEE DANNY, THEN?
I MIGHT.
JUST THINKING ABOUT IT, I'VE GOT A TIP ON A HORSE IN THE TWO-THIRTY. IF I PUT HALF THE CASH I'VE GOT LEFT ON THAT, I'LL WIN ENOUGH FOR A FIRST CLASS TICKET--MAYBE BE ABLE TO DO THE TRIP IN STYLE...
KEV...
I KNOW WHAT YOU'RE THINKING, BOB. I KNOW.
BUT THIS ONE'S A FUCKING *CERT*...

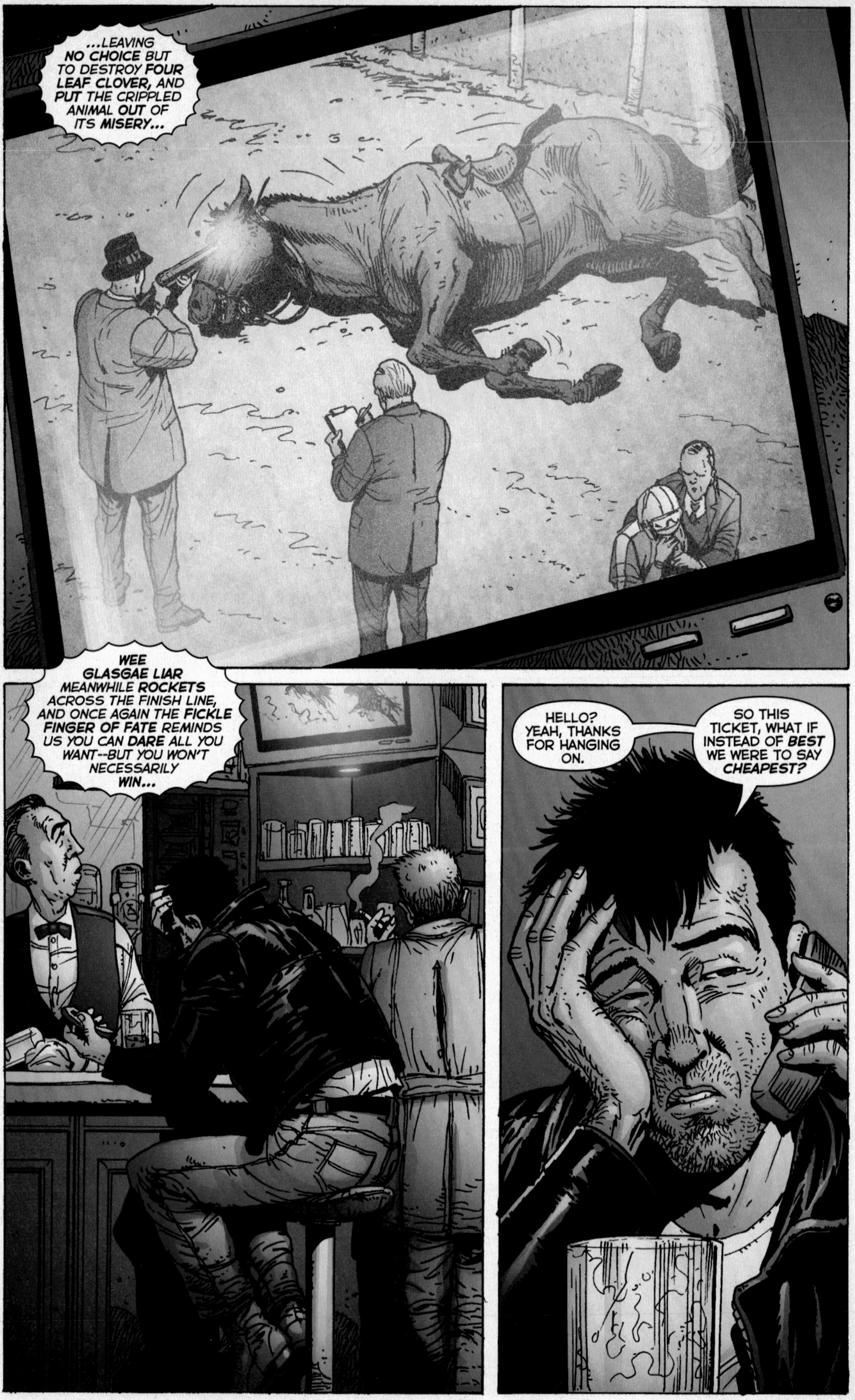
...LEAVING NO CHOICE BUT TO DESTROY FOUR LEAF CLOVER, AND PUT THE CRIPPLED ANIMAL OUT OF ITS MISERY...
WEE GLASGAE LIAR MEANWHILE ROCKETS ACROSS THE FINISH LINE, AND ONCE AGAIN THE FICKLE FINGER OF FATE REMINDS US YOU CAN DARE ALL YOU WANT--BUT YOU WON'T NECESSARILY WIN...
HELLO? YEAH, THANKS FOR HANGING ON.
SO THIS TICKET, WHAT IF INSTEAD OF BEST WE WERE TO SAY CHEAPEST?

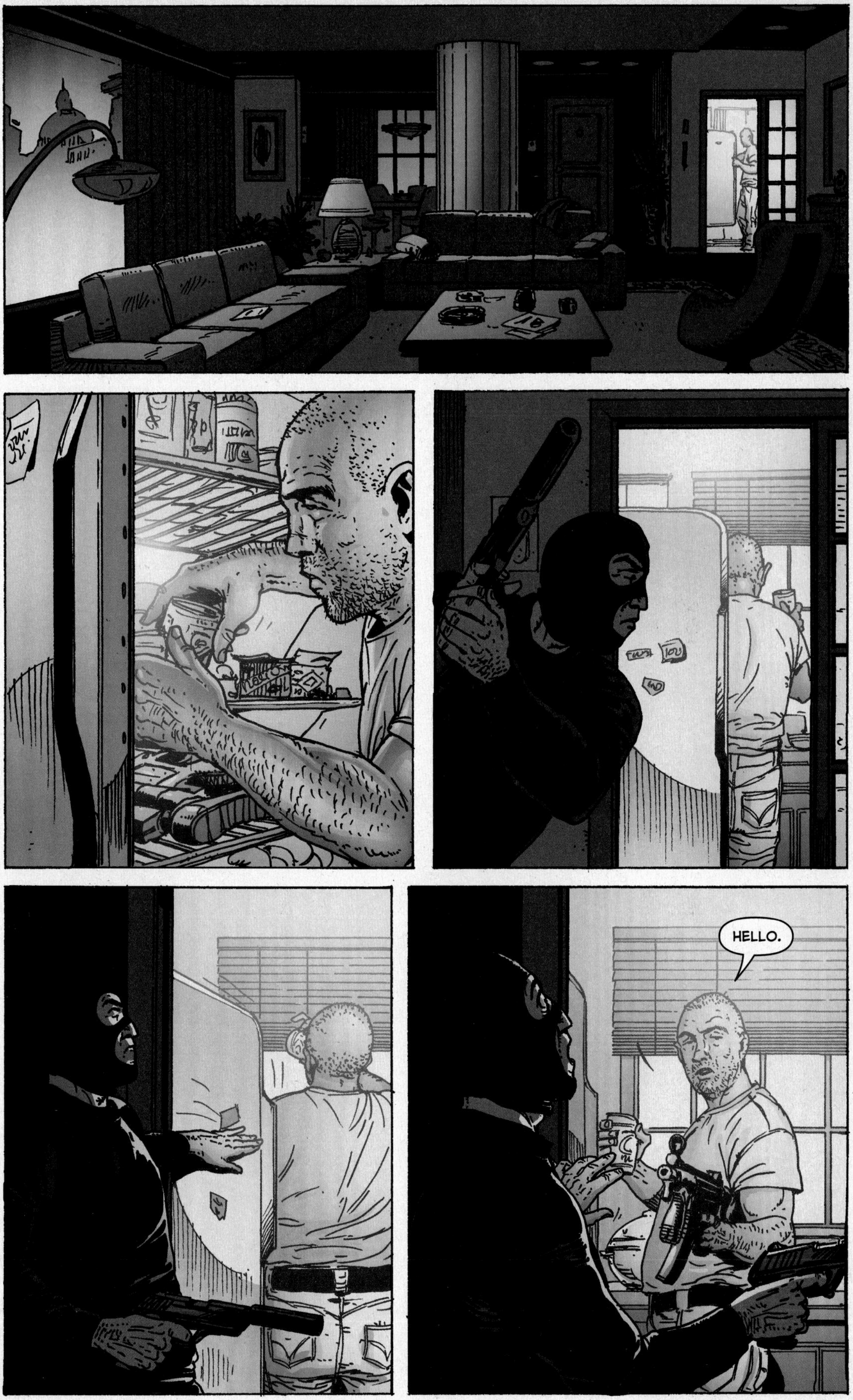
HELLO.

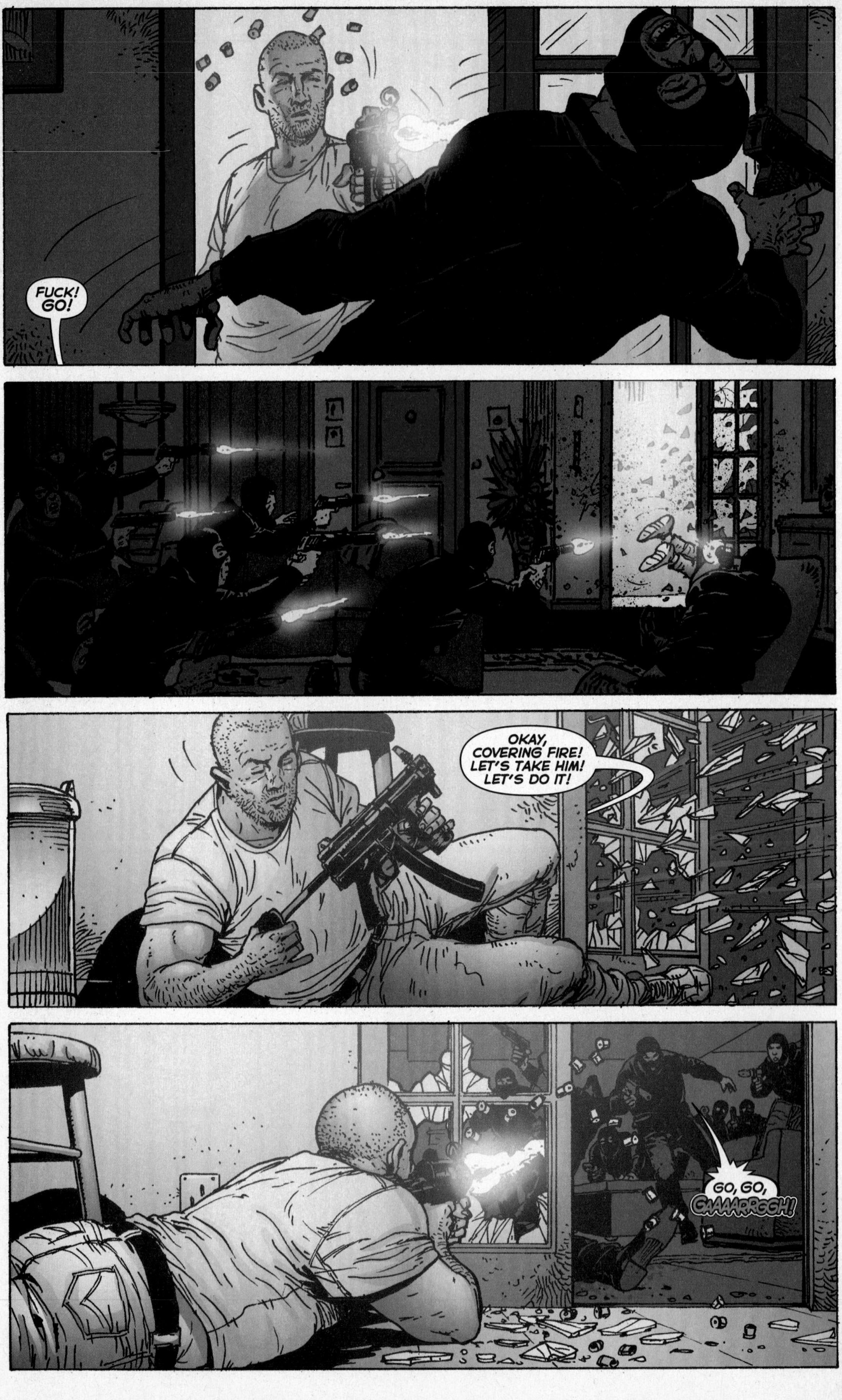
FUCK! GO!
OKAY, COVERING FIRE! LET'S TAKE HIM! LET'S DO IT!
GO, GO, GAAAARRGGH!

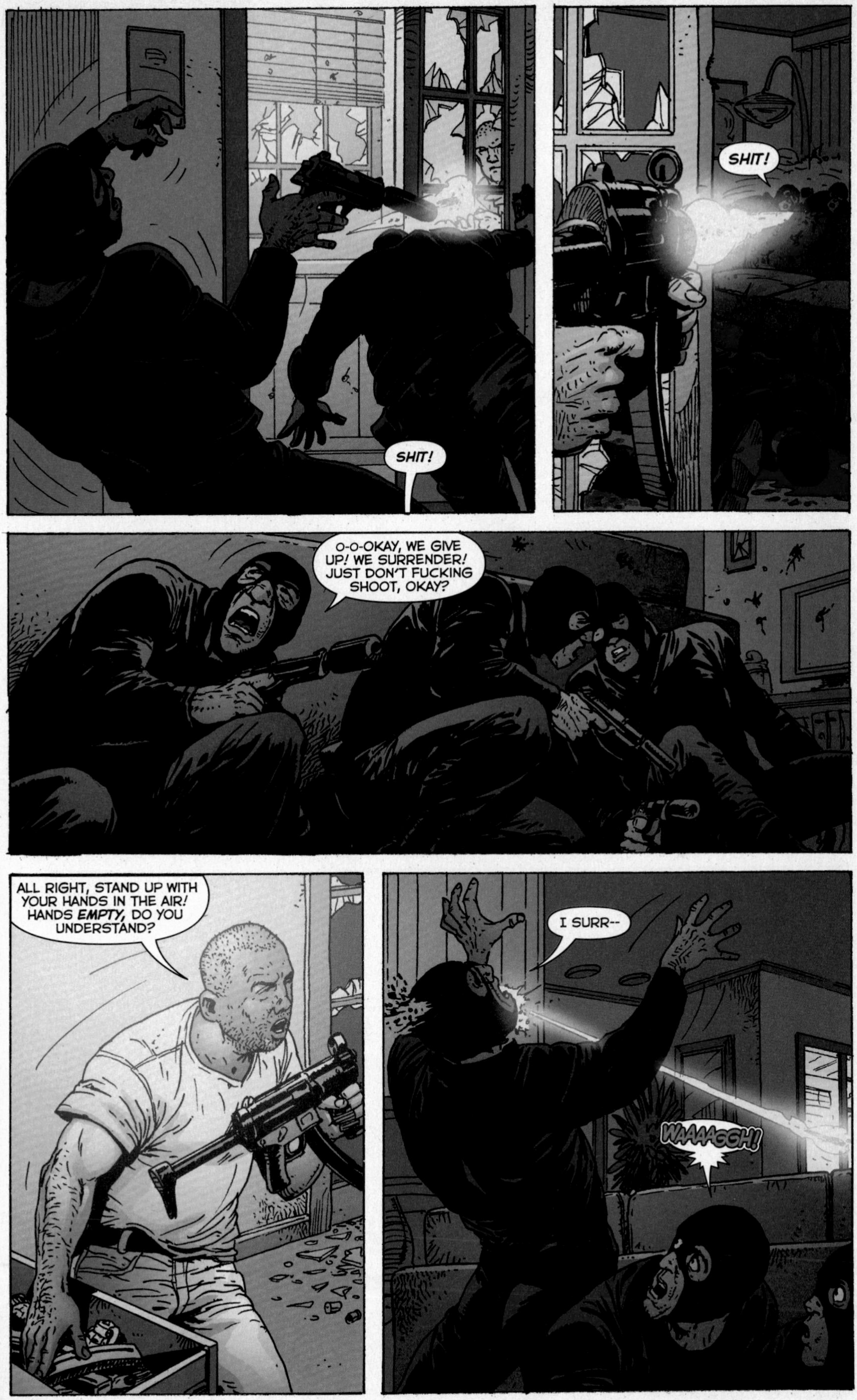
SHIT!
SHIT!
O-O-OKAY, WE GIVE UP! WE SURRENDER! JUST DON'T FUCKING SHOOT, OKAY?
ALL RIGHT, STAND UP WITH YOUR HANDS IN THE AIR! HANDS EMPTY, DO YOU UNDERSTAND?
I SURR--
WAAAAGGH!

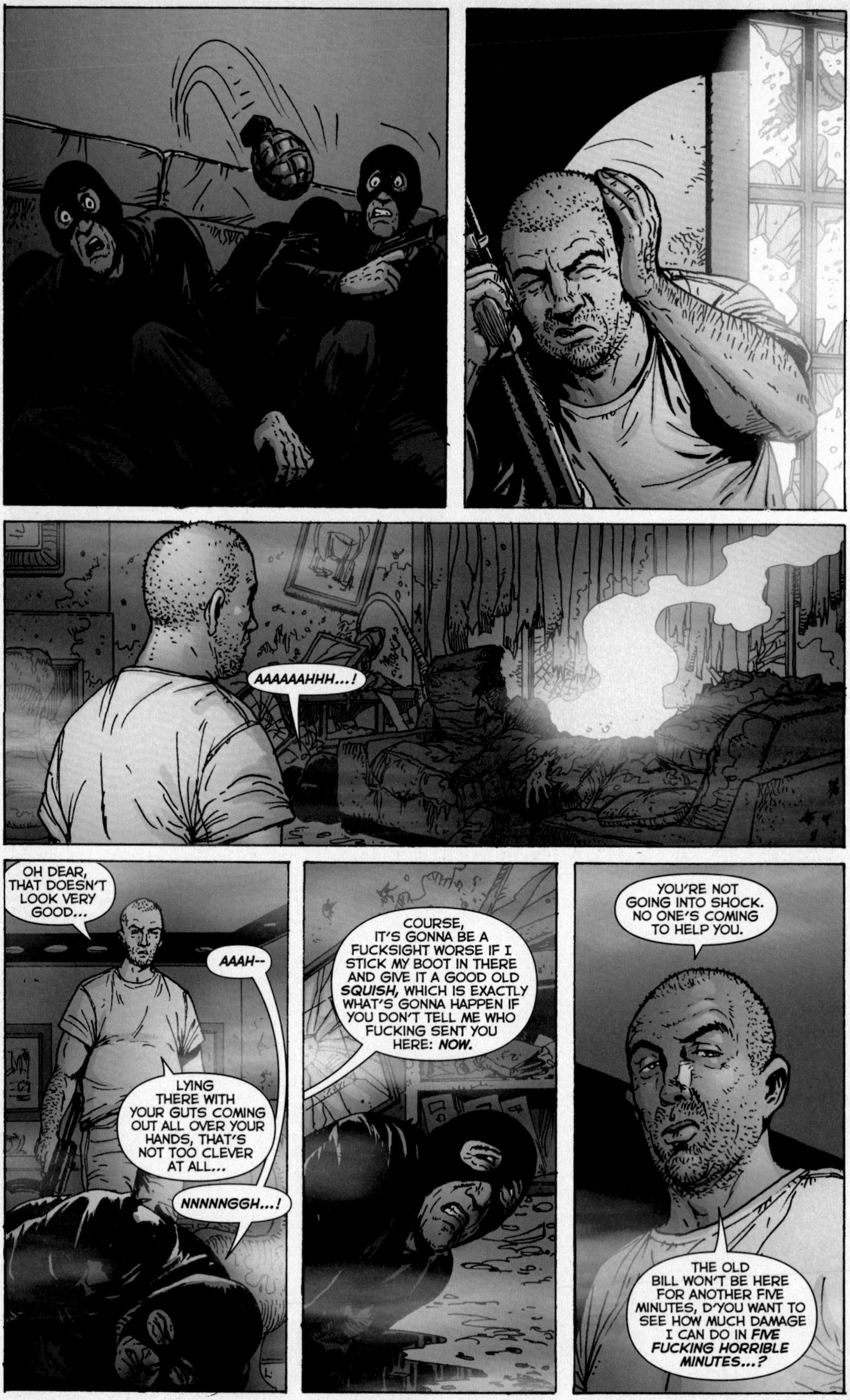
AAAAAAHHH...!
OH DEAR, THAT DOESN'T LOOK VERY GOOD...
AAAH--
LYING THERE WITH YOUR GUTS COMING OUT ALL OVER YOUR HANDS, THAT'S NOT TOO CLEVER AT ALL...
NNNNNGGH...!
COURSE, IT'S GONNA BE A FUCKSIGHT WORSE IF I STICK MY BOOT IN THERE AND GIVE IT A GOOD OLD SQUISH, WHICH IS EXACTLY WHAT'S GONNA HAPPEN IF YOU DON'T TELL ME WHO FUCKING SENT YOU HERE: NOW.
YOU'RE NOT GOING INTO SHOCK. NO ONE'S COMING TO HELP YOU.
THE OLD BILL WON'T BE HERE FOR ANOTHER FIVE MINUTES, D'YOU WANT TO SEE HOW MUCH DAMAGE I CAN DO IN FIVE FUCKING HORRIBLE MINUTES...?

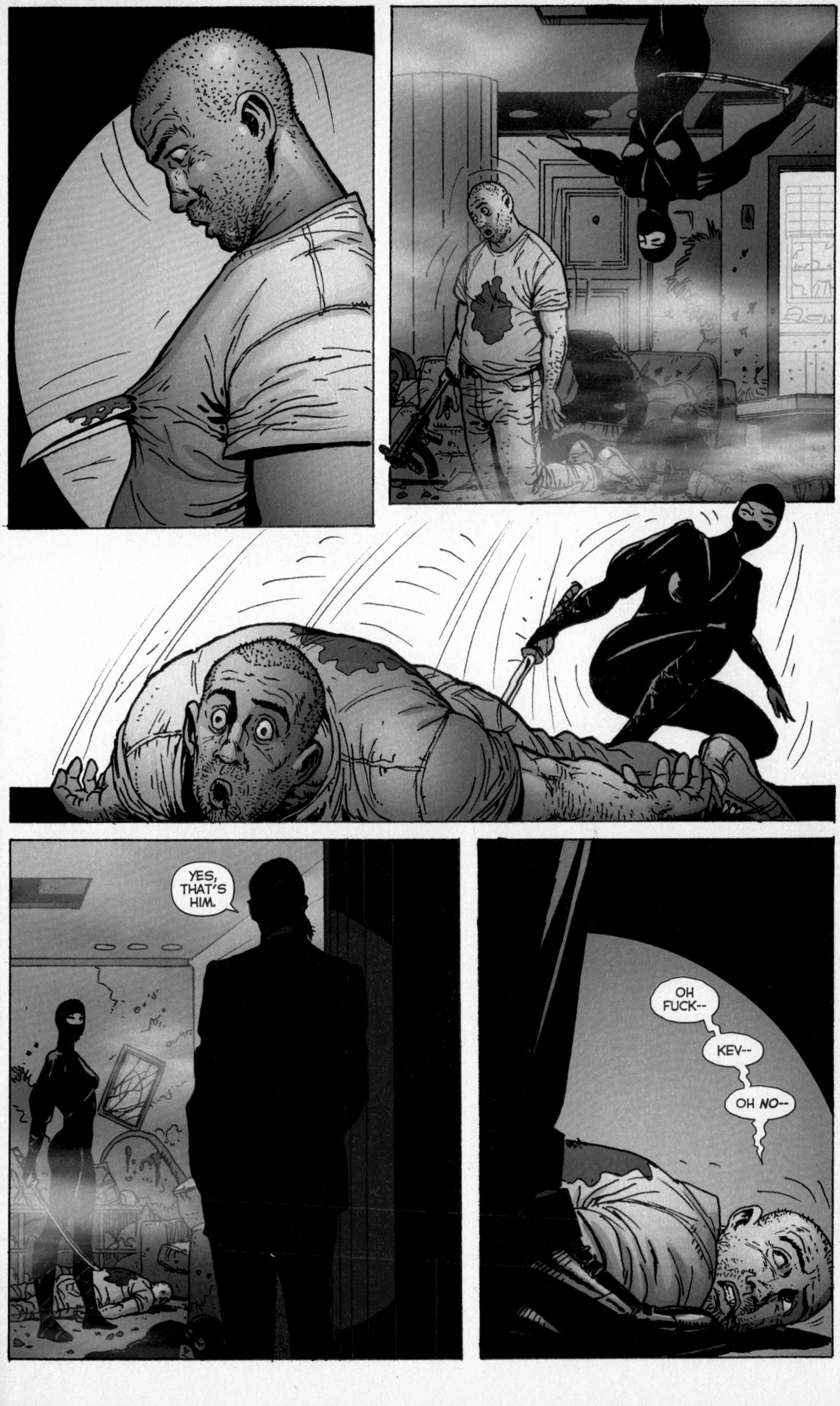
YES, THAT'S HIM.
OH FUCK--
KEV--
OH NO--

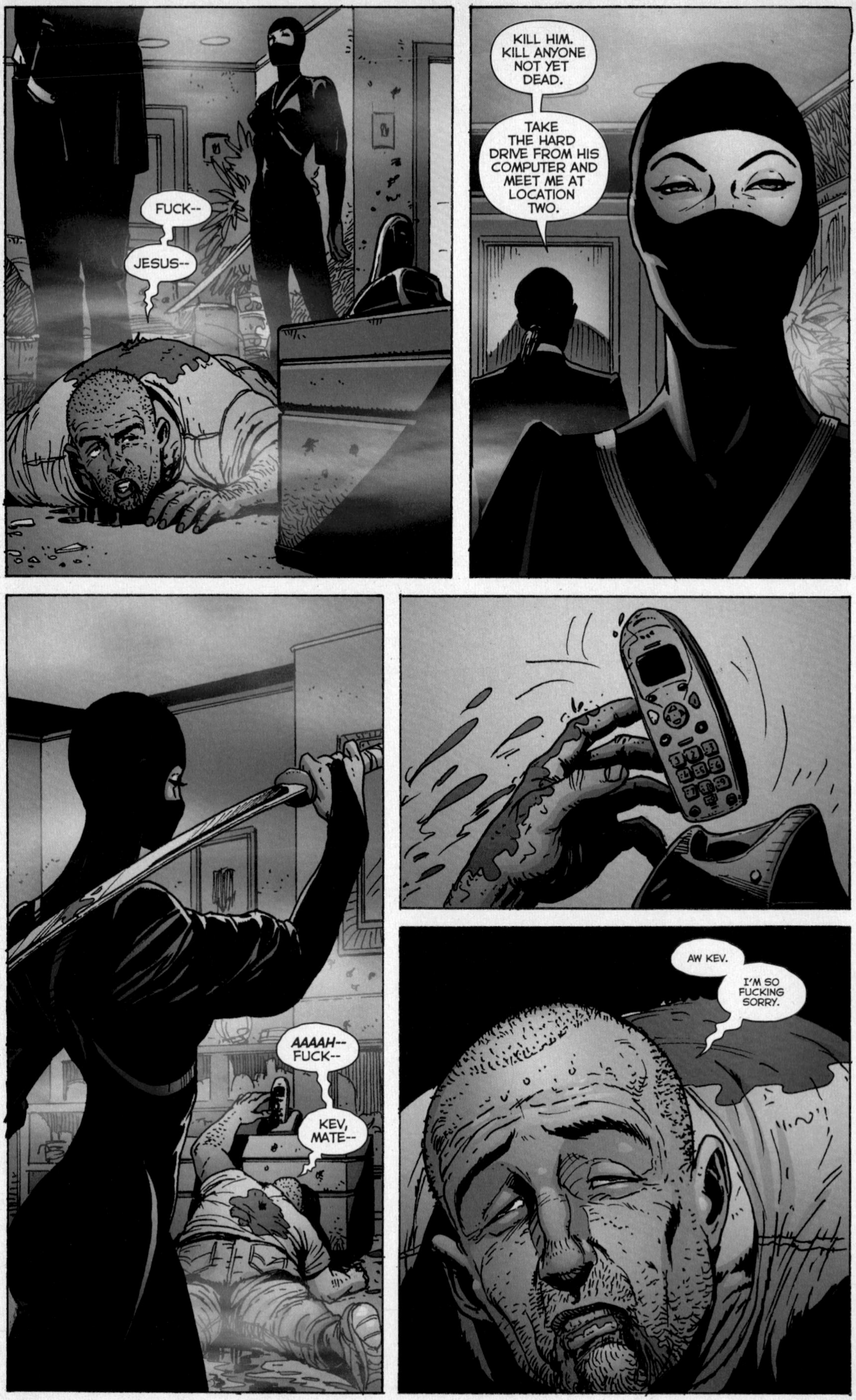
FUCK--
JESUS--
KILL HIM. KILL ANYONE NOT YET DEAD.
TAKE THE HARD DRIVE FROM HIS COMPUTER AND MEET ME AT LOCATION TWO.
AAAAH-- FUCK--
KEV, MATE--
AW KEV.
I'M SO FUCKING SORRY.

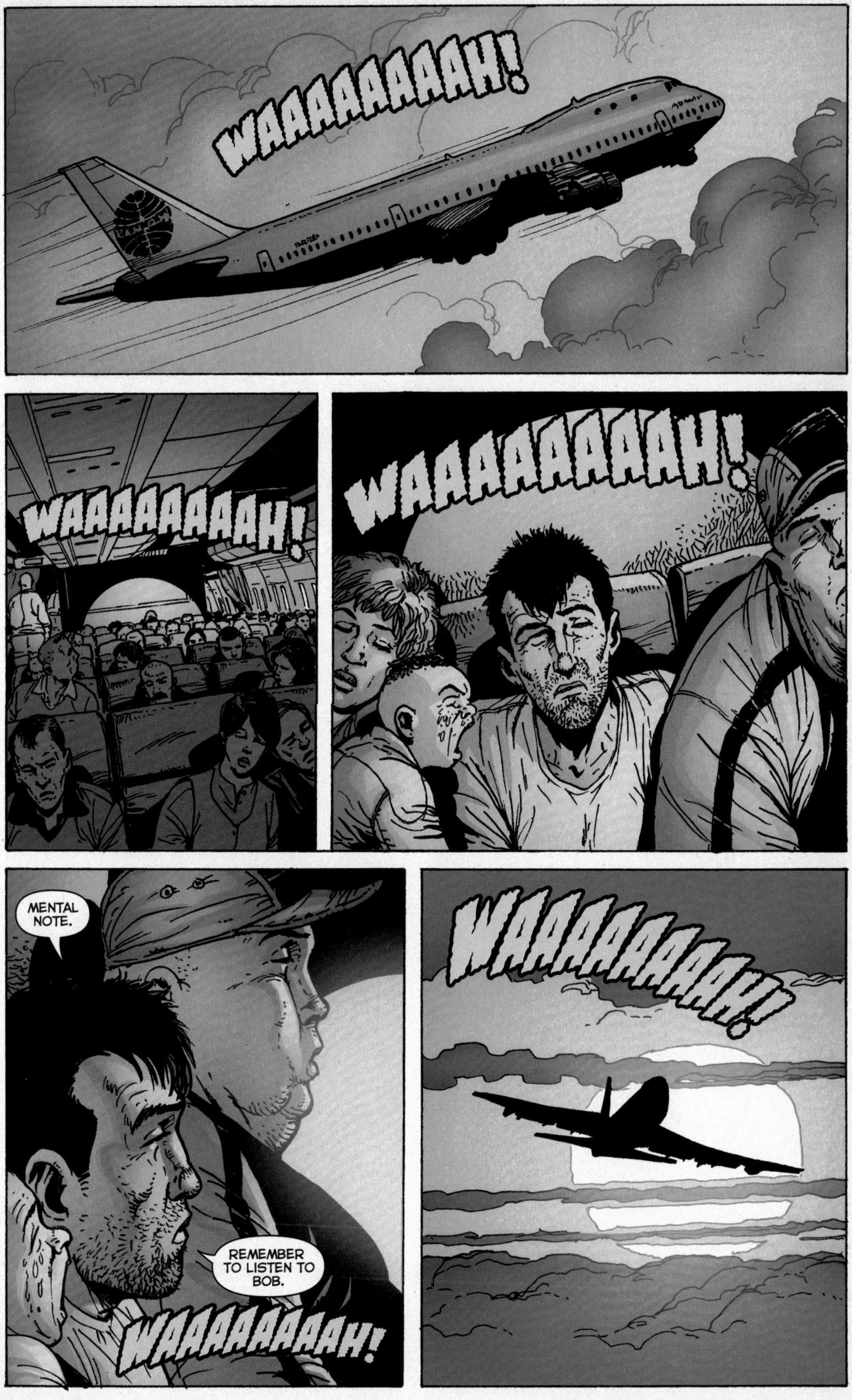

WAAAAAAAAH!
WAAAAAAAAAH!
WAAAAAAAAAAH!
MENTAL NOTE.
REMEMBER TO LISTEN TO BOB.
WAAAAAAAAH!
WAAAAAAAAAAH!

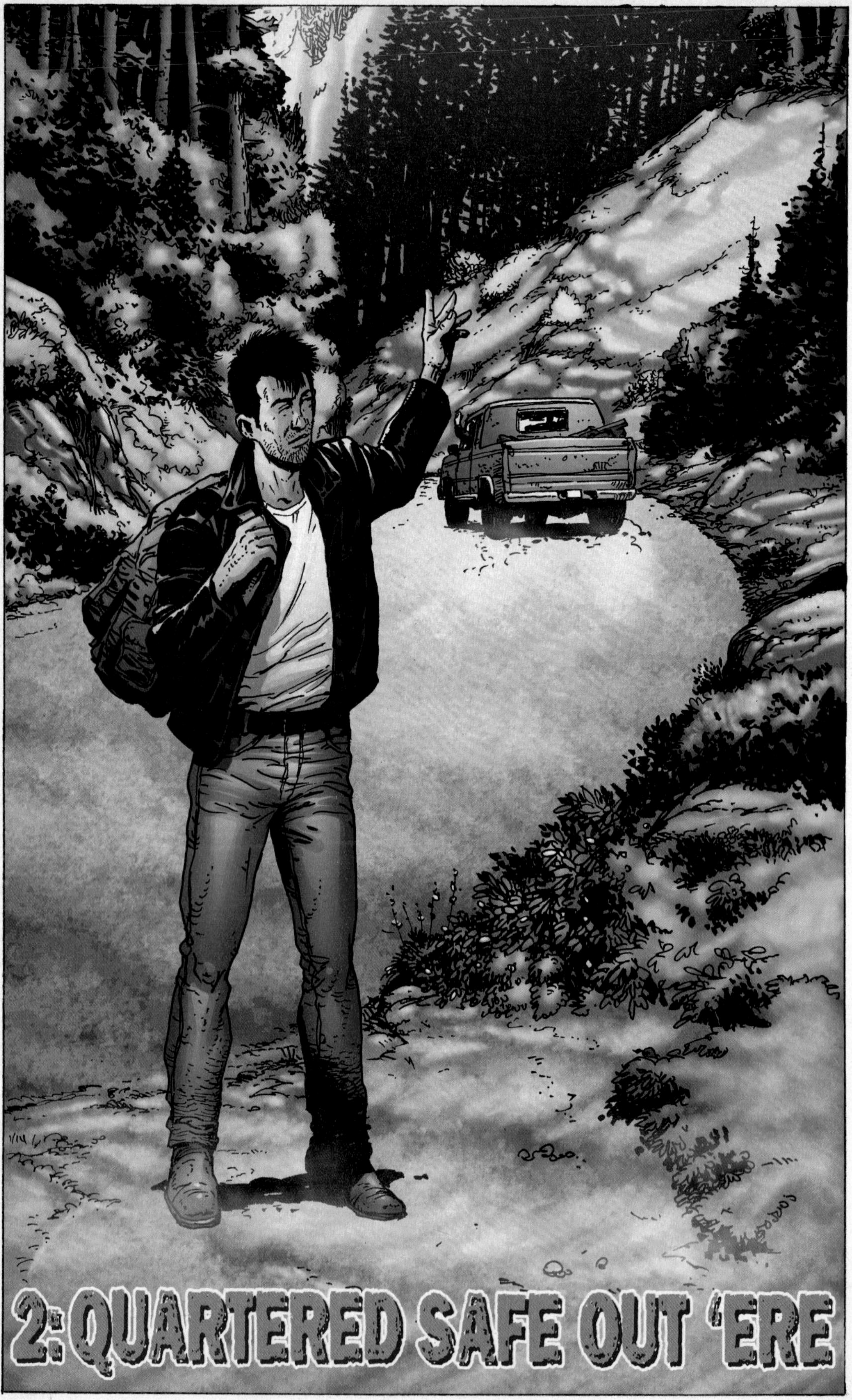
2: QUARTERED SAFE OUT 'ERE

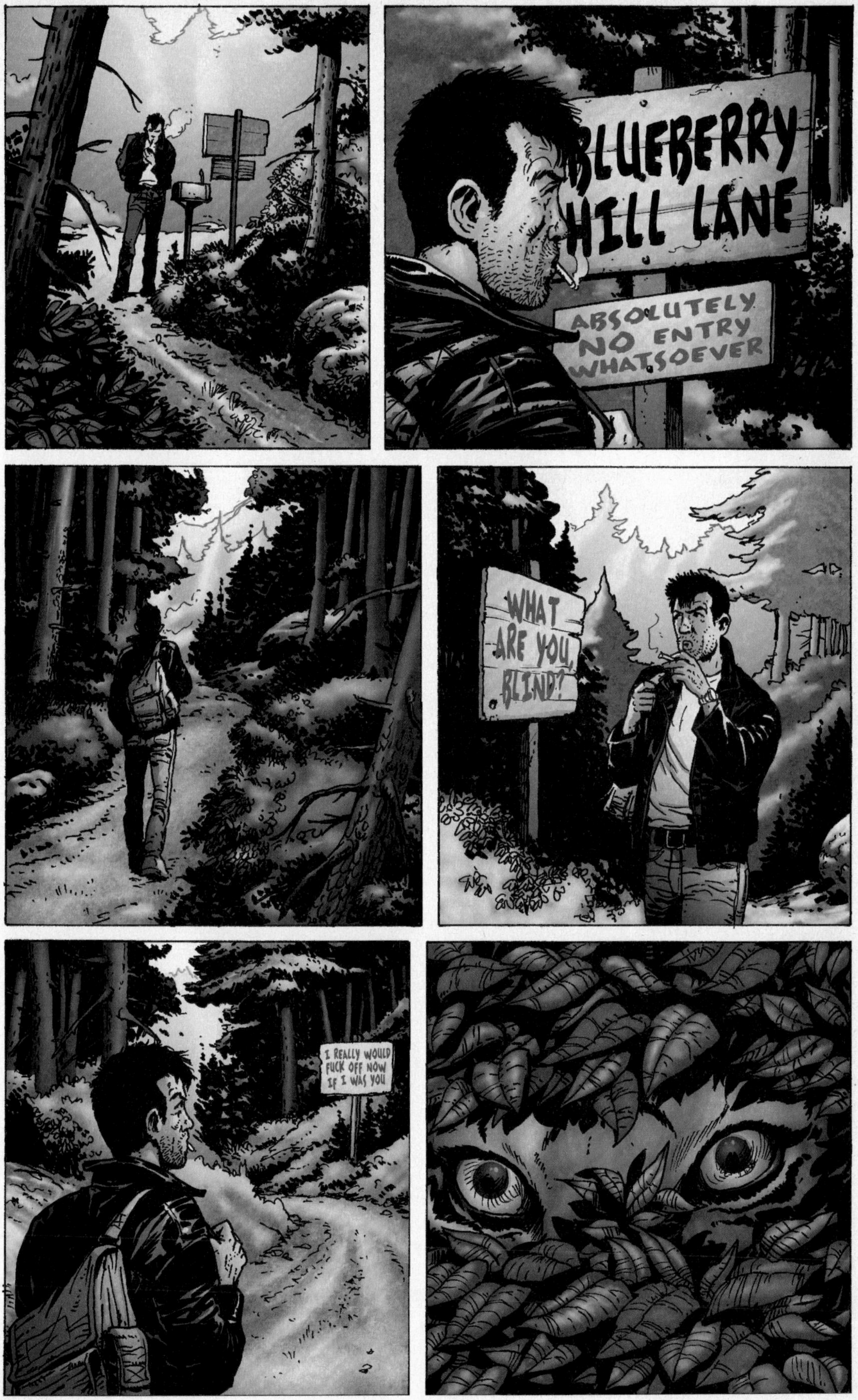
BLUEBERRY HILL LANE
ABSOLUTELY NO ENTRY WHATSOEVER
WHAT ARE YOU, BLIND?
I REALLY WOULD FUCK OFF NOW IF I WAS YOU

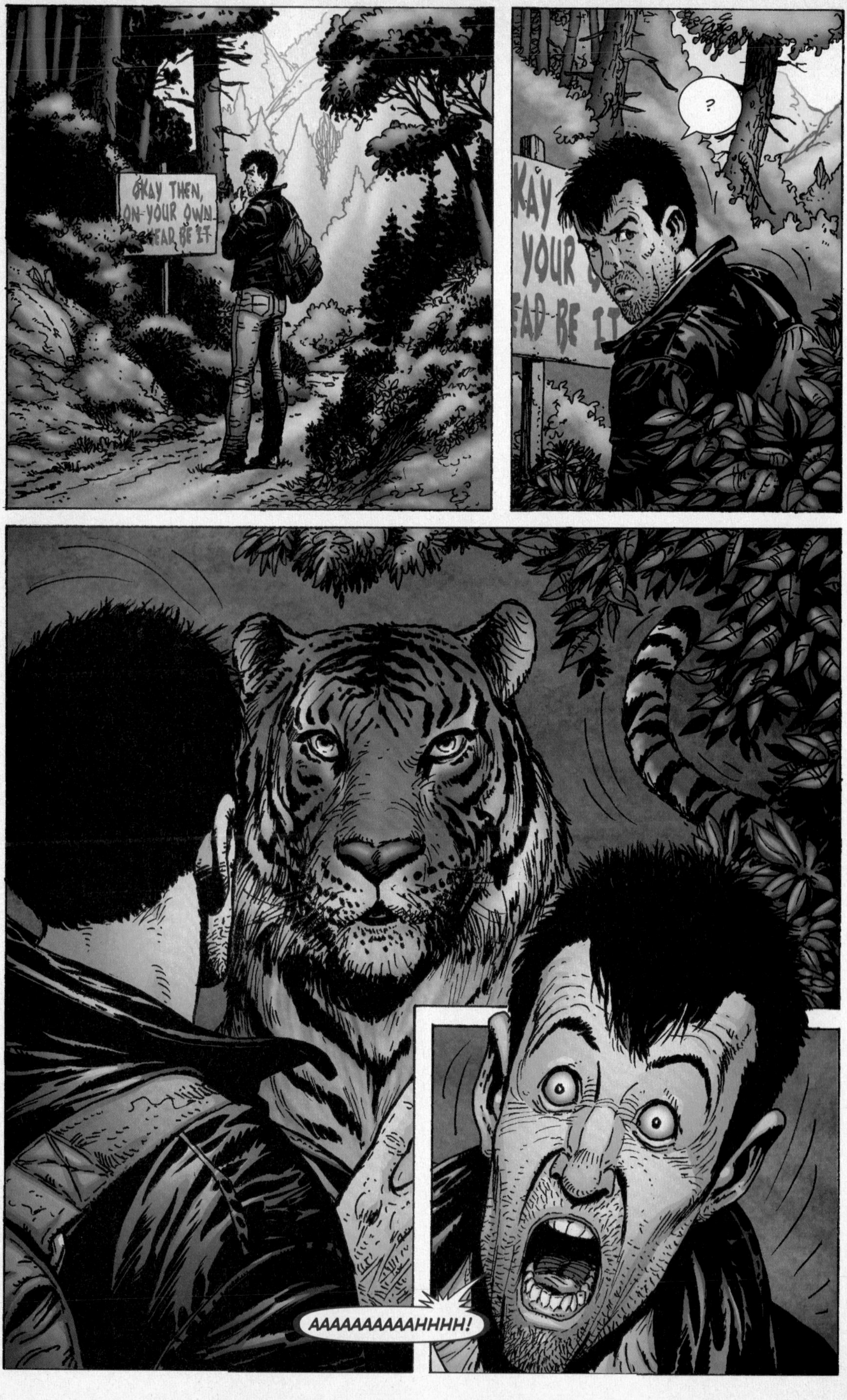

OKAY THEN,
ON YOUR OWN
HEAD BE IT
?
AAAAAAAAAAHHHH!

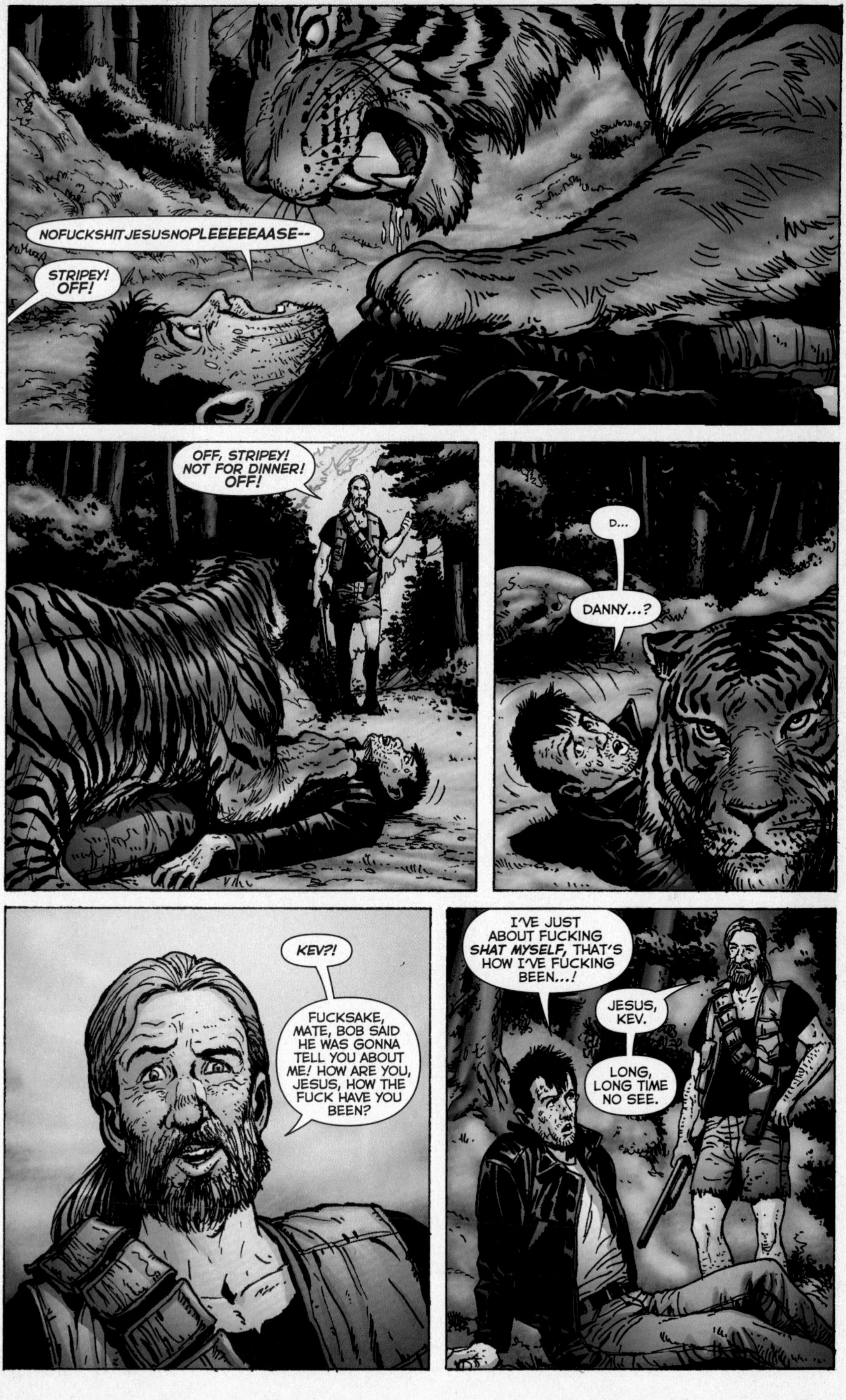
NOFUCKSHITJESUSNOPLEEEEEAASE--
STRIPEY! OFF!
OFF, STRIPEY! NOT FOR DINNER! OFF!
D...
DANNY...?
KEV?!
FUCKSAKE, MATE, BOB SAID HE WAS GONNA TELL YOU ABOUT ME! HOW ARE YOU, JESUS, HOW THE FUCK HAVE YOU BEEN?
I'VE JUST ABOUT FUCKING *SHAT MYSELF,* THAT'S HOW I'VE FUCKING BEEN...!
JESUS, KEV.
LONG, LONG TIME NO SEE.

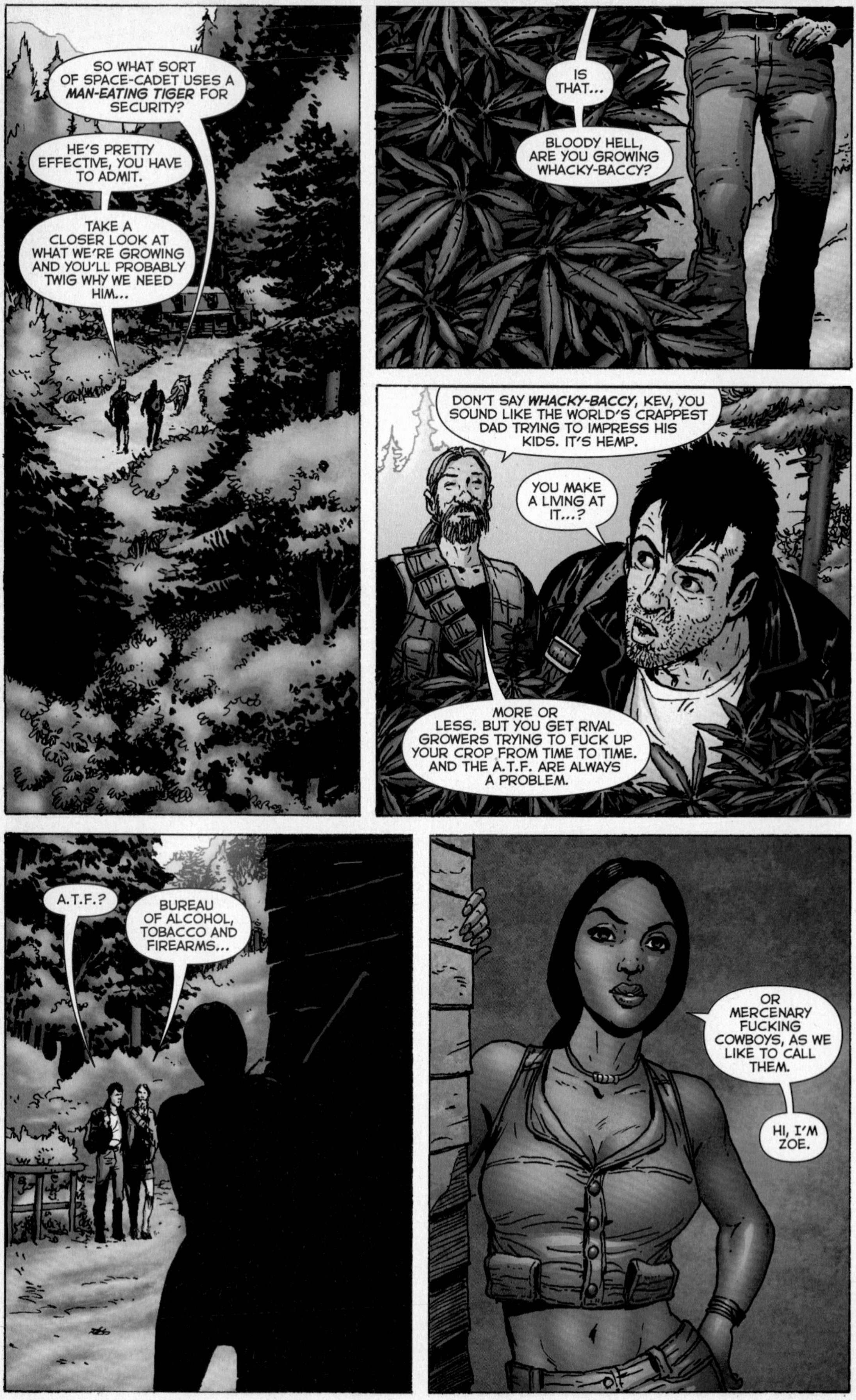
SO WHAT SORT OF SPACE-CADET USES A MAN-EATING TIGER FOR SECURITY?
HE'S PRETTY EFFECTIVE, YOU HAVE TO ADMIT.
TAKE A CLOSER LOOK AT WHAT WE'RE GROWING AND YOU'LL PROBABLY TWIG WHY WE NEED HIM...
IS THAT...
BLOODY HELL, ARE YOU GROWING WHACKY-BACCY?
DON'T SAY WHACKY-BACCY, KEV, YOU SOUND LIKE THE WORLD'S CRAPPEST DAD TRYING TO IMPRESS HIS KIDS. IT'S HEMP.
YOU MAKE A LIVING AT IT...?
MORE OR LESS. BUT YOU GET RIVAL GROWERS TRYING TO FUCK UP YOUR CROP FROM TIME TO TIME. AND THE A.T.F. ARE ALWAYS A PROBLEM.
A.T.F.?
BUREAU OF ALCOHOL, TOBACCO AND FIREARMS...
OR MERCENARY FUCKING COWBOYS, AS WE LIKE TO CALL THEM.
HI, I'M ZOE.

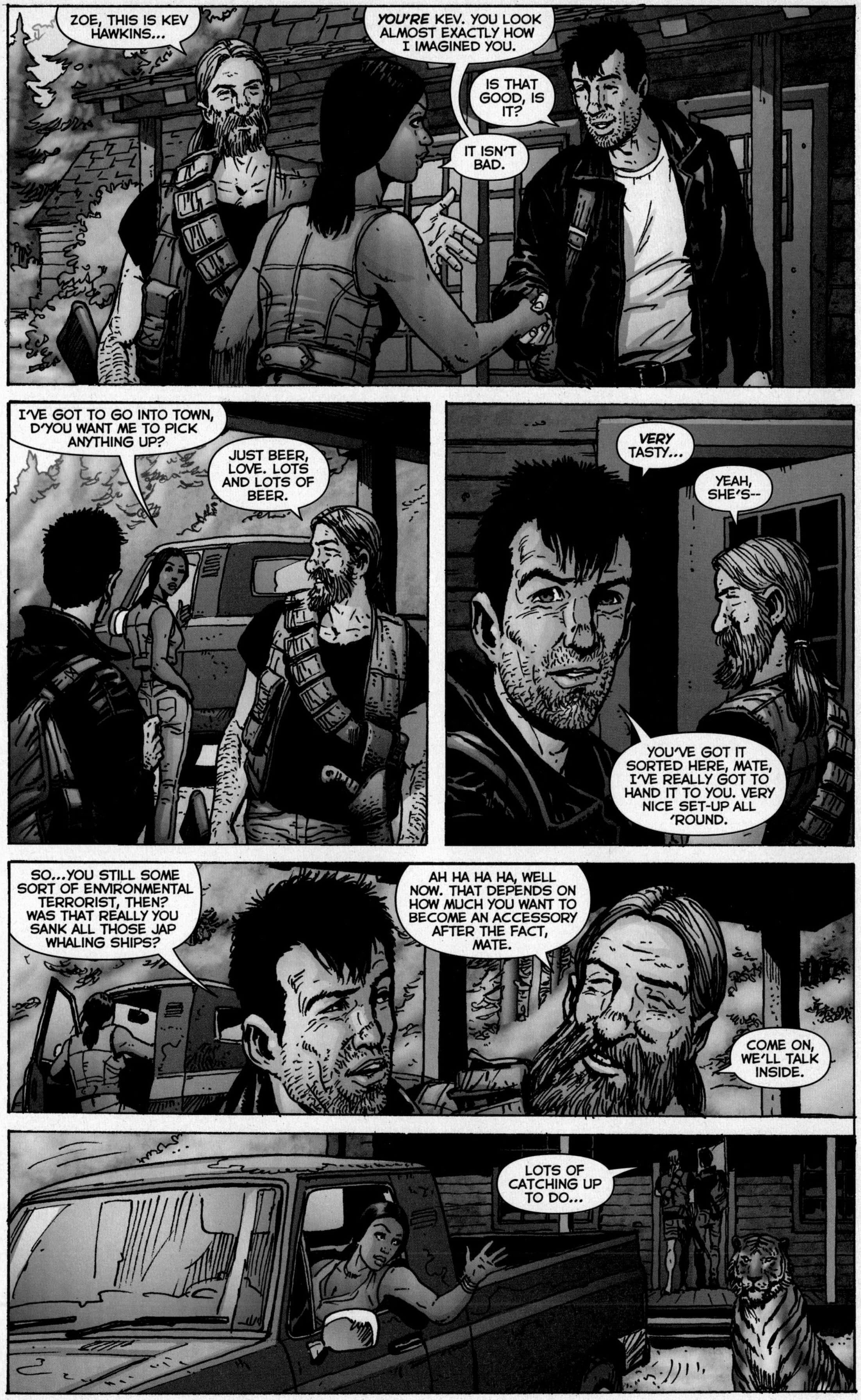
ZOE, THIS IS KEV HAWKINS...
YOU'RE KEV. YOU LOOK ALMOST EXACTLY HOW I IMAGINED YOU.
IS THAT GOOD, IS IT?
IT ISN'T BAD.
I'VE GOT TO GO INTO TOWN, D'YOU WANT ME TO PICK ANYTHING UP?
JUST BEER, LOVE. LOTS AND LOTS OF BEER.
VERY TASTY...
YEAH, SHE'S--
YOU'VE GOT IT SORTED HERE, MATE, I'VE REALLY GOT TO HAND IT TO YOU. VERY NICE SET-UP ALL 'ROUND.
SO...YOU STILL SOME SORT OF ENVIRONMENTAL TERRORIST, THEN? WAS THAT REALLY YOU SANK ALL THOSE JAP WHALING SHIPS?
AH HA HA HA, WELL NOW. THAT DEPENDS ON HOW MUCH YOU WANT TO BECOME AN ACCESSORY AFTER THE FACT, MATE.
COME ON, WE'LL TALK INSIDE.
LOTS OF CATCHING UP TO DO...

...BLOODY PARAS USED TO KICK THE CRAP OUT OF US EVERY TIME THEY WERE STATIONED NEAR US, THERE WERE THESE TWO BASTARDS IN PARTICULAR ALWAYS USED TO HAVE IT IN FOR ME...

THEY NEVER *GOT ME*, BUT THEM AND THEIR MATES USED TO CHASE ME ALL OVER THE PLACE. I CLIMBED A SODDING CHURCH STEEPLE ONCE TO GET AWAY FROM THEM.

SO ANYWAY, I'VE PASSED SELECTION AND I'M WANDERING AROUND STIRLING LINES HAVING A LOOK AT EVERYTHING, AND WHO DO I COME FACE TO FACE WITH...?

OH, LET ME GUESS.

THEY'D BOTH PASSED ABOUT A YEAR BEFORE I DID. BET YOU CAN'T GUESS WHO THEY WERE, THOUGH.

I WOULDN'T HAVE A CLUE...

BOB AND MICK.

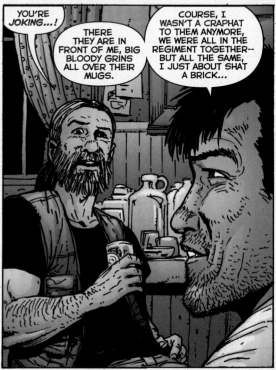

YOU'RE JOKING...!

THERE THEY ARE IN FRONT OF ME, BIG BLOODY GRINS ALL OVER THEIR MUGS.

COURSE, I WASN'T A CRAPHAT TO THEM ANYMORE, WE WERE ALL IN THE REGIMENT TOGETHER-- BUT ALL THE SAME, I JUST ABOUT SHAT A BRICK...

OH, PARDON MY FRENCH, LOVE...

DON'T SWEAT IT. YOU CAN SAY FUCK TOO, IF YOU LIKE.

GETTING A BIT LOST WITH ALL THIS ARMY TALK, THOUGH.

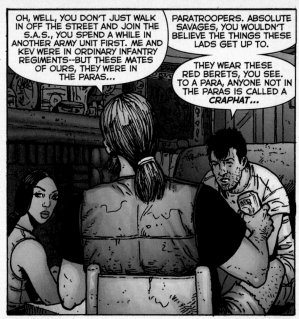

OH, WELL, YOU DON'T JUST WALK IN OFF THE STREET AND JOIN THE S.A.S., YOU SPEND A WHILE IN ANOTHER ARMY UNIT FIRST. ME AND KEV WERE IN ORDINARY INFANTRY REGIMENTS--BUT THESE MATES OF OURS, THEY WERE IN THE PARAS...

PARATROOPERS. ABSOLUTE SAVAGES, YOU WOULDN'T BELIEVE THE THINGS THESE LADS GET UP TO.

THEY WEAR THESE RED BERETS, YOU SEE. TO A PARA, ANYONE NOT IN THE PARAS IS CALLED A *CRAPHAT*...

AND WHAT SORT OF THINGS DO THEY DO?

HA! OH, JESUS.

HERE, TELL HER ABOUT *FRECKLE*, KEV.

AW, I'M NOT TELLING HER ABOUT *THAT*...!

WHAT IS IT?

YOU DON'T WANT TO KNOW, LOVE. HONESTLY.

TELL ME...!

NO, REALLY, IT'S BLOODY HORRIBLE. YOU WON'T THANK ME.

COME ON, KEV, I'M A BIG GIRL. *TELL ME*...

YOU'RE IN THE PUB WITH YOUR MATES AND YOU PUT A TURD ON THE TABLE BETWEEN TWO BEERMATS, AND YOU HIT IT AS HARD AS YOU CAN AND THE ONE WITH THE LEAST SHIT ON HIM HAS TO GET THE NEXT ROUND IN.

UH. YOU ASKED FOR IT.

UH.

SEE, NOW YOU'RE NEVER GOING TO LOOK AT ME THE SAME WAY AGAIN. I'M ALWAYS GOING TO BE THE BLOKE WHO TOLD YOU ABOUT FRECKLE.

THAT IS *SO* DISGUSTING...

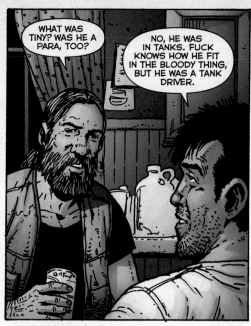

WHAT WAS TINY? WAS HE A PARA, TOO?

NO, HE WAS IN TANKS. FUCK KNOWS HOW HE FIT IN THE BLOODY THING, BUT HE WAS A TANK DRIVER.

*HHHHFFF*IT'S FUNNY LISTENING TO THE TWO OF YOU TALK ABOUT THIS STUFF. ALL THESE DIFFERENT BRANCHES, IT MAKES THE ARMY SOUND LIKE A WHOLE SOCIETY, OR SOMETHING.

OR EVEN A FAMILY.

YEAH, WITH THE PARAS AS THE WIFEBEATING DAD...

WHAT ABOUT YOU GUYS? THE S.A.S.?

WE'D BE... MMM...

WE'D BE THAT QUIET COUSIN YOU'RE NEVER QUITE SURE ABOUT. ONLY LATER ON YOU FIND OUT HE'S BRUCE WILLIS IN *DIE HARD.*

GIVE US A BLAST ON THAT, THEN...

YOU WANT TO WATCH THAT, KEV, YOU'VE HAD A BIT TO DRINK.

IT WAS NEVER REALLY YOUR POISON ANYWAY, YOU'RE GOING TO GIVE YOURSELF A WHITEY...

HA.

BOLLOCKS.

KEV?
YOU SURE, MATE?
FINE.
FINE.
HAWKINS.
DON'T BOTHER LOOKING 'ROUND, YOU IMBECILE. YOU CAN'T SEE ME, I'M SITTING IN THE BACK OF YOUR HEAD.
IT'S ME. IT'S THE BOSS. I'M SITTING HERE INSIDE YOUR SKULL WITH THAT EVER-SO-FETCHING BULLETHOLE YOU PUT BETWEEN MY EYES, AND I'M LOOKING AT YOUR PITIFUL LITTLE PEBBLE OF A BRAIN.
D'YOU KNOW WHAT I THINK I'LL DO, HAWKINS? I'M GOING TO STRAP ON MY GIANT BLACK DILDO OF DOOM AND I'M GOING TO FUCK YOUR BRAIN COMPLETELY IN HALF, YES, THAT'S WHAT I'M GOING TO DO...
FUCK OFF, FUCK RIGHT OFF, YOU'RE NOT EVEN BLOODY THERE...
OH, AREN'T I?
IT'S JUST PARANOIA FROM THAT SHIT I SMOKED, IT'S NOT REAL...
WELL, MAYBE IF YOU HADN'T SMOKED THREE JOINTS JUST TO IMPRESS ZOE, YOU WOULDN'T BE IN THIS WRETCHED CONDITION--
BUT YOU DID SO YOU ARE WHICH MEANS YOU GET TO LISTEN TO ME...
FUCK OFF...!

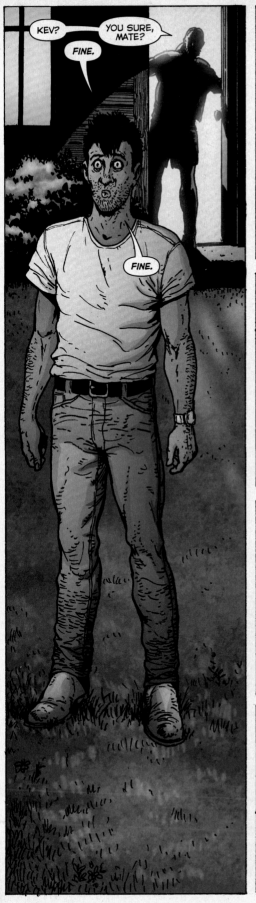

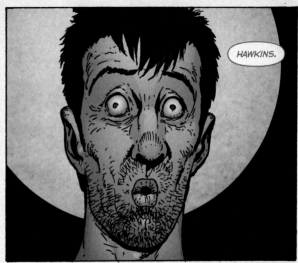

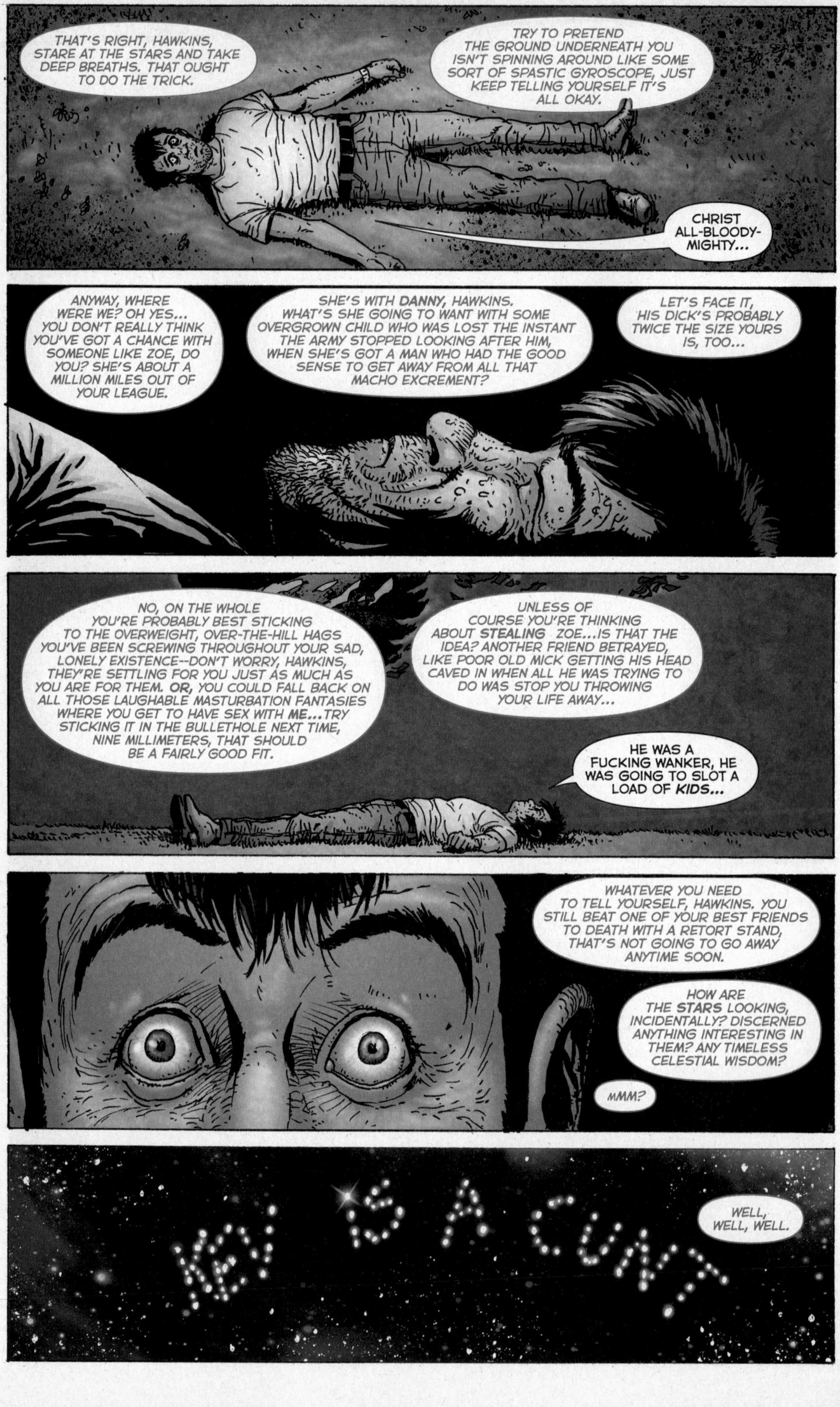
THAT'S RIGHT, HAWKINS, STARE AT THE STARS AND TAKE DEEP BREATHS. THAT OUGHT TO DO THE TRICK.
TRY TO PRETEND THE GROUND UNDERNEATH YOU ISN'T SPINNING AROUND LIKE SOME SORT OF SPASTIC GYROSCOPE, JUST KEEP TELLING YOURSELF IT'S ALL OKAY.
CHRIST ALL-BLOODY-MIGHTY...
ANYWAY, WHERE WERE WE? OH YES... YOU DON'T REALLY THINK YOU'VE GOT A CHANCE WITH SOMEONE LIKE ZOE, DO YOU? SHE'S ABOUT A MILLION MILES OUT OF YOUR LEAGUE.
SHE'S WITH **DANNY,** HAWKINS. WHAT'S SHE GOING TO WANT WITH SOME OVERGROWN CHILD WHO WAS LOST THE INSTANT THE ARMY STOPPED LOOKING AFTER HIM, WHEN SHE'S GOT A MAN WHO HAD THE GOOD SENSE TO GET AWAY FROM ALL THAT MACHO EXCREMENT?
LET'S FACE IT, HIS DICK'S PROBABLY TWICE THE SIZE YOURS IS, TOO...
NO, ON THE WHOLE YOU'RE PROBABLY BEST STICKING TO THE OVERWEIGHT, OVER-THE-HILL HAGS YOU'VE BEEN SCREWING THROUGHOUT YOUR SAD, LONELY EXISTENCE--DON'T WORRY, HAWKINS, THEY'RE SETTLING FOR YOU JUST AS MUCH AS YOU ARE FOR THEM. **OR,** YOU COULD FALL BACK ON ALL THOSE LAUGHABLE MASTURBATION FANTASIES WHERE YOU GET TO HAVE SEX WITH **ME...**TRY STICKING IT IN THE BULLETHOLE NEXT TIME, NINE MILLIMETERS, THAT SHOULD BE A FAIRLY GOOD FIT.
UNLESS OF COURSE YOU'RE THINKING ABOUT **STEALING** ZOE...IS THAT THE IDEA? ANOTHER FRIEND BETRAYED, LIKE POOR OLD MICK GETTING HIS HEAD CAVED IN WHEN ALL HE WAS TRYING TO DO WAS STOP YOU THROWING YOUR LIFE AWAY...
HE WAS A FUCKING WANKER, HE WAS GOING TO SLOT A LOAD OF **KIDS...**
WHATEVER YOU NEED TO TELL YOURSELF, HAWKINS. YOU STILL BEAT ONE OF YOUR BEST FRIENDS TO DEATH WITH A RETORT STAND, THAT'S NOT GOING TO GO AWAY ANYTIME SOON.
HOW ARE THE **STARS** LOOKING, INCIDENTALLY? DISCERNED ANYTHING INTERESTING IN THEM? ANY TIMELESS CELESTIAL WISDOM?
MMM?
KEV IS A CUNT
WELL, WELL, WELL.

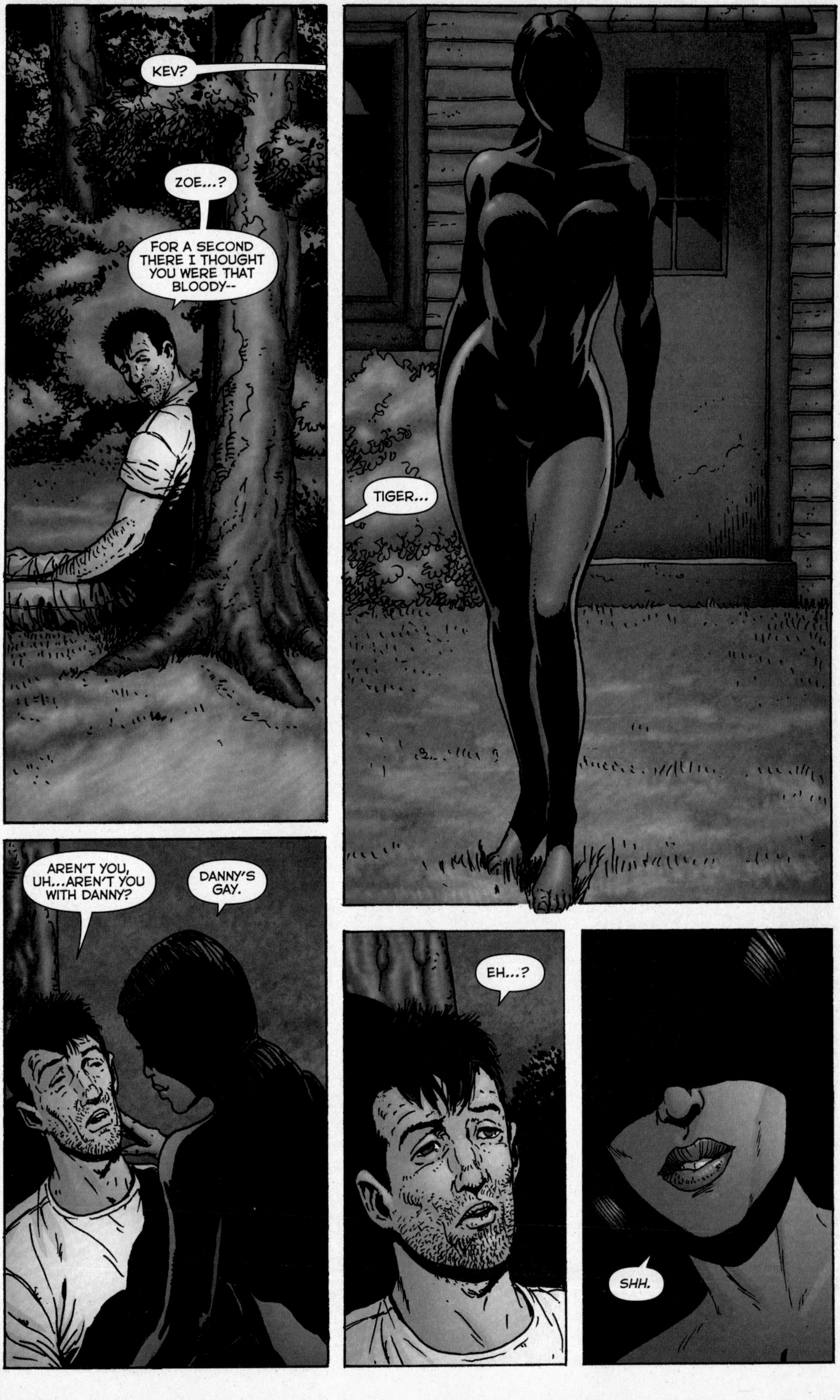
KEV?
ZOE...?
FOR A SECOND THERE I THOUGHT YOU WERE THAT BLOODY--
TIGER...
AREN'T YOU, UH...AREN'T YOU WITH DANNY?
DANNY'S GAY.
EH...?
SHH.

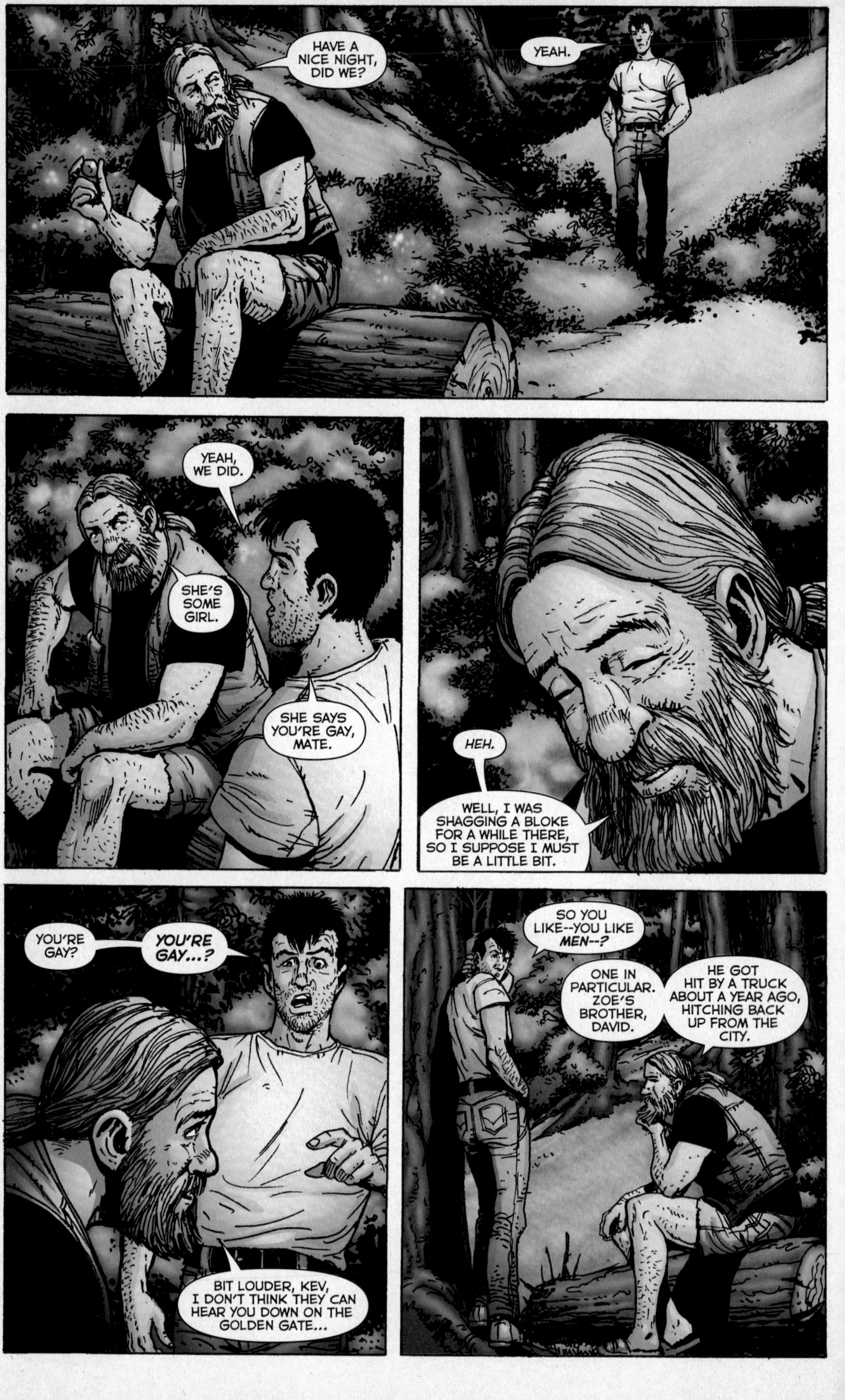
HAVE A NICE NIGHT, DID WE?
YEAH.
YEAH, WE DID.
SHE'S SOME GIRL.
SHE SAYS YOU'RE GAY, MATE.
HEH.
WELL, I WAS SHAGGING A BLOKE FOR A WHILE THERE, SO I SUPPOSE I MUST BE A LITTLE BIT.
YOU'RE GAY?
YOU'RE GAY...?
BIT LOUDER, KEV, I DON'T THINK THEY CAN HEAR YOU DOWN ON THE GOLDEN GATE...
SO YOU LIKE--YOU LIKE MEN--?
ONE IN PARTICULAR. ZOE'S BROTHER, DAVID.
HE GOT HIT BY A TRUCK ABOUT A YEAR AGO, HITCHING BACK UP FROM THE CITY.

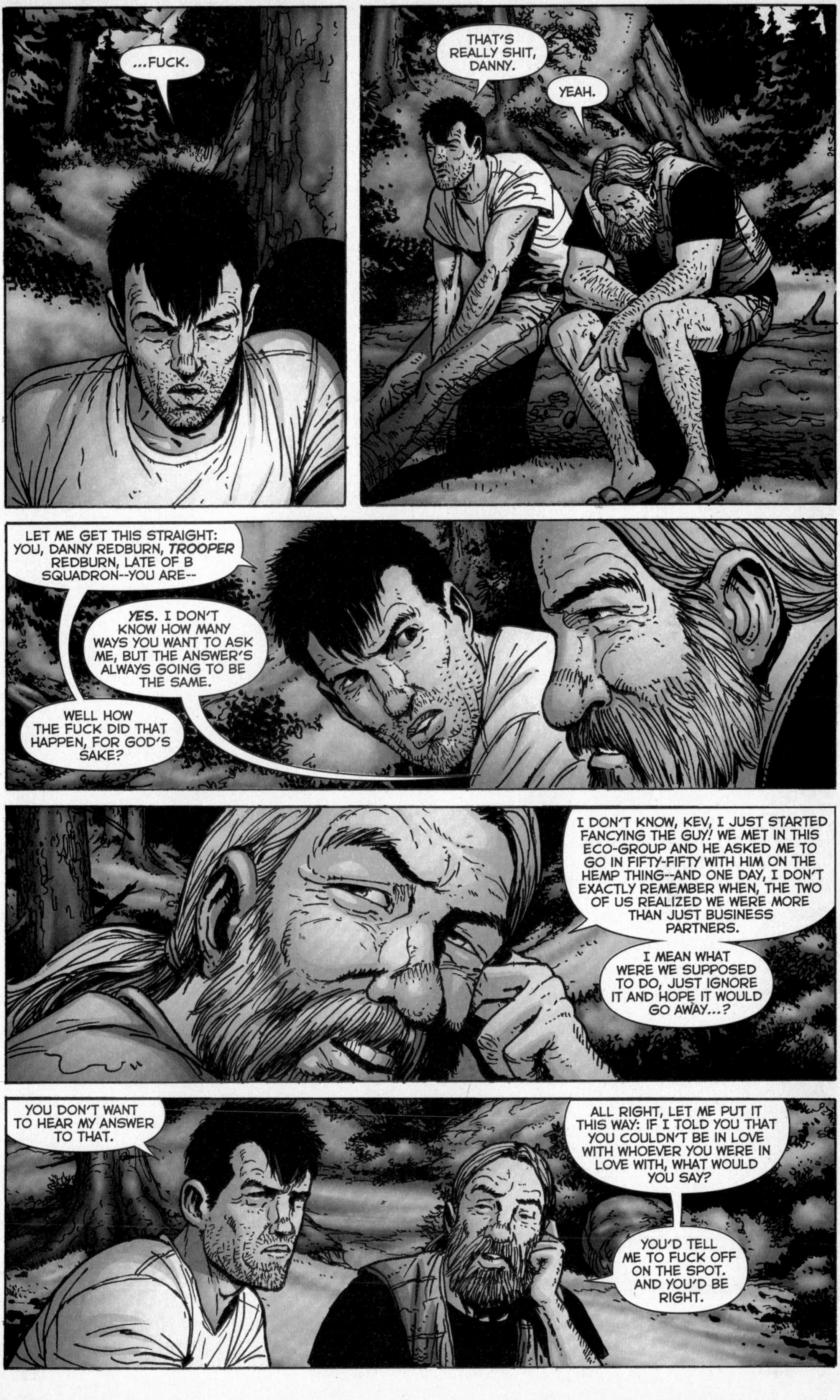
...FUCK.
THAT'S REALLY SHIT, DANNY.
YEAH.
LET ME GET THIS STRAIGHT: YOU, DANNY REDBURN, *TROOPER* REDBURN, LATE OF B SQUADRON--YOU ARE--
YES. I DON'T KNOW HOW MANY WAYS YOU WANT TO ASK ME, BUT THE ANSWER'S ALWAYS GOING TO BE THE SAME.
WELL HOW THE FUCK DID THAT HAPPEN, FOR GOD'S SAKE?
I DON'T KNOW, KEV, I JUST STARTED FANCYING THE GUY! WE MET IN THIS ECO-GROUP AND HE ASKED ME TO GO IN FIFTY-FIFTY WITH HIM ON THE HEMP THING--AND ONE DAY, I DON'T EXACTLY REMEMBER WHEN, THE TWO OF US REALIZED WE WERE MORE THAN JUST BUSINESS PARTNERS.
I MEAN WHAT WERE WE SUPPOSED TO DO, JUST IGNORE IT AND HOPE IT WOULD GO AWAY...?
YOU DON'T WANT TO HEAR MY ANSWER TO THAT.
ALL RIGHT, LET ME PUT IT THIS WAY: IF I TOLD YOU THAT YOU COULDN'T BE IN LOVE WITH WHOEVER YOU WERE IN LOVE WITH, WHAT WOULD YOU SAY?
YOU'D TELL ME TO FUCK OFF ON THE SPOT. AND YOU'D BE RIGHT.

IT'S NOT THE SAME.

WHY, BECAUSE WITH YOU IT'D BE A BIRD?

IT'S JUST DIFFERENT, THAT'S ALL.

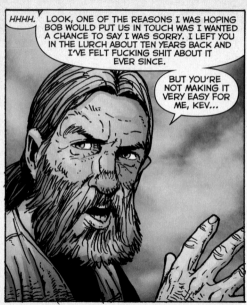

HHHH. LOOK, ONE OF THE REASONS I WAS HOPING BOB WOULD PUT US IN TOUCH WAS I WANTED A CHANCE TO SAY I WAS SORRY. I LEFT YOU IN THE LURCH ABOUT TEN YEARS BACK AND I'VE FELT FUCKING SHIT ABOUT IT EVER SINCE.

BUT YOU'RE NOT MAKING IT VERY EASY FOR ME, KEV...

WHAT'RE YOU TALKING ABOUT?

YOU KNOW, STRIPEY EATING THE GOVERNMENT BLOKE. AND ME LEGGING IT.

OH, BOLLOCKS TO THAT.

YOU WERE ABSOLUTELY RIGHT ABOUT THAT. IF I'D HAD ANY SENSE I'D HAVE FUCKED OFF RIGHT ALONG WITH YOU, I KNOW THAT NOW.

BUT... THIS...

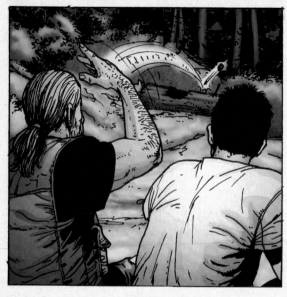

YOU AIMING AT THE HOLE?

YEAH.

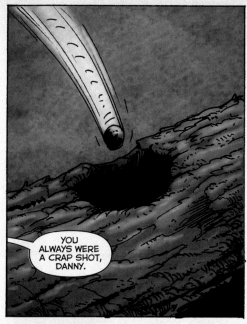

YOU ALWAYS WERE A CRAP SHOT, DANNY.

I FAILED TO LEARN FROM THE MASTER.

D'YOU REMEMBER THAT TIME IN, WHERE WAS IT IN AFRICA, WHERE WE WERE TRAINING UP THOSE MILITIA LADS?

YOUR LOT WERE DIABOLICAL, YOU COULDN'T DO ANYTHING WITH THEM...

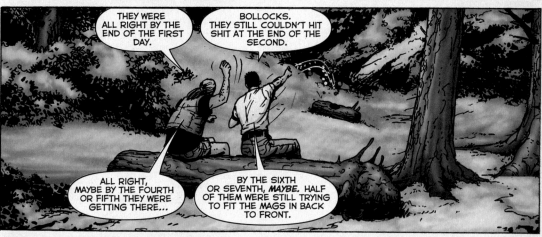

THEY WERE ALL RIGHT BY THE END OF THE FIRST DAY.

BOLLOCKS. THEY STILL COULDN'T HIT SHIT AT THE END OF THE SECOND.

ALL RIGHT, MAYBE BY THE FOURTH OR FIFTH THEY WERE GETTING THERE...

BY THE SIXTH OR SEVENTH, *MAYBE*. HALF OF THEM WERE STILL TRYING TO FIT THE MAGS IN BACK TO FRONT.

D'YOU REMEMBER WHAT THEY DID ON THE LAST DAY?

YEAH.

THEY STEAMED INTO THE NEXT VILLAGE, JUST DOWN THE ROAD...

AND THEY KILLED EVERY MAN, WOMAN AND CHILD THEY COULD FIND.

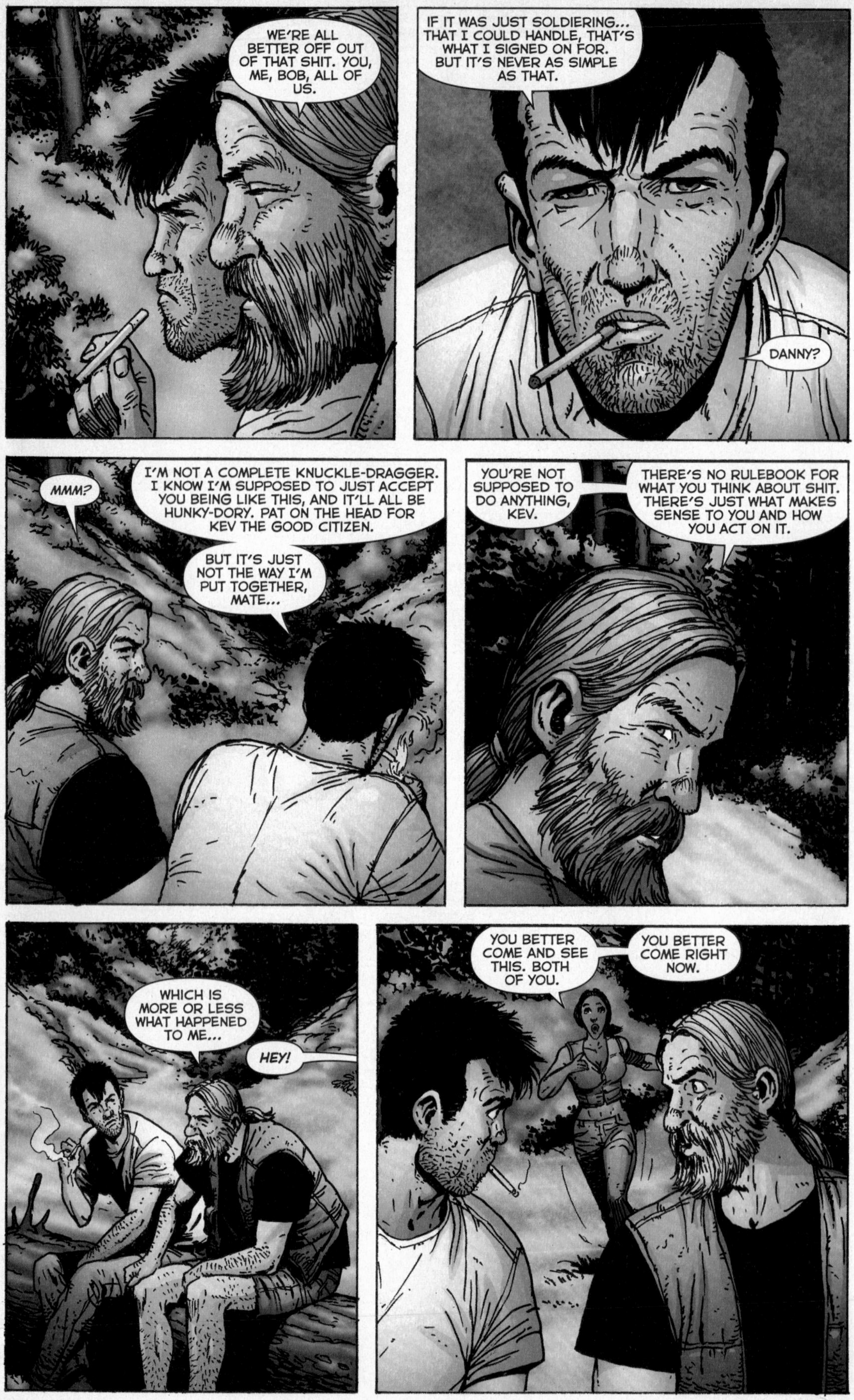

WE'RE ALL BETTER OFF OUT OF THAT SHIT. YOU, ME, BOB, ALL OF US.
IF IT WAS JUST SOLDIERING... THAT I COULD HANDLE, THAT'S WHAT I SIGNED ON FOR. BUT IT'S NEVER AS SIMPLE AS THAT.
DANNY?
MMM?
I'M NOT A COMPLETE KNUCKLE-DRAGGER. I KNOW I'M SUPPOSED TO JUST ACCEPT YOU BEING LIKE THIS, AND IT'LL ALL BE HUNKY-DORY. PAT ON THE HEAD FOR KEV THE GOOD CITIZEN.
BUT IT'S JUST NOT THE WAY I'M PUT TOGETHER, MATE...
YOU'RE NOT SUPPOSED TO DO ANYTHING, KEV.
THERE'S NO RULEBOOK FOR WHAT YOU THINK ABOUT SHIT. THERE'S JUST WHAT MAKES SENSE TO YOU AND HOW YOU ACT ON IT.
WHICH IS MORE OR LESS WHAT HAPPENED TO ME...
HEY!
YOU BETTER COME AND SEE THIS. BOTH OF YOU.
YOU BETTER COME RIGHT NOW.

THIS WAS ON THE B.B.C. WEBSITE. I DOWNLOADED IT.

I'M SORRY, GUYS.

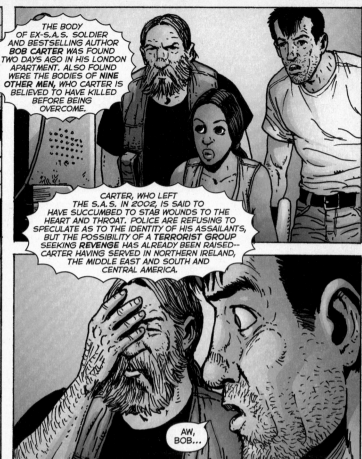

THE BODY OF EX-S.A.S. SOLDIER AND BESTSELLING AUTHOR *BOB CARTER* WAS FOUND TWO DAYS AGO IN HIS LONDON APARTMENT. ALSO FOUND WERE THE BODIES OF *NINE OTHER MEN*, WHO CARTER IS BELIEVED TO HAVE KILLED BEFORE BEING OVERCOME.

CARTER, WHO LEFT THE S.A.S. IN 2002, IS SAID TO HAVE SUCCUMBED TO STAB WOUNDS TO THE HEART AND THROAT. POLICE ARE REFUSING TO SPECULATE AS TO THE IDENTITY OF HIS ASSAILANTS, BUT THE POSSIBILITY OF A *TERRORIST GROUP* SEEKING *REVENGE* HAS ALREADY BEEN RAISED-- CARTER HAVING SERVED IN NORTHERN IRELAND, THE MIDDLE EAST AND SOUTH AND CENTRAL AMERICA.

AW, BOB...

AW NO, MATE, NO, NO...

IS IT *PIRA?*

IN A RELATED STORY, *MICHAEL SEBASTIAN*, A SENIOR OFFICIAL AT *M.I.5*, WAS ALSO FOUND DEAD YESTERDAY: *DECAPITATED IN HIS CAR* OUTSIDE HIS HOME IN WESTMINSTER...

AN M.I.5 SPOKESMAN WOULD NOT COMMENT ON A POSSIBLE *LINK* BETWEEN THE TWO MURDERS--BUT SEBASTIAN IS REPUTED TO HAVE SPENT TIME WITH THE S.A.S. AS A LIAISON OFFICER...

FUCK.

SPORT PLAYER WEATHER PLAYER RADIO
News Player
NEWS HEADLINES
NEWS

PLAYER SIZE | NORMAL VIDEO & TEXT | NORMAL VIDEO ONLY | DOUBLE VIDEO ONLY | FULL SIZE VIDEO ONLY

SPECIAL COVERAGE

WHAT?

I *KNEW* I'D SEEN THAT ARSEHOLE BEFORE SOMEWHERE...!

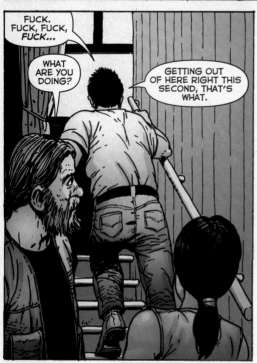

FUCK. FUCK, FUCK, *FUCK...*

WHAT ARE YOU DOING?

GETTING OUT OF HERE RIGHT THIS SECOND, THAT'S WHAT.

WHY...?

BECAUSE OTHERWISE I'M GOING TO BRING A TON OF SHIT DOWN ON YOUR HEADS. I'M GOING TO GET THE PAIR OF YOU KILLED.

BOB AND THAT SEBASTIAN NOBBER WERE ALL THAT WAS LEFT OF THE BIGGEST GANGFUCK IN THE HISTORY OF THE REGIMENT-- ALL EXCEPT FOR GUESS BLOODY WHO...

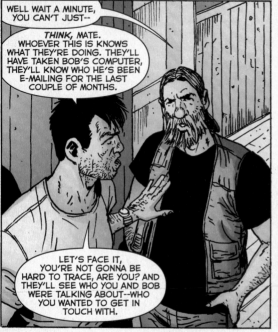

WELL WAIT A MINUTE, YOU CAN'T JUST--

THINK, MATE. WHOEVER THIS IS KNOWS WHAT THEY'RE DOING. THEY'LL HAVE TAKEN BOB'S COMPUTER, THEY'LL KNOW WHO HE'S BEEN E-MAILING FOR THE LAST COUPLE OF MONTHS.

LET'S FACE IT, YOU'RE NOT GONNA BE HARD TO TRACE, ARE YOU? AND THEY'LL SEE WHO YOU AND BOB WERE TALKING ABOUT--WHO YOU WANTED TO GET IN TOUCH WITH.

THEY COULD BE ON THEIR WAY HERE RIGHT NOW, YOU SHOULD BOTH GET THE FUCK OUT AND NOT COME BACK FOR ABOUT A MONTH...

WAIT!

EH?

I'M NOT LETTING YOU JUST WALK OUT OF HERE TO YOUR DEATH, YOU ARSEHOLE! THERE'S NO WAY YOU'RE GOING TO TAKE THESE CUNTS ON BY YOURSELF, NO FUCKING WAY IN HELL!

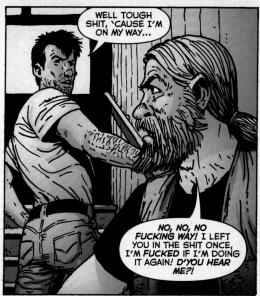

WELL TOUGH SHIT, 'CAUSE I'M ON MY WAY...

NO, NO, NO FUCKING WAY! I LEFT YOU IN THE SHIT ONCE, I'M FUCKED IF I'M DOING IT AGAIN! D'YOU HEAR ME?!

DANNY, THIS HAS GOT NOTHING TO DO WITH THAT, FOR FUCK'S SAKE! THIS IS--YOU DON'T EVEN WANT TO KNOW WHAT THIS IS, BELIEVE ME!

I'M GOING, OKAY? END OF STORY. I'M GOING.

THEN YOU'RE FUCKING WELL GOING THROUGH ME.

DON'T BE A PRICK, DANNY, WE BOTH KNOW HOW THAT ONE WOULD END UP.

AND WHAT ABOUT ZOE? DID YOU THINK TO ASK HER BEFORE YOU INCLUDED HER IN YOUR LITTLE SUICIDE PACT?

DANNY AND I ARE PARTNERS, KEV. THIS IS OUR PLACE.

OH, FUCK ME...!

ALL RIGHT. LOOK.

I'VE GOT SOME FILES IN MY BAG THAT BOB GAVE ME, SOME STUFF THAT MIGHT HELP WITH THIS. LET ME GO AND GET THEM AND WE'LL TALK ABOUT IT, OKAY?

JUST GIVE ME ONE MINUTE.

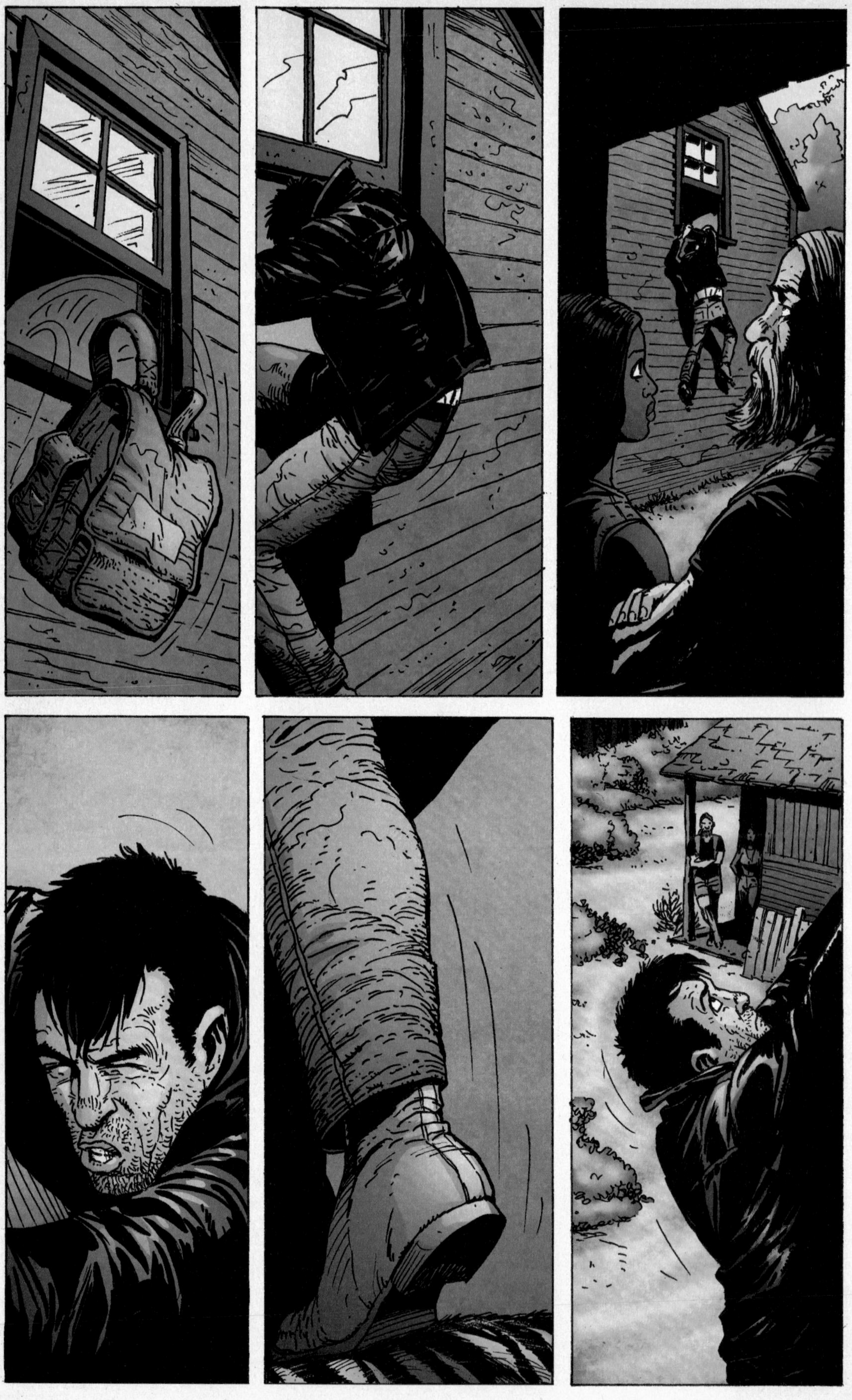

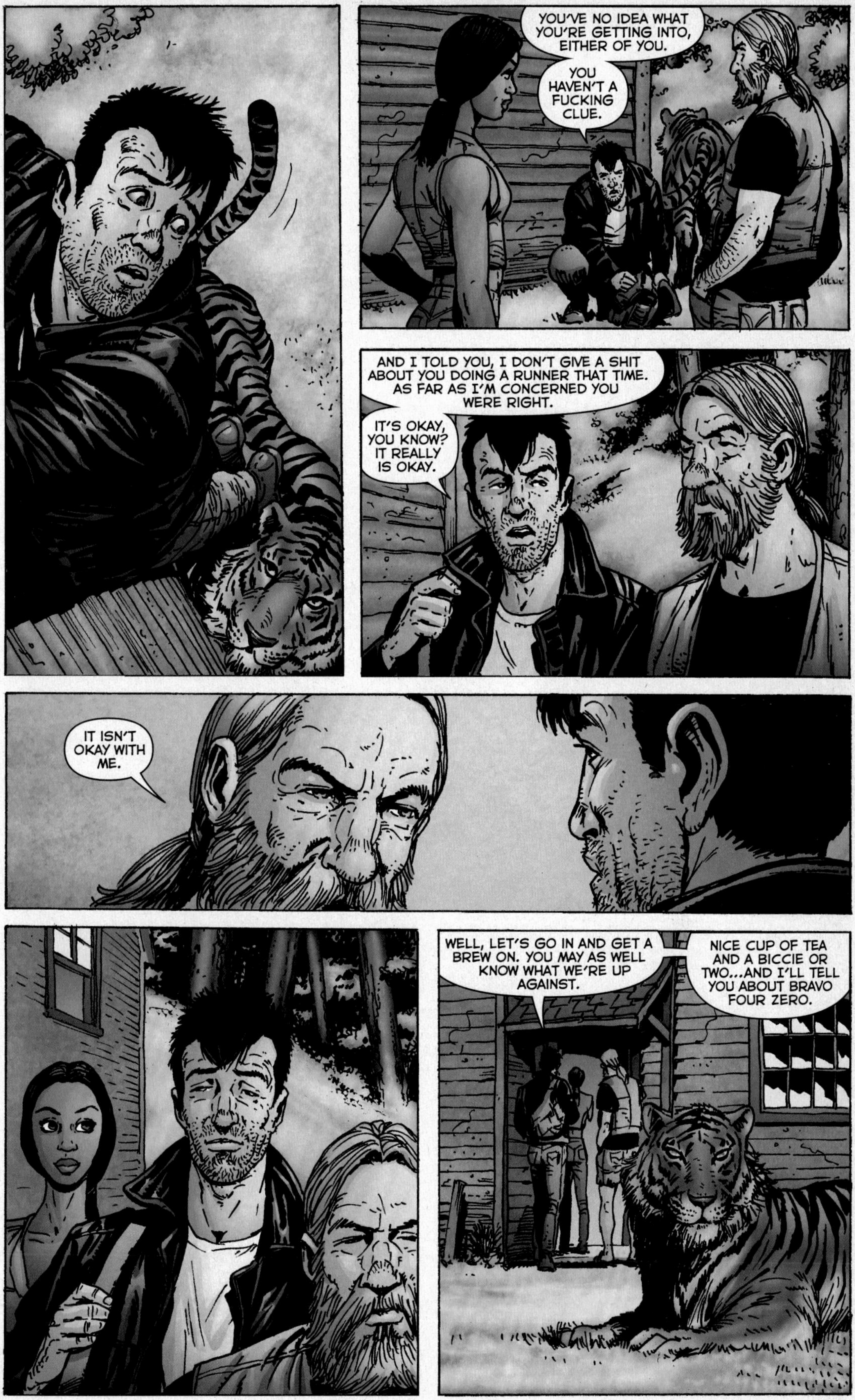
YOU'VE NO IDEA WHAT YOU'RE GETTING INTO, EITHER OF YOU.
YOU HAVEN'T A FUCKING CLUE.
AND I TOLD YOU, I DON'T GIVE A SHIT ABOUT YOU DOING A RUNNER THAT TIME. AS FAR AS I'M CONCERNED YOU WERE RIGHT.
IT'S OKAY, YOU KNOW? IT REALLY IS OKAY.
IT ISN'T OKAY WITH ME.
WELL, LET'S GO IN AND GET A BREW ON. YOU MAY AS WELL KNOW WHAT WE'RE UP AGAINST.
NICE CUP OF TEA AND A BICCIE OR TWO...AND I'LL TELL YOU ABOUT BRAVO FOUR ZERO.

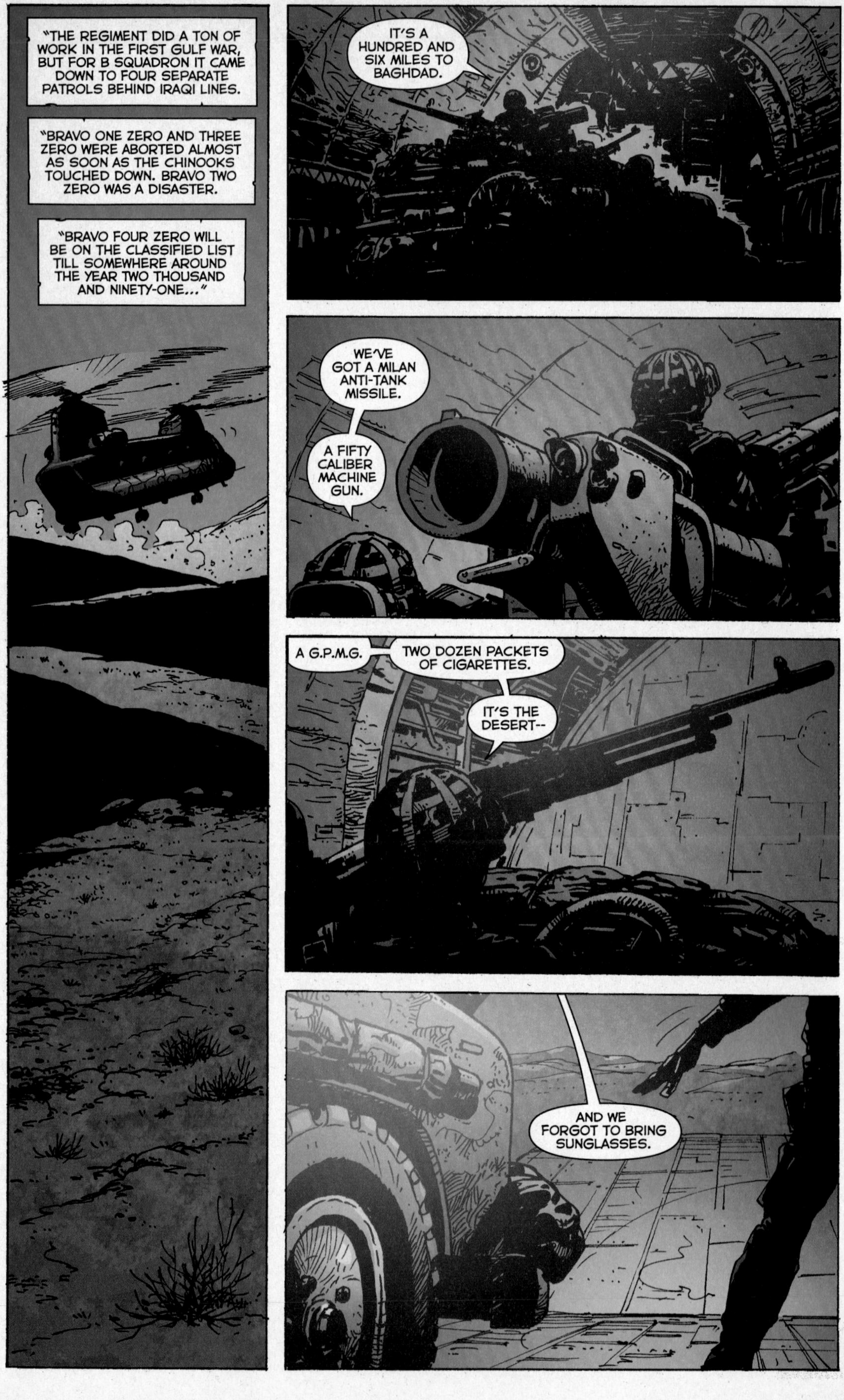
"THE REGIMENT DID A TON OF WORK IN THE FIRST GULF WAR, BUT FOR B SQUADRON IT CAME DOWN TO FOUR SEPARATE PATROLS BEHIND IRAQI LINES.
"BRAVO ONE ZERO AND THREE ZERO WERE ABORTED ALMOST AS SOON AS THE CHINOOKS TOUCHED DOWN. BRAVO TWO ZERO WAS A DISASTER.
"BRAVO FOUR ZERO WILL BE ON THE CLASSIFIED LIST TILL SOMEWHERE AROUND THE YEAR TWO THOUSAND AND NINETY-ONE..."
IT'S A HUNDRED AND SIX MILES TO BAGHDAD.
WE'VE GOT A MILAN ANTI-TANK MISSILE.
A FIFTY CALIBER MACHINE GUN.
A G.P.M.G.
TWO DOZEN PACKETS OF CIGARETTES.
IT'S THE DESERT--
AND WE FORGOT TO BRING SUNGLASSES.

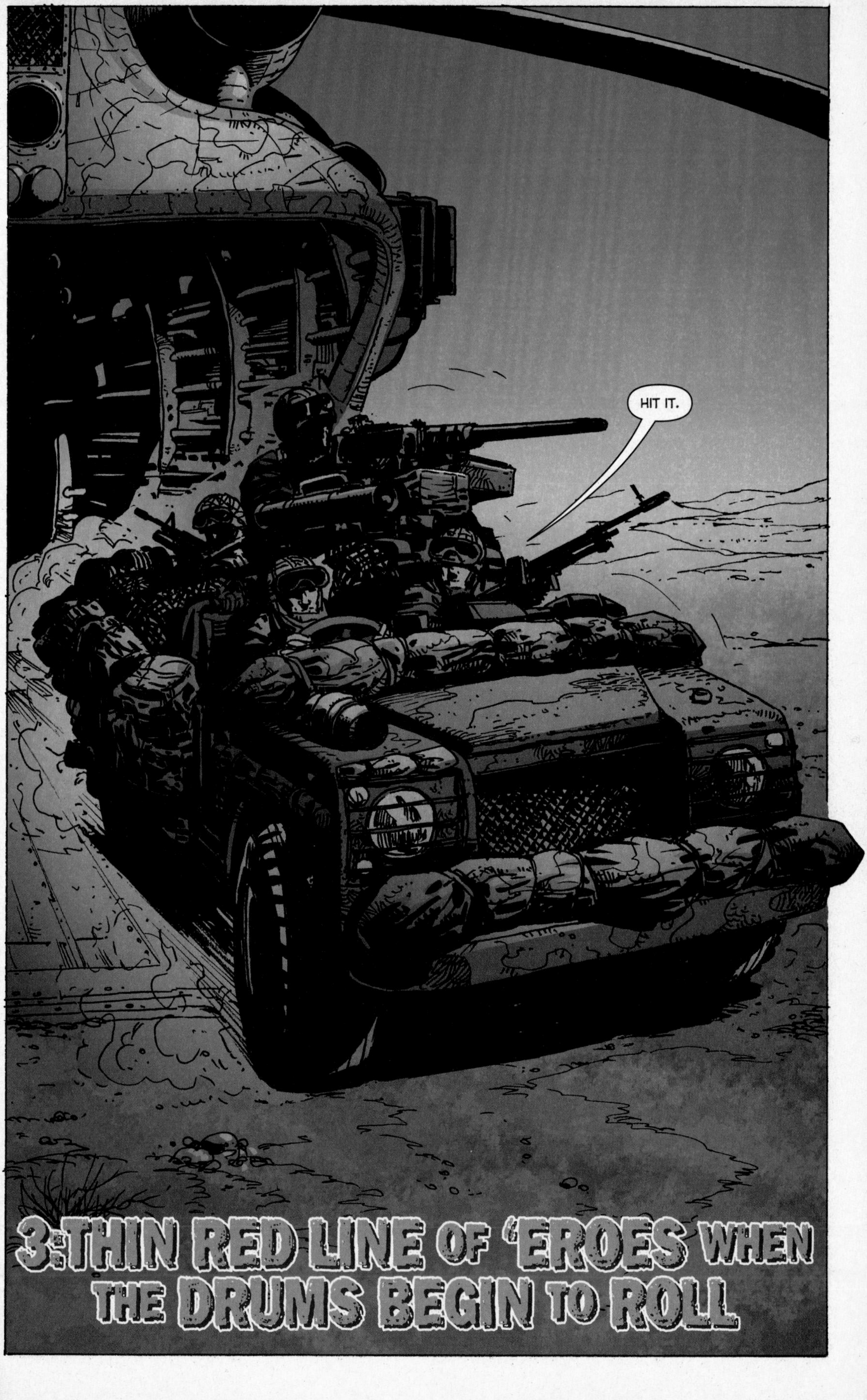
HIT IT.
3: THIN RED LINE OF 'EROES WHEN THE DRUMS BEGIN TO ROLL

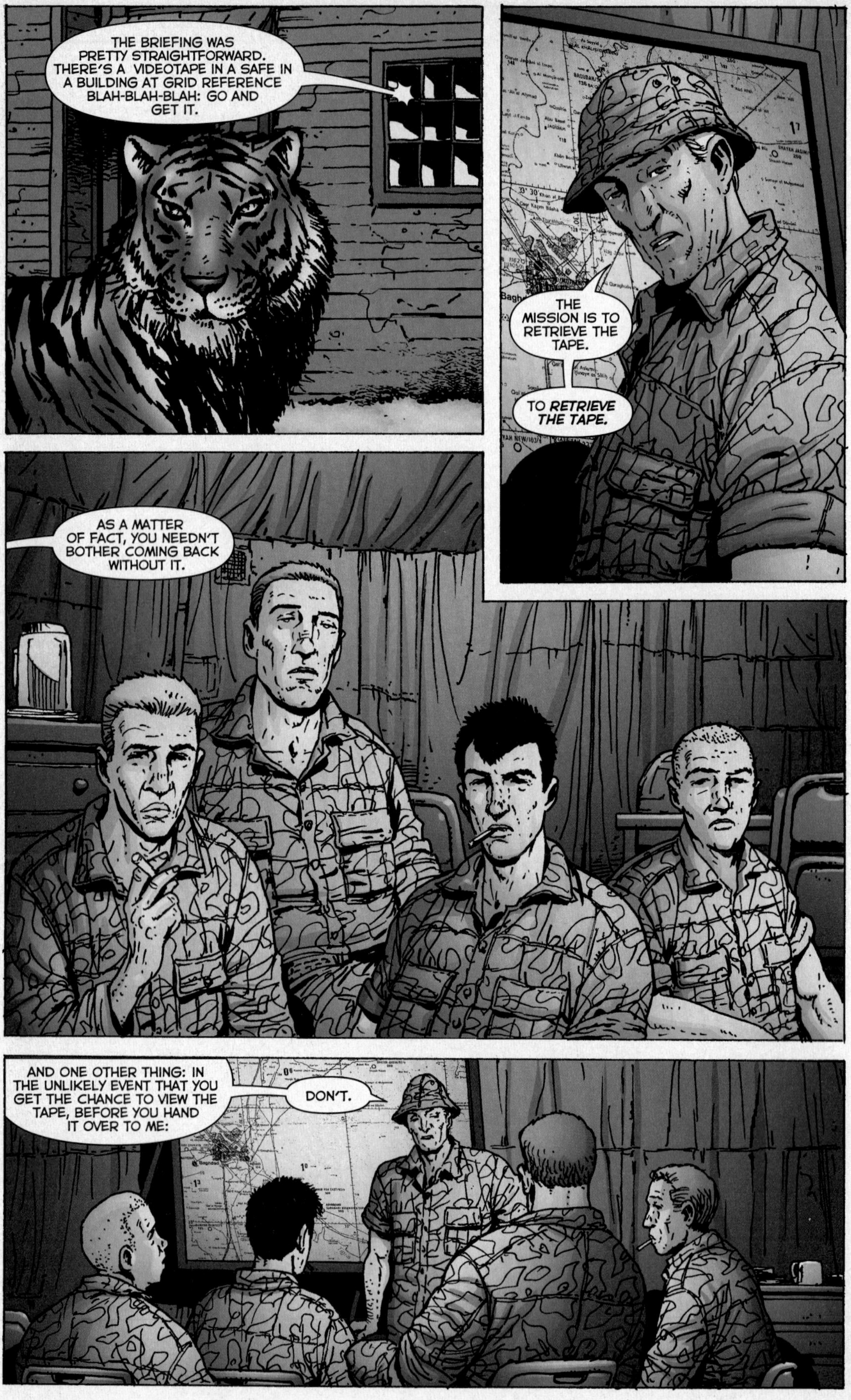
THE BRIEFING WAS PRETTY STRAIGHTFORWARD. THERE'S A VIDEOTAPE IN A SAFE IN A BUILDING AT GRID REFERENCE BLAH-BLAH-BLAH: GO AND GET IT.
THE MISSION IS TO RETRIEVE THE TAPE.
TO *RETRIEVE THE TAPE.*
AS A MATTER OF FACT, YOU NEEDN'T BOTHER COMING BACK WITHOUT IT.
AND ONE OTHER THING: IN THE UNLIKELY EVENT THAT YOU GET THE CHANCE TO VIEW THE TAPE, BEFORE YOU HAND IT OVER TO ME:
DON'T.

RIGHT. TINY, SCALEY KIT. OUR CALLSIGN'S BRAVO FOUR ZERO.

MICK, YOU MAKE SURE WE'RE PROPERLY TOOLED UP. I WANT 203s ALL 'ROUND AND ALL THE GRENADES YOU CAN FIND.

KEV-- TRANSPORT. GO AND GRAB US A DECENT ONE-TEN BEFORE THOSE A SQUADRON NOBBERS NICK THE LOT.

QUESTIONS?

WONDER WHAT'S ON IT?

YOUR MUM WANKING OFF A HORSE, KEV.

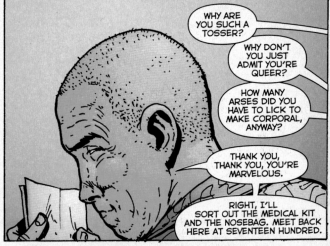

WHY ARE YOU SUCH A TOSSER?

WHY DON'T YOU JUST ADMIT YOU'RE QUEER?

HOW MANY ARSES DID YOU HAVE TO LICK TO MAKE CORPORAL, ANYWAY?

THANK YOU, THANK YOU, YOU'RE MARVELOUS.

RIGHT, I'LL SORT OUT THE MEDICAL KIT AND THE NOSEBAG. MEET BACK HERE AT SEVENTEEN HUNDRED.

THIS WAS LATE JANUARY OF NINETY-ONE. THE COALITION WAS KICKING THE SHIT OUT OF IRAQ WITH AIRSTRIKES, BUT THE GROUND TROOPS STILL HADN'T GONE IN.

THERE WAS A VERY GOOD REASON FOR THAT, AS WE WERE ABOUT TO FIND OUT...

THE *TAPE?*

THE. TAPE.

WE DIDN'T KNOW IT YET, BUT WE WERE ABOUT TO START A WAR.

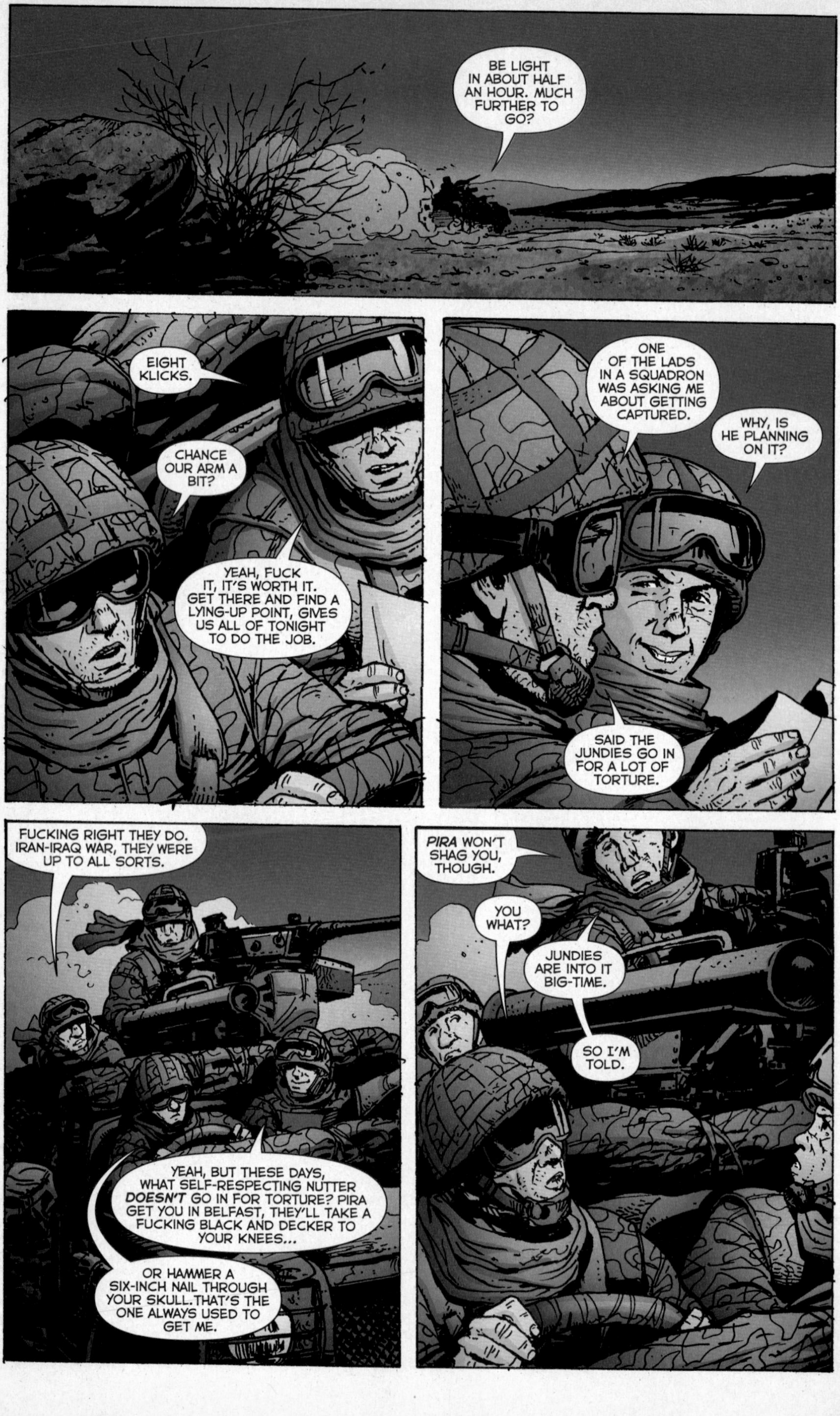
BE LIGHT IN ABOUT HALF AN HOUR. MUCH FURTHER TO GO?
EIGHT KLICKS.
CHANCE OUR ARM A BIT?
YEAH, FUCK IT, IT'S WORTH IT. GET THERE AND FIND A LYING-UP POINT, GIVES US ALL OF TONIGHT TO DO THE JOB.
ONE OF THE LADS IN A SQUADRON WAS ASKING ME ABOUT GETTING CAPTURED.
WHY, IS HE PLANNING ON IT?
SAID THE JUNDIES GO IN FOR A LOT OF TORTURE.
FUCKING RIGHT THEY DO. IRAN-IRAQ WAR, THEY WERE UP TO ALL SORTS.
YEAH, BUT THESE DAYS, WHAT SELF-RESPECTING NUTTER DOESN'T GO IN FOR TORTURE? PIRA GET YOU IN BELFAST, THEY'LL TAKE A FUCKING BLACK AND DECKER TO YOUR KNEES...
OR HAMMER A SIX-INCH NAIL THROUGH YOUR SKULL. THAT'S THE ONE ALWAYS USED TO GET ME.
PIRA WON'T SHAG YOU, THOUGH.
YOU WHAT?
JUNDIES ARE INTO IT BIG-TIME.
SO I'M TOLD.

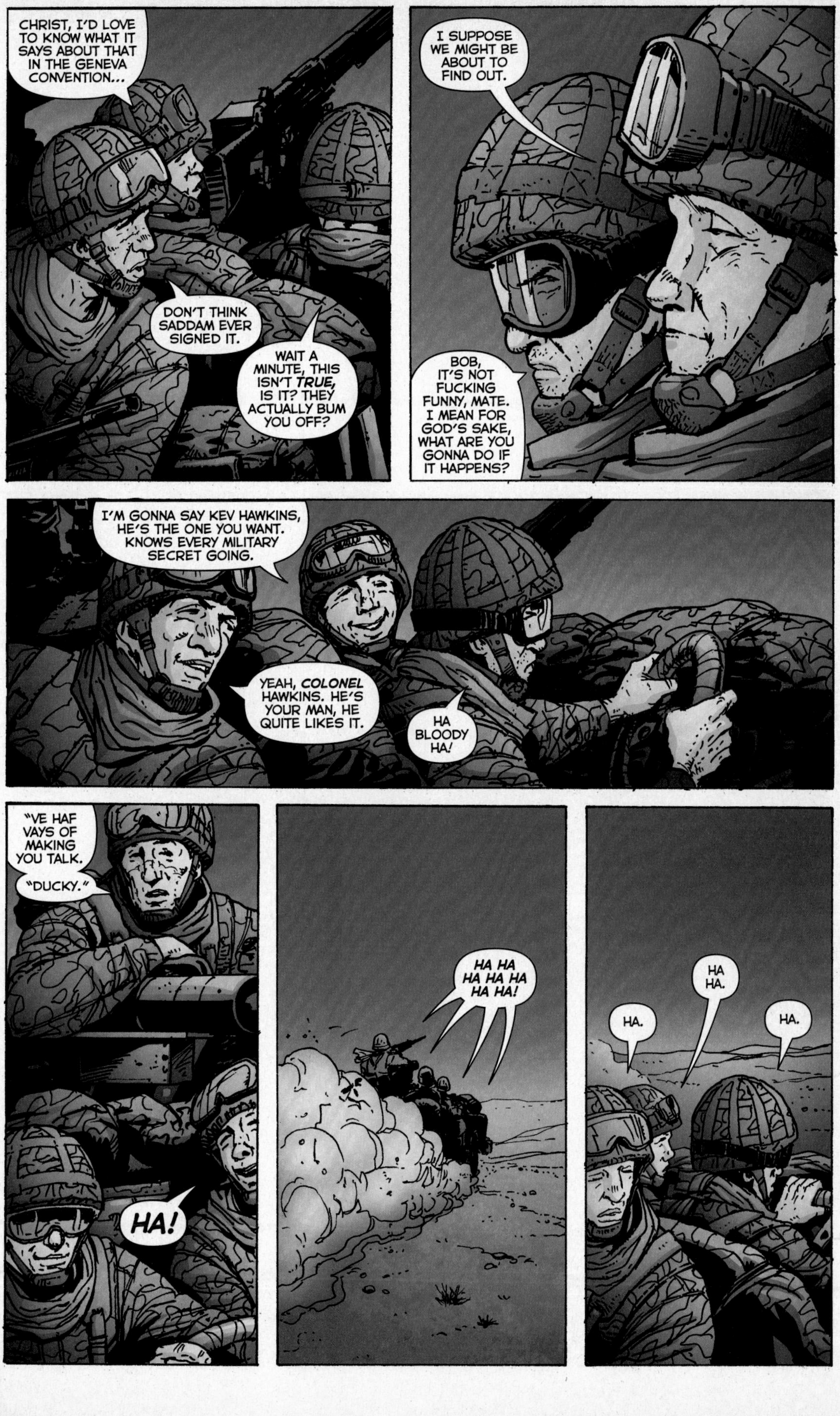
CHRIST, I'D LOVE TO KNOW WHAT IT SAYS ABOUT THAT IN THE GENEVA CONVENTION...
DON'T THINK SADDAM EVER SIGNED IT.
WAIT A MINUTE, THIS ISN'T TRUE, IS IT? THEY ACTUALLY BUM YOU OFF?
I SUPPOSE WE MIGHT BE ABOUT TO FIND OUT.
BOB, IT'S NOT FUCKING FUNNY, MATE. I MEAN FOR GOD'S SAKE, WHAT ARE YOU GONNA DO IF IT HAPPENS?
I'M GONNA SAY KEV HAWKINS, HE'S THE ONE YOU WANT. KNOWS EVERY MILITARY SECRET GOING.
YEAH, COLONEL HAWKINS. HE'S YOUR MAN, HE QUITE LIKES IT.
HA BLOODY HA!
"VE HAF VAYS OF MAKING YOU TALK.
"DUCKY."
HA!
HA HA HA HA HA HA HA!
HA.
HA HA.
HA.

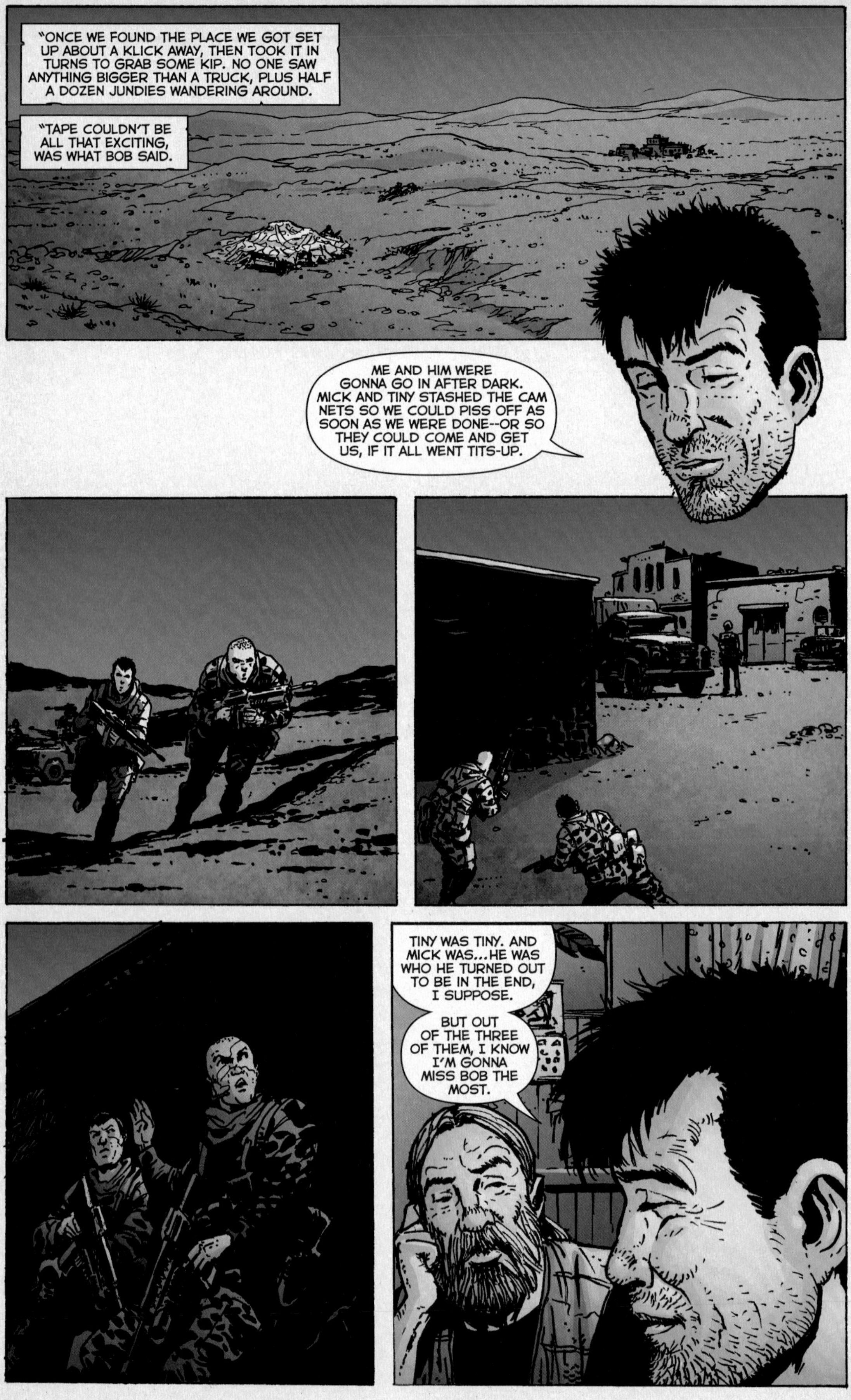
"ONCE WE FOUND THE PLACE WE GOT SET UP ABOUT A KLICK AWAY, THEN TOOK IT IN TURNS TO GRAB SOME KIP. NO ONE SAW ANYTHING BIGGER THAN A TRUCK, PLUS HALF A DOZEN JUNDIES WANDERING AROUND.
"TAPE COULDN'T BE ALL THAT EXCITING, WAS WHAT BOB SAID.
ME AND HIM WERE GONNA GO IN AFTER DARK. MICK AND TINY STASHED THE CAM NETS SO WE COULD PISS OFF AS SOON AS WE WERE DONE--OR SO THEY COULD COME AND GET US, IF IT ALL WENT TITS-UP.
TINY WAS TINY. AND MICK WAS...HE WAS WHO HE TURNED OUT TO BE IN THE END, I SUPPOSE.
BUT OUT OF THE THREE OF THEM, I KNOW I'M GONNA MISS BOB THE MOST.

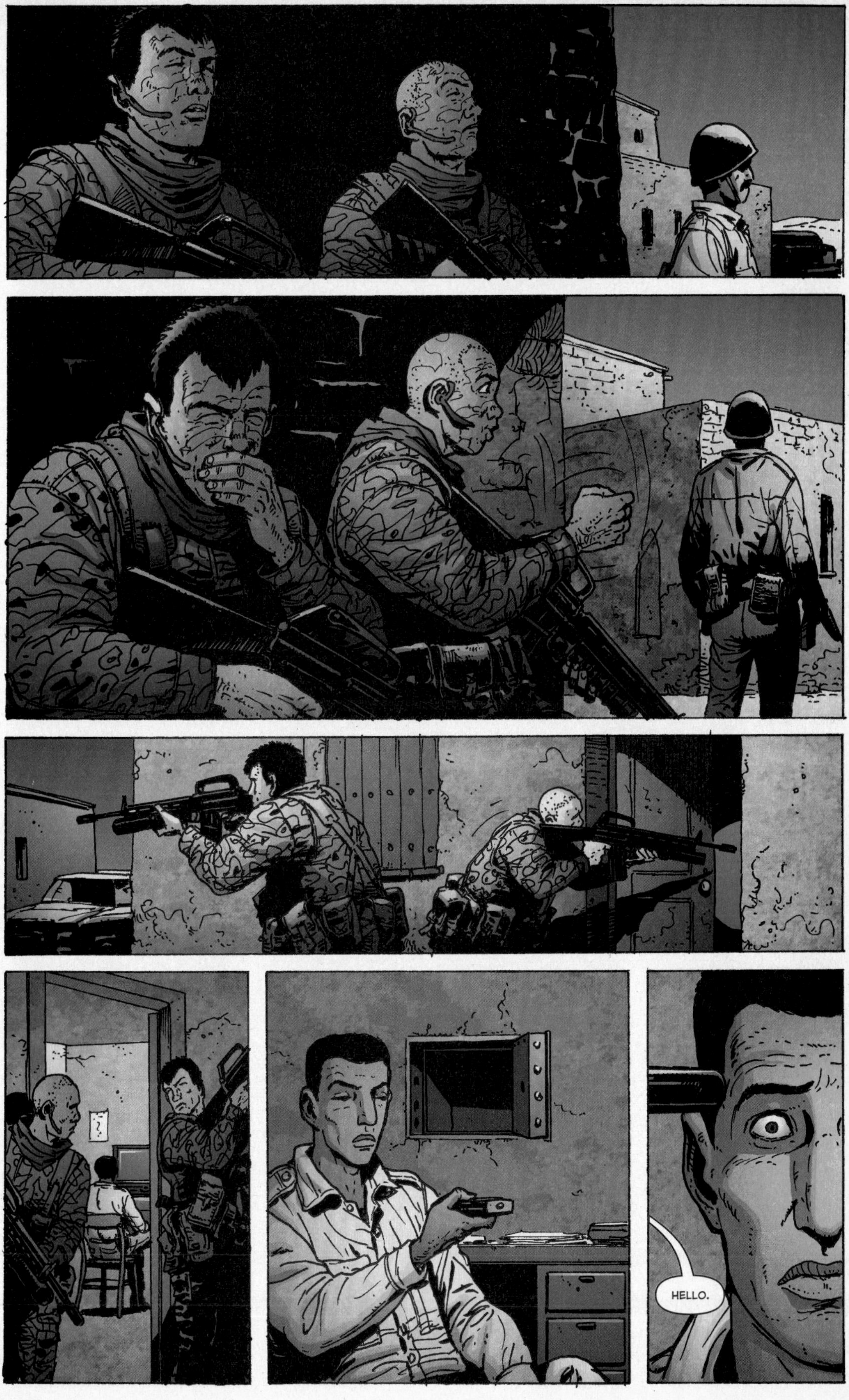
HELLO.

UH--NNNHH--

SHH

I--I SPEAK ENGLISH--!

DON'T.

OTHER TWO ROOMS ARE CLEAR.

NOD YES OR SHAKE YOUR HEAD NO: DOES THE TAPE YOU'RE WATCHING BELONG IN THAT SAFE?

GOOD MAN.

GET UP. KEEP YOUR HANDS IN SIGHT. WALK TO THE T.V. AND EJECT THE TAPE, DO YOU UNDERSTAND?

GOOD M--

HERE...

HOLD ON A SECOND, SUNSHINE.

IS THAT MAGGIE THATCHER?

YEAH...

AND THAT'S... SADDAM?

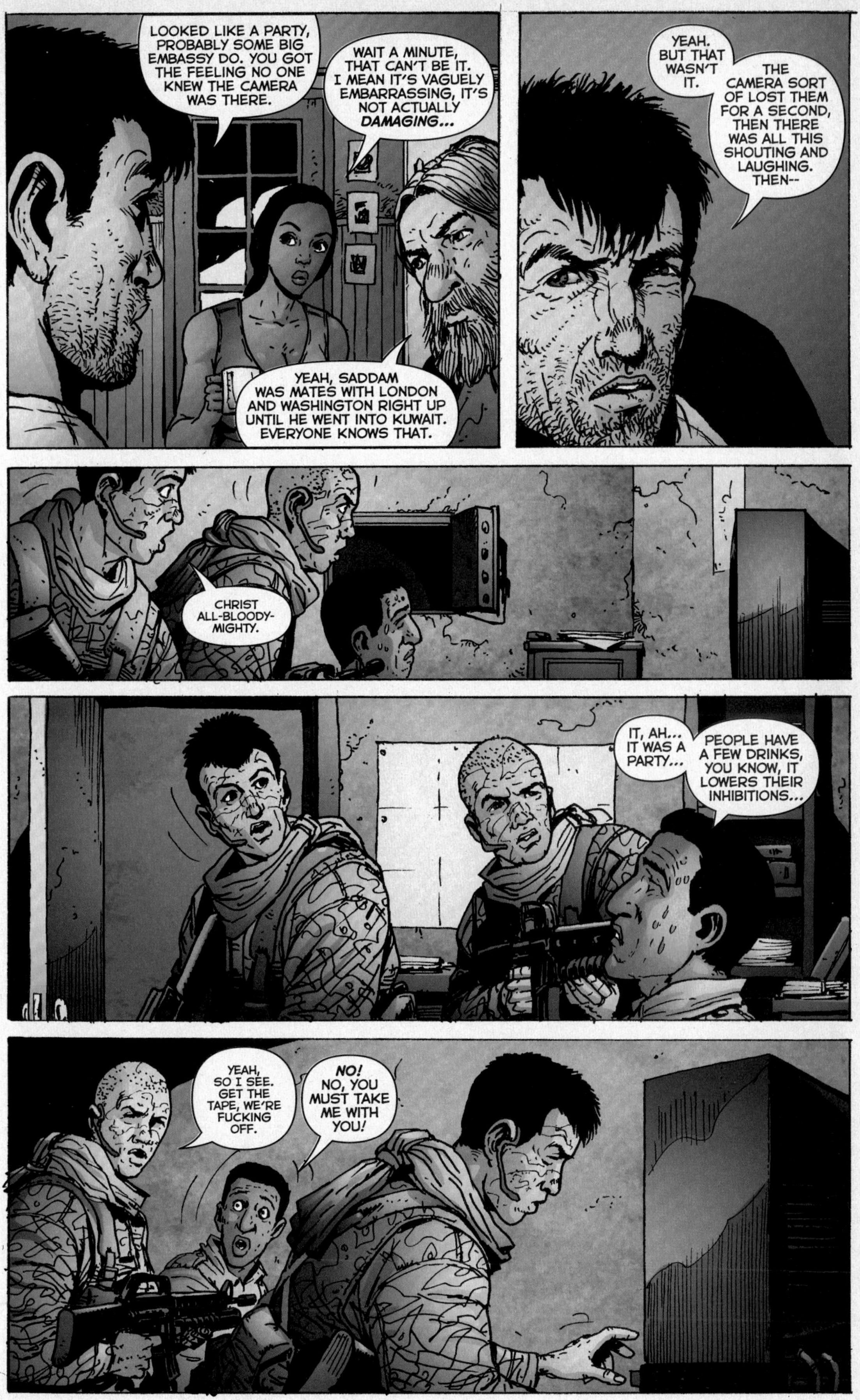
LOOKED LIKE A PARTY, PROBABLY SOME BIG EMBASSY DO. YOU GOT THE FEELING NO ONE KNEW THE CAMERA WAS THERE.
WAIT A MINUTE, THAT CAN'T BE IT. I MEAN IT'S VAGUELY EMBARRASSING, IT'S NOT ACTUALLY *DAMAGING...*
YEAH, SADDAM WAS MATES WITH LONDON AND WASHINGTON RIGHT UP UNTIL HE WENT INTO KUWAIT. EVERYONE KNOWS THAT.
YEAH. BUT THAT WASN'T IT.
THE CAMERA SORT OF LOST THEM FOR A SECOND, THEN THERE WAS ALL THIS SHOUTING AND LAUGHING. THEN--
CHRIST ALL-BLOODY-MIGHTY.
IT, AH... IT WAS A PARTY...
PEOPLE HAVE A FEW DRINKS, YOU KNOW, IT LOWERS THEIR INHIBITIONS...
YEAH, SO I SEE. GET THE TAPE, WE'RE FUCKING OFF.
NO! NO, YOU MUST TAKE ME WITH YOU!

SHUT UP, YOU--

PLEASE, PLEASE, I IMPLORE YOU! IT WAS I WHO CONTACTED YOUR LEADERS, I WHO PROVIDED THE INTELLIGENCE THAT BROUGHT YOU HERE!

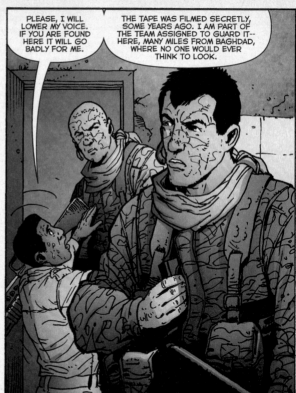

PLEASE, I WILL LOWER MY VOICE. IF YOU ARE FOUND HERE IT WILL GO BADLY FOR ME.

THE TAPE WAS FILMED SECRETLY, SOME YEARS AGO. I AM PART OF THE TEAM ASSIGNED TO GUARD IT-- HERE, MANY MILES FROM BAGHDAD, WHERE NO ONE WOULD EVER THINK TO LOOK.

SADDAM HAS WARNED YOUR LEADERS: SHOULD THE INVASION OF IRAQ COMMENCE, THE TAPE WILL BE RELEASED! ALL THE WORLD WILL GAZE UPON HIM, GIVING IT TO THE IRON LADY IN THE STYLE OF DOGS!

DO YOU SEE NOW? DO YOU SEE?

SO WHAT'S YOUR GAME?

I WANT SADDAM GONE, LIKE SO MANY OF MY PEOPLE! IF THE WEST INVADES, IRAQ WILL BE A PARADISE ON EARTH!

JUST CURIOUS.

UNNHH!

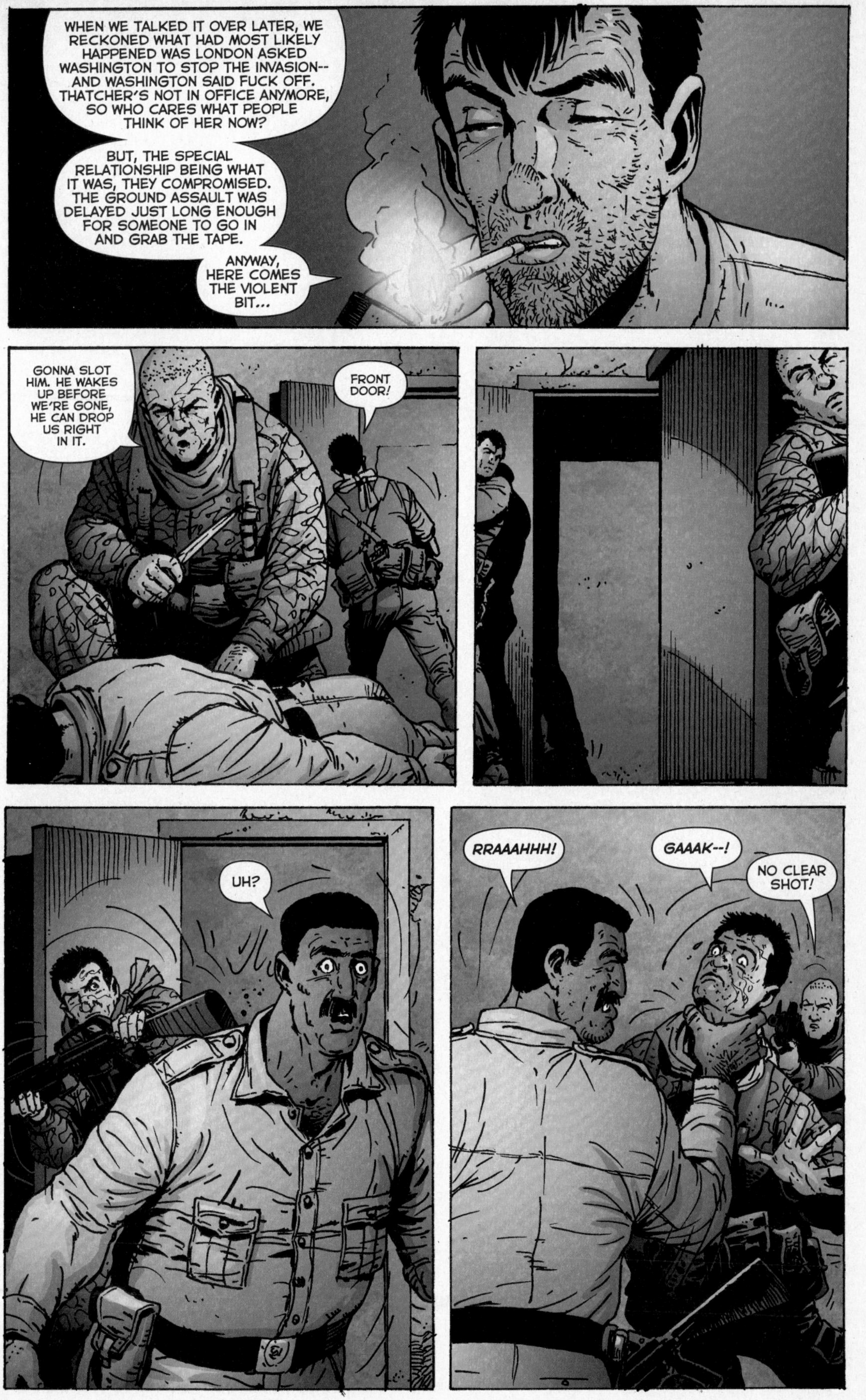
WHEN WE TALKED IT OVER LATER, WE RECKONED WHAT HAD MOST LIKELY HAPPENED WAS LONDON ASKED WASHINGTON TO STOP THE INVASION-- AND WASHINGTON SAID FUCK OFF. THATCHER'S NOT IN OFFICE ANYMORE, SO WHO CARES WHAT PEOPLE THINK OF HER NOW?
BUT, THE SPECIAL RELATIONSHIP BEING WHAT IT WAS, THEY COMPROMISED. THE GROUND ASSAULT WAS DELAYED JUST LONG ENOUGH FOR SOMEONE TO GO IN AND GRAB THE TAPE.
ANYWAY, HERE COMES THE VIOLENT BIT...
GONNA SLOT HIM. HE WAKES UP BEFORE WE'RE GONE, HE CAN DROP US RIGHT IN IT.
FRONT DOOR!
UH?
RRAAAHHH!
GAAAK--!
NO CLEAR SHOT!

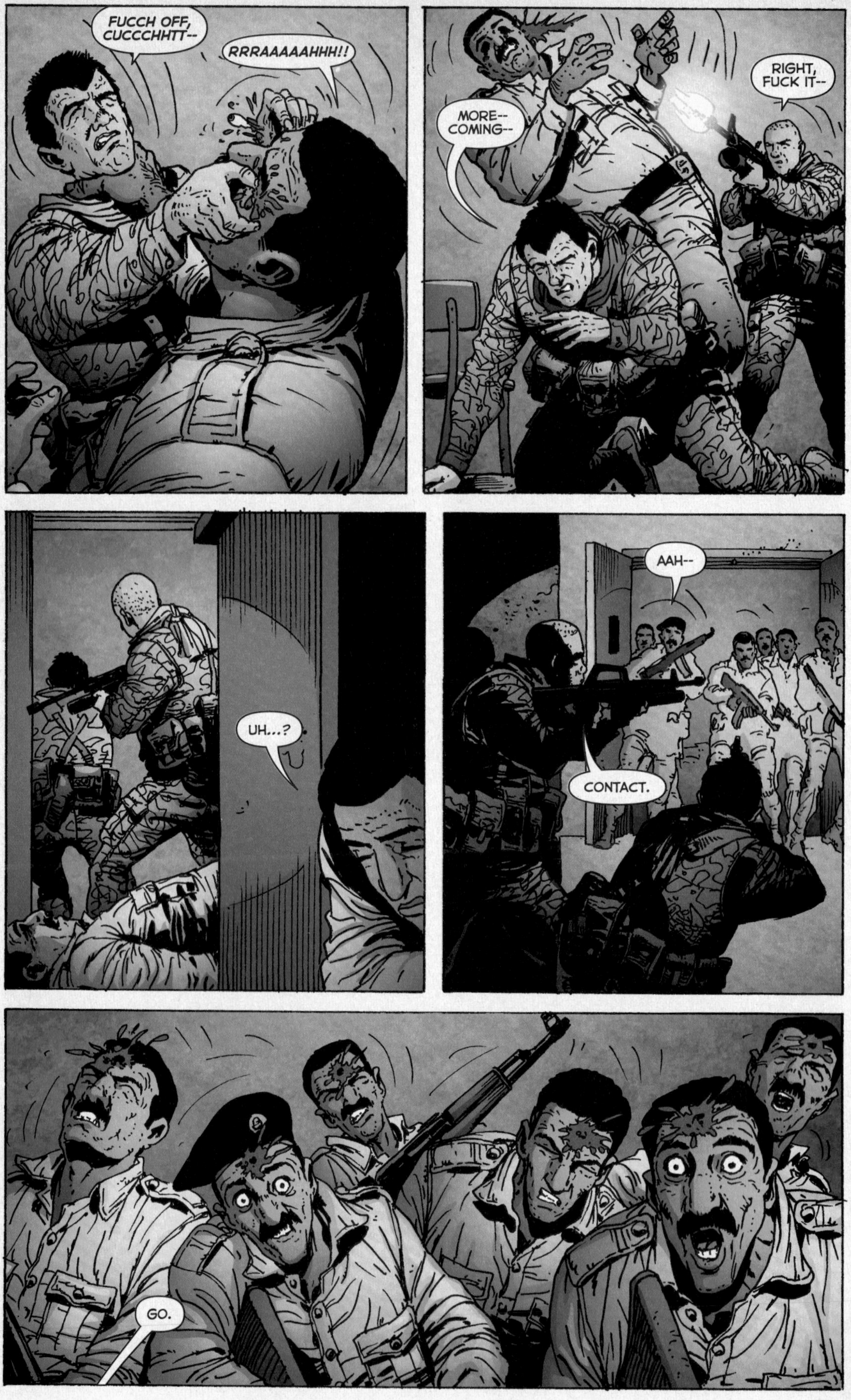
FUCCH OFF, CUCCCHHTT--
RRRAAAAAHHH!!
MORE-- COMING--
RIGHT, FUCK IT--
UH...?
AAH--
CONTACT.
GO.

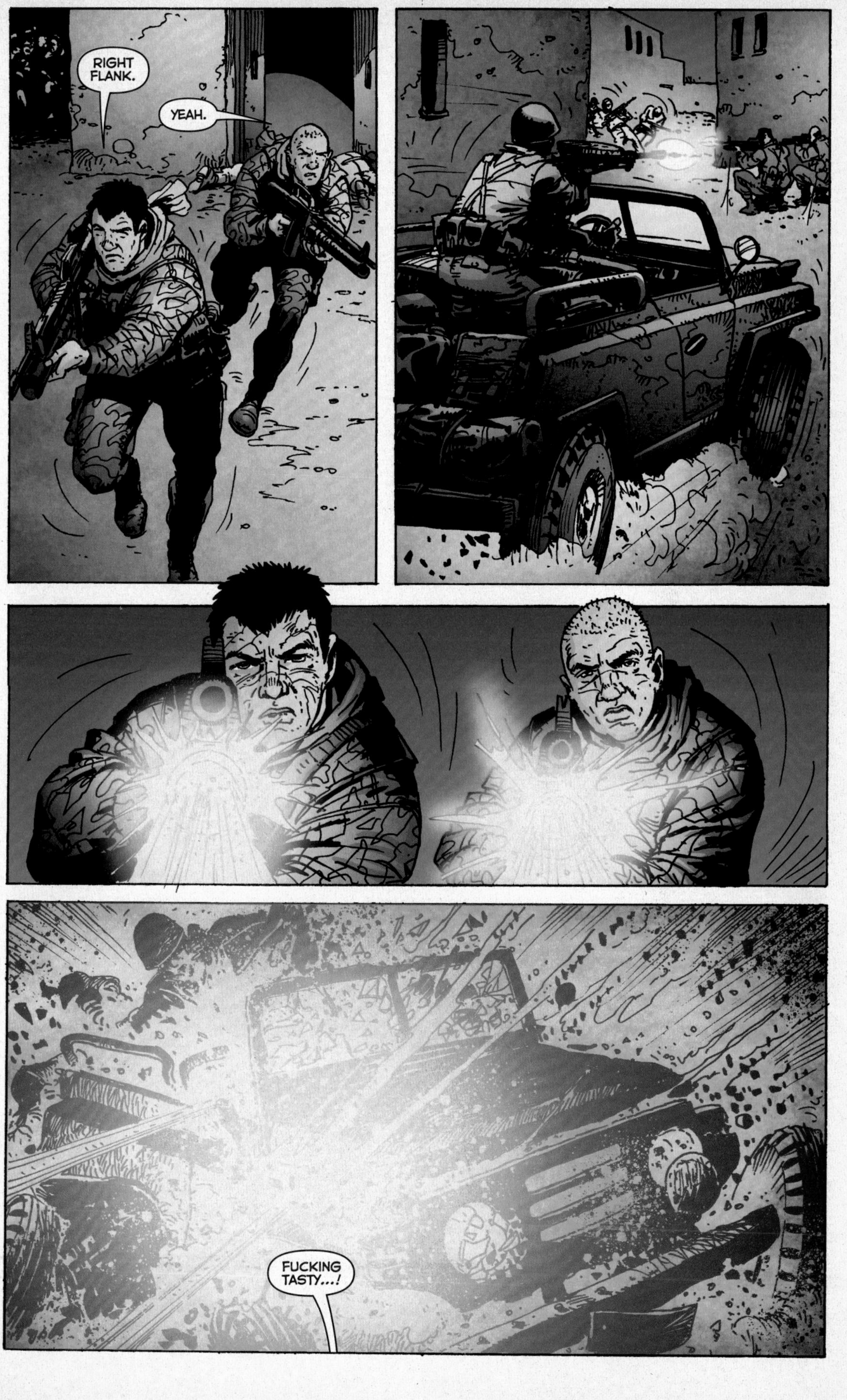
RIGHT FLANK.
YEAH.
FUCKING TASTY...!

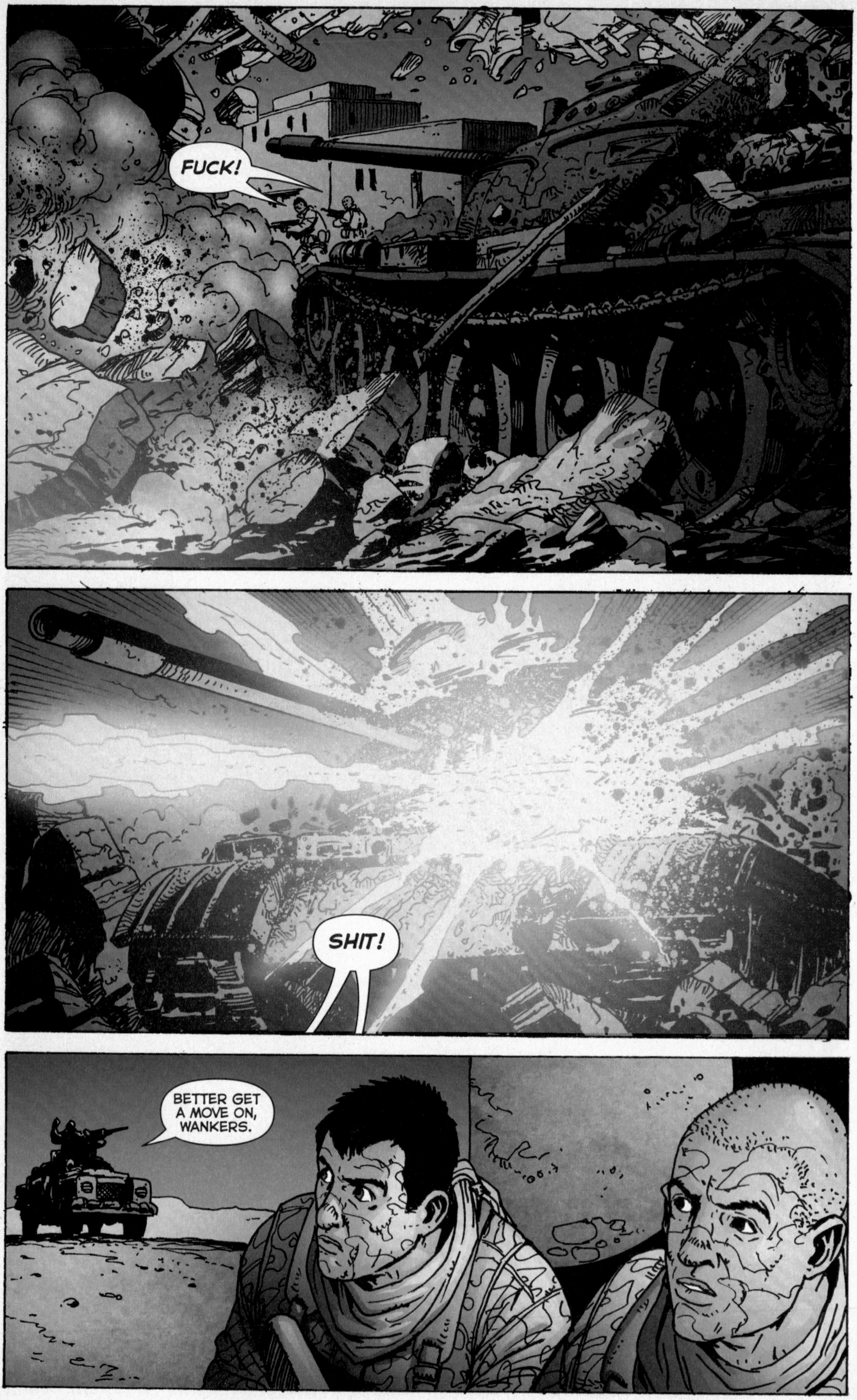
FUCK!
SHIT!
BETTER GET A MOVE ON, WANKERS.

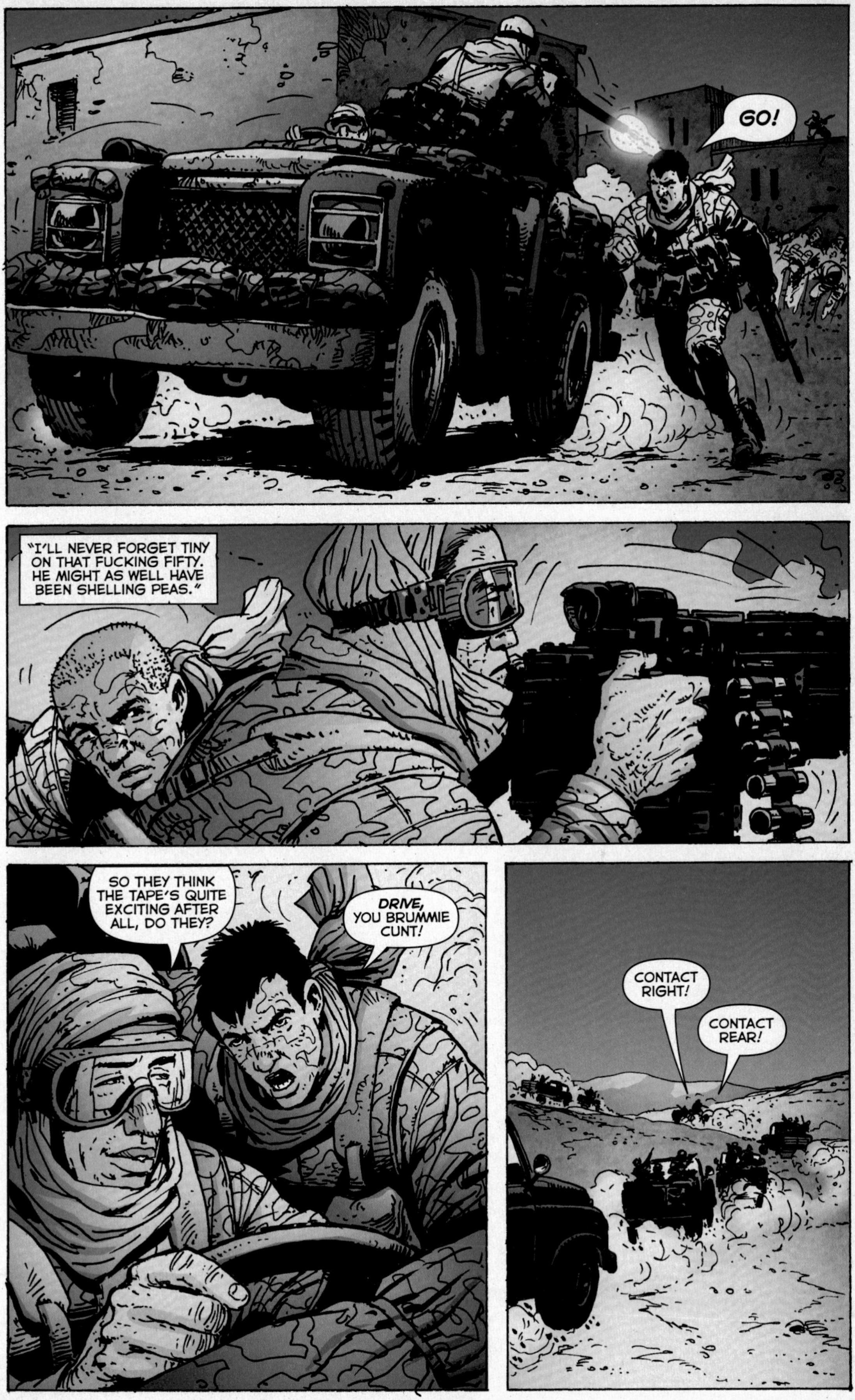
GO!
"I'LL NEVER FORGET TINY ON THAT FUCKING FIFTY. HE MIGHT AS WELL HAVE BEEN SHELLING PEAS."
SO THEY THINK THE TAPE'S QUITE EXCITING AFTER ALL, DO THEY?
DRIVE, YOU BRUMMIE CUNT!
CONTACT RIGHT!
CONTACT REAR!

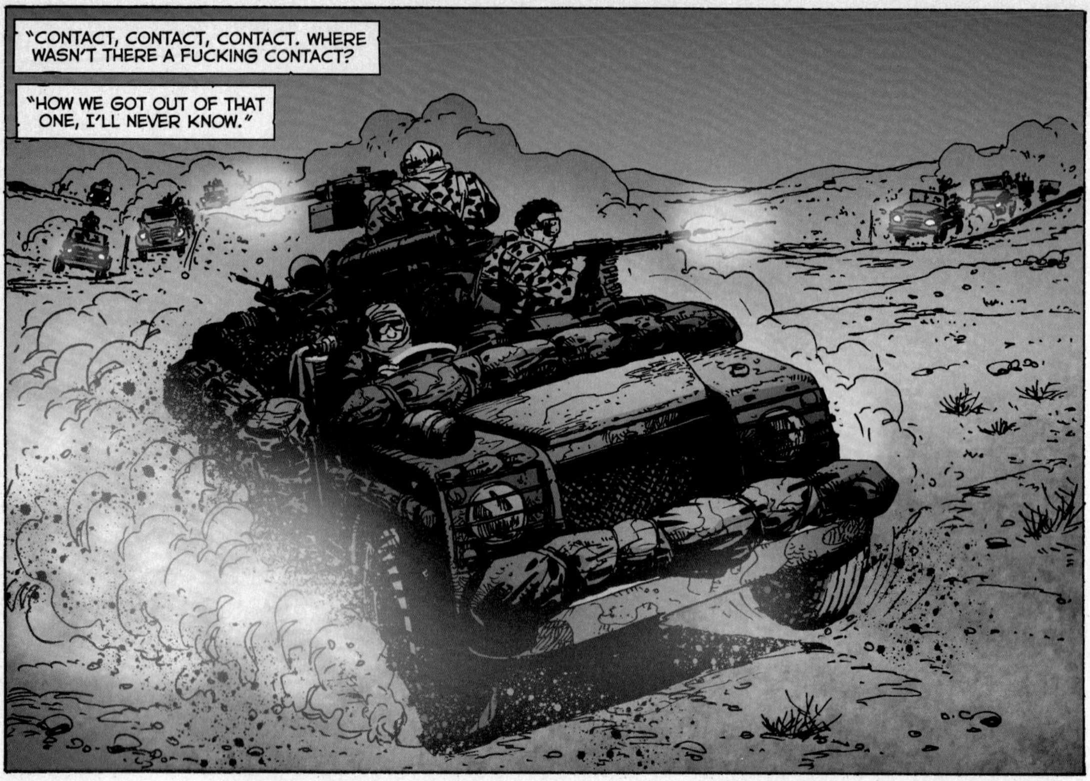
"CONTACT, CONTACT, CONTACT. WHERE WASN'T THERE A FUCKING CONTACT?
"HOW WE GOT OUT OF THAT ONE, I'LL NEVER KNOW."

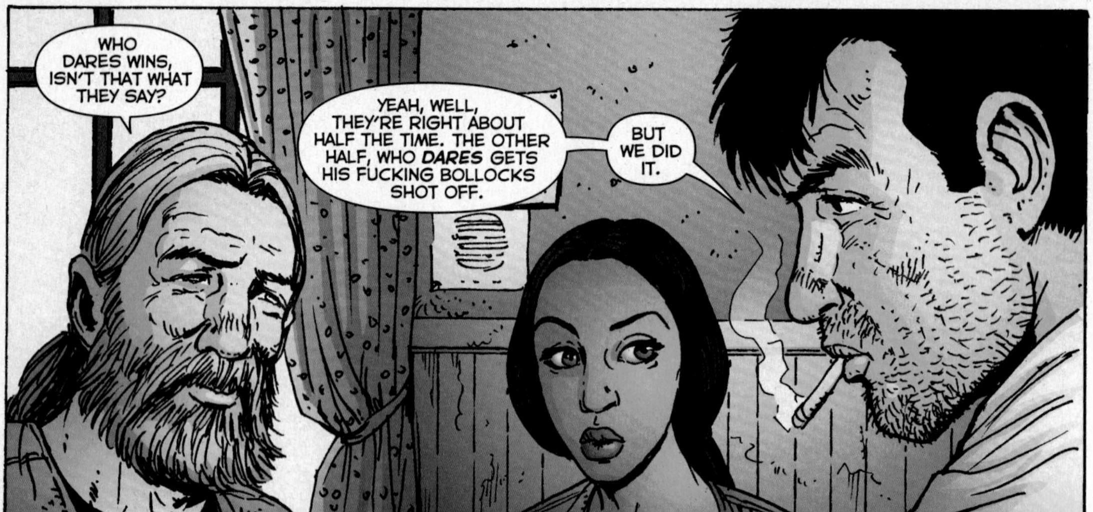
WHO DARES WINS, ISN'T THAT WHAT THEY SAY?
YEAH, WELL, THEY'RE RIGHT ABOUT HALF THE TIME. THE OTHER HALF, WHO *DARES* GETS HIS FUCKING BOLLOCKS SHOT OFF.
BUT WE DID IT.

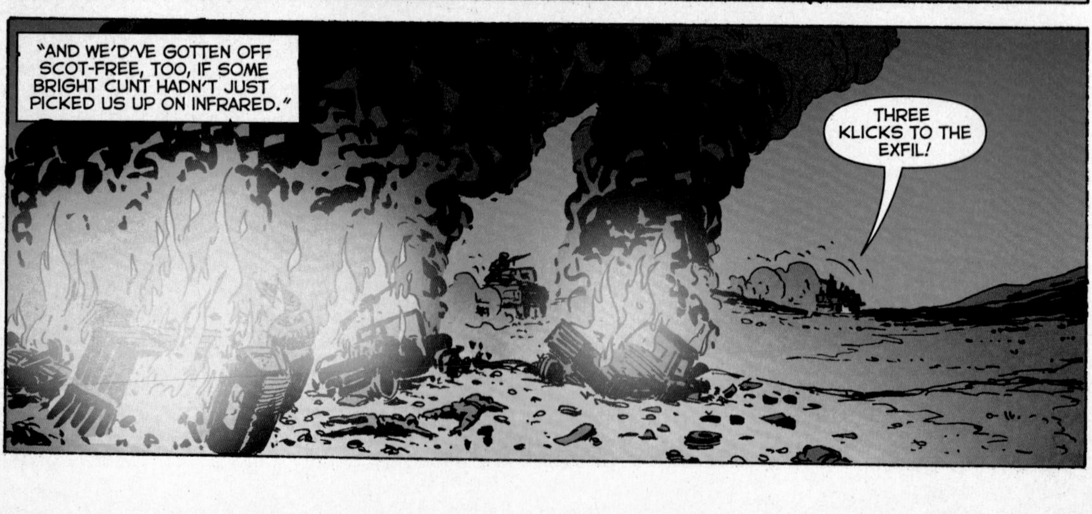
"AND WE'D'VE GOTTEN OFF SCOT-FREE, TOO, IF SOME BRIGHT CUNT HADN'T JUST PICKED US UP ON INFRARED."
THREE KLICKS TO THE EXFIL!

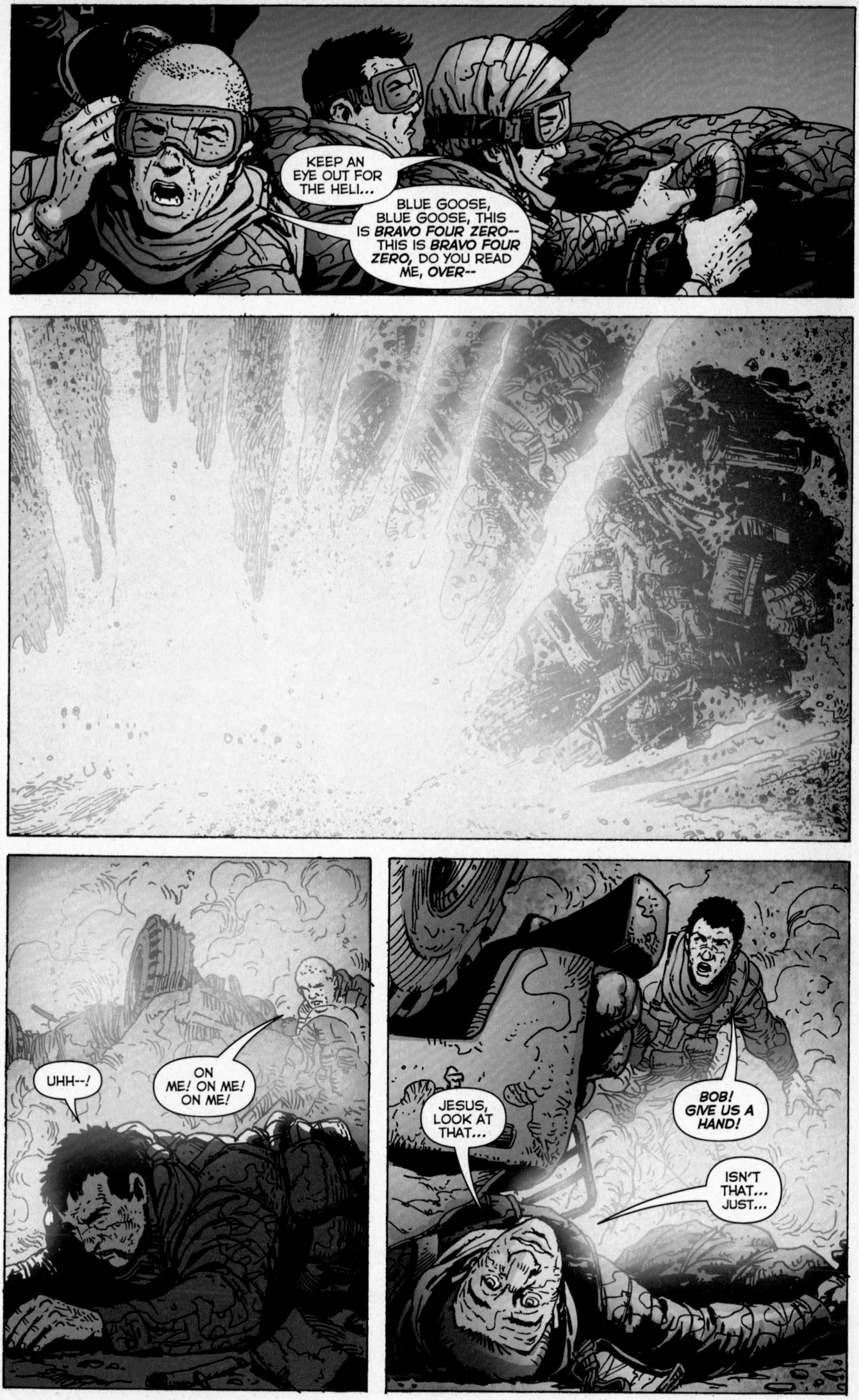
KEEP AN EYE OUT FOR THE HELI...
BLUE GOOSE, BLUE GOOSE, THIS IS BRAVO FOUR ZERO-- THIS IS BRAVO FOUR ZERO, DO YOU READ ME, OVER--
UHH--!
ON ME! ON ME! ON ME!
BOB! GIVE US A HAND!
JESUS, LOOK AT THAT...
ISN'T THAT... JUST...

...FUCKING TYPICAL...
THE NEXT YANK I MEET, I'M JUST GONNA FUCKING SLOT HIM.
RIGHT, MY ARM'S FUCKED. STICK MICK OVER MY BACK AND LET'S PISS OFF OUT OF IT SHARPISH.
TINY...?
FUCKING HELL! TINY!
KEV?
MY ARSE IS SOAKING WET. AND I DON'T THINK IT'S ME.
OH, BOLLOCKS.

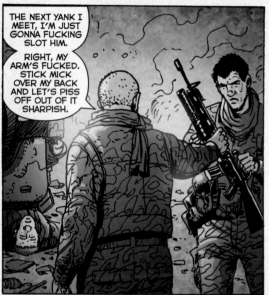

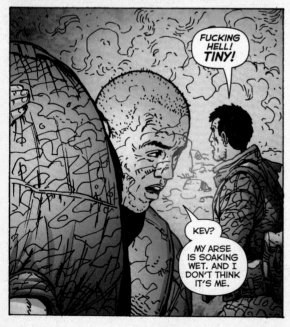

FEMORAL ARTERY. I TIED MY BELT 'ROUND IT, BUT ALL THAT DID WAS SLOW THE BLEEDING.

SO IT CAME DOWN TO MICK OR TINY.

"IN LIGHT OF LAST YEAR THAT WOULD HAVE BEEN AN EASY ONE, BUT ALL WE KNEW AT THE TIME WAS TINY WAS MISSING--MICK WAS DEFINITELY GOING TO DIE.

"BOB WAS PATROL COMMANDER, SO IT WAS HIS DECISION. WHEN HE FOUND OUT WHAT DID HAPPEN TO TINY, I HAD TO STOP HIM FROM SLOTTING HIMSELF ON THE SPOT.

"NOT THAT WE EVER TOLD ANYONE THAT LITTLE DETAIL...

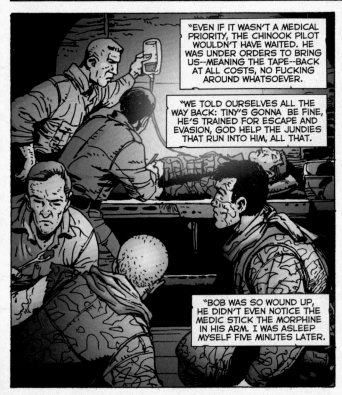

"EVEN IF IT WASN'T A MEDICAL PRIORITY, THE CHINOOK PILOT WOULDN'T HAVE WAITED. HE WAS UNDER ORDERS TO BRING US--MEANING THE TAPE--BACK AT ALL COSTS, NO FUCKING AROUND WHATSOEVER.

"WE TOLD OURSELVES ALL THE WAY BACK: TINY'S GONNA BE FINE, HE'S TRAINED FOR ESCAPE AND EVASION, GOD HELP THE JUNDIES THAT RUN INTO HIM, ALL THAT.

"BOB WAS SO WOUND UP, HE DIDN'T EVEN NOTICE THE MEDIC STICK THE MORPHINE IN HIS ARM. I WAS ASLEEP MYSELF FIVE MINUTES LATER.

"BRAVO FOUR ZERO--

"OVER AND OUT."

WHAT DID HAPPEN TO...

THE JUNDIES GOT HIM.

HE BROKE BOTH LEGS IN THE CRASH. THEY FOUND HIM AT THE BOTTOM OF A WADI.

THEY KNOCKED THE LIVING FUCK OUT OF HIM EVERY DAY FOR THREE WEEKS. LET HIS WOUNDS GET INFECTED, THEN SLAPPED RED HOT KNIVES UP AGAINST THEM. AT ONE STAGE THEY BROKE HIS JAW, SO THEY BROUGHT IN SOME BOY THEY SAID WAS A DENTIST, AND HE PULLED HALF OF TINY'S TEETH OUT WITH PLIERS.

THEN THE WAR ENDED AND THEY HANDED HIM OVER TO THE RED CROSS.

"NOT THAT WE KNEW THAT AT THE TIME. MICK AND BOB WERE FUCKED, BUT ALL I COULD THINK ABOUT WAS MOUNTING SOME KIND OF RESCUE MISSION.

"I SHOULD'VE KNOWN NOT TO TAKE THE PISS."

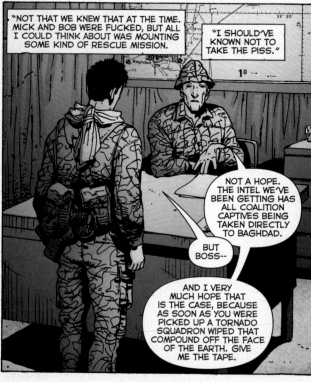

NOT A HOPE. THE INTEL WE'VE BEEN GETTING HAS ALL COALITION CAPTIVES BEING TAKEN DIRECTLY TO BAGHDAD.

BUT BOSS--

AND I VERY MUCH HOPE THAT IS THE CASE, BECAUSE AS SOON AS YOU WERE PICKED UP A TORNADO SQUADRON WIPED THAT COMPOUND OFF THE FACE OF THE EARTH. GIVE ME THE TAPE.

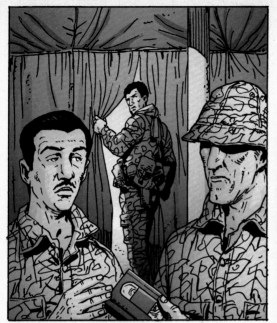

WHAT I ONLY JUST TWIGGED TODAY--WHEN YOU SHOWED US THAT THING ON THE NEWS, ZOE-- IS THAT THE BLOKE THE BOSS GAVE THE TAPE TO WAS THIS SEBASTIAN WANKER.

WHOEVER IT IS FOUND OUT HE HAD IT, SLOTTED HIM FOR IT, SLOTTED BOB TOO.

THE IRAQI BLOKE WOULD'VE DIED WHEN THE AIRSTRIKE WENT IN. SADDAM'S GRABBING HIS ANKLES AS WE SPEAK. LEAVING YOURS TRULY AS THE ONLY ONE WHO KNOWS WHAT'S ON THE TAPE.

WE DON'T KNOW WHO THIS IS...BUT WE KNOW WHO THEY FUCKING WELL WANT.

SO DANNY, MATE?

YOU SURE YOU STILL WANT ME TO STAY?

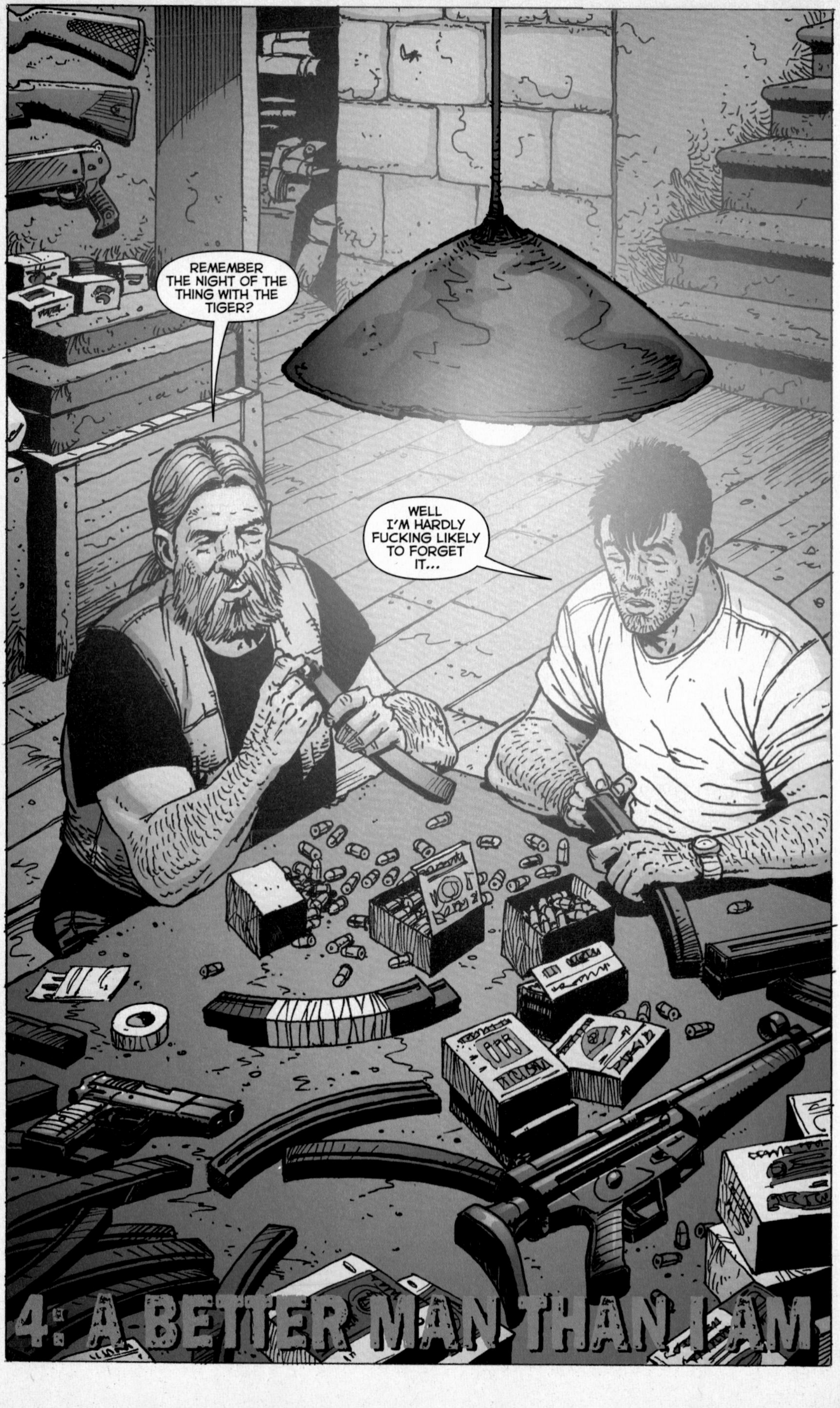
REMEMBER THE NIGHT OF THE THING WITH THE TIGER?
WELL I'M HARDLY FUCKING LIKELY TO FORGET IT...
4: A BETTER MAN THAN I AM

WELL YEAH, OBVIOUSLY...

DANNY, IF YOU'RE STILL FEELING GUILTY ABOUT THAT JUST KNOCK IT ON THE HEAD, MATE. AS FAR AS I'M CONCERNED IT'S ALL SINS FORGIVEN.

THAT'S NOT WHAT--

WHERE DID YOU GET ALL THIS STUFF, ANYWAY?

LAND OF THE FREE, MATE. BETWEEN THE POT AND MY ILLUSTRIOUS PAST, I THOUGHT IT MIGHT COME IN HANDY ONE DAY.

YOU'VE A FUCKING *TON* OF C4...

YEAH, I THINK IT ACTUALLY IS ABOUT A TON. GREEN BERET SERGEANT IN PORTLAND WAS GETTING RID OF IT CHEAP.

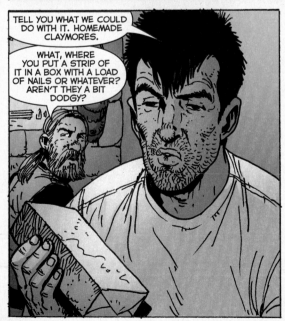

TELL YOU WHAT WE COULD DO WITH IT. HOMEMADE CLAYMORES.

WHAT, WHERE YOU PUT A STRIP OF IT IN A BOX WITH A LOAD OF NAILS OR WHATEVER? AREN'T THEY A BIT DODGY?

NOT IF YOU DO IT RIGHT.

TINY SHOWED ME, HE WAS ALWAYS THE DEMS MAN IN OUR GANG.

SO ABOUT THAT NIGHT...

DANNY, FOR FUCK'S SAKE--

D'YOU REMEMBER AFTER STRIPEY ATE THE BLOKE, I FOUND AN ORANGE ON THE FLOOR OF THE CELLAR?

YEAH...

AND I WAS EATING IT, AND I OFFERED YOU A BIT AND YOU DIDN'T WANT ANY?

YEAH...

WELL I DIDN'T REALLY THINK ABOUT IT TILL AFTERWARDS, BUT I COULD NEVER WORK OUT WHY THERE WOULD HAVE BEEN AN ORANGE THERE IN THE FIRST PLACE...

I DUNNO, MATE, IT WASN'T MINE.

THERE YOU GO. THAT'S MADE READY, SAFETY ON.

OH, THANKS.

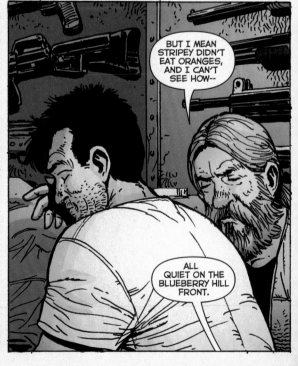

BUT I MEAN STRIPEY DIDN'T EAT ORANGES, AND I CAN'T SEE HOW--

ALL QUIET ON THE BLUEBERRY HILL FRONT.

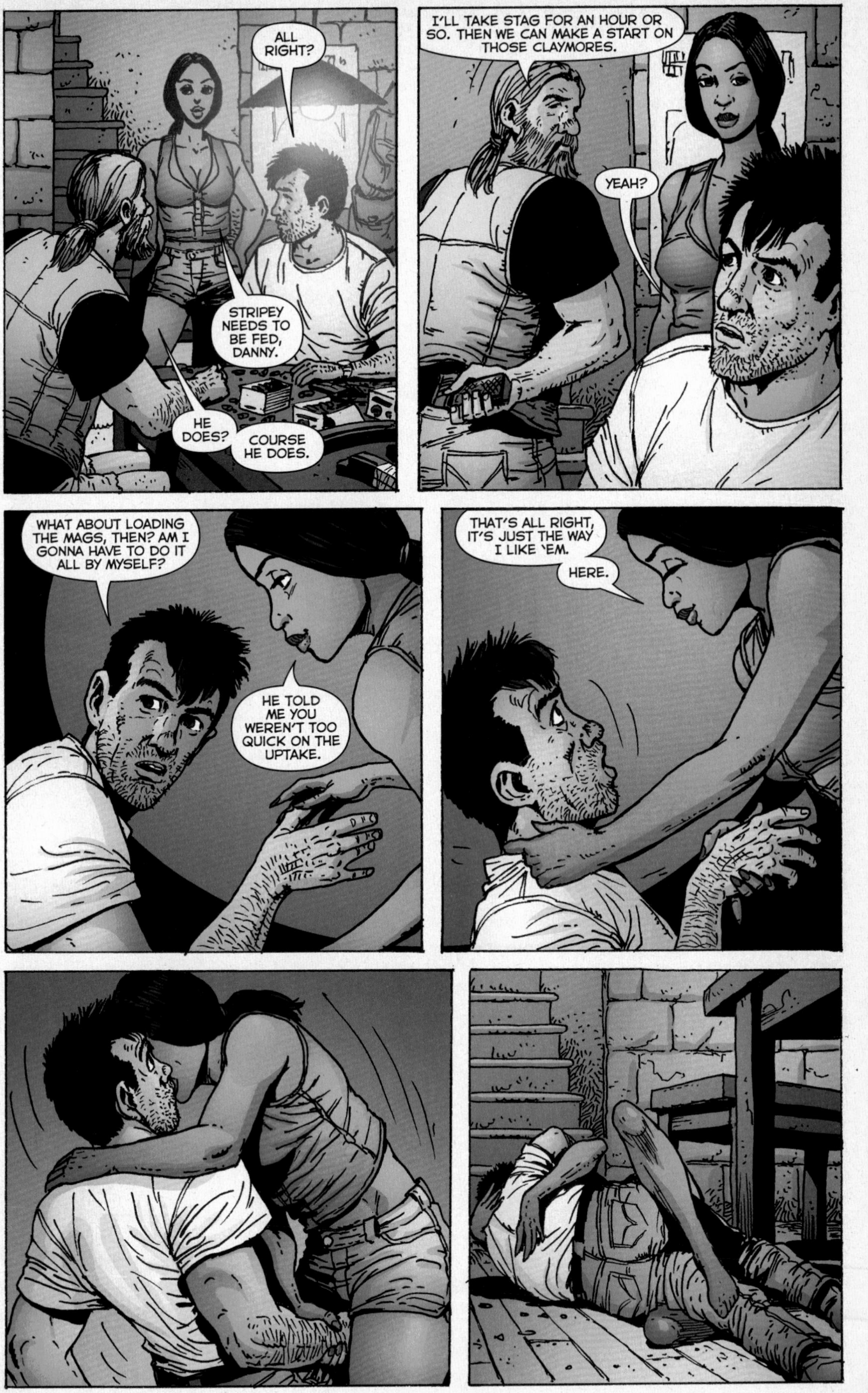
ALL RIGHT?
STRIPEY NEEDS TO BE FED, DANNY.
HE DOES?
COURSE HE DOES.
I'LL TAKE STAG FOR AN HOUR OR SO. THEN WE CAN MAKE A START ON THOSE CLAYMORES.
YEAH?
WHAT ABOUT LOADING THE MAGS, THEN? AM I GONNA HAVE TO DO IT ALL BY MYSELF?
HE TOLD ME YOU WEREN'T TOO QUICK ON THE UPTAKE.
THAT'S ALL RIGHT, IT'S JUST THE WAY I LIKE 'EM.
HERE.

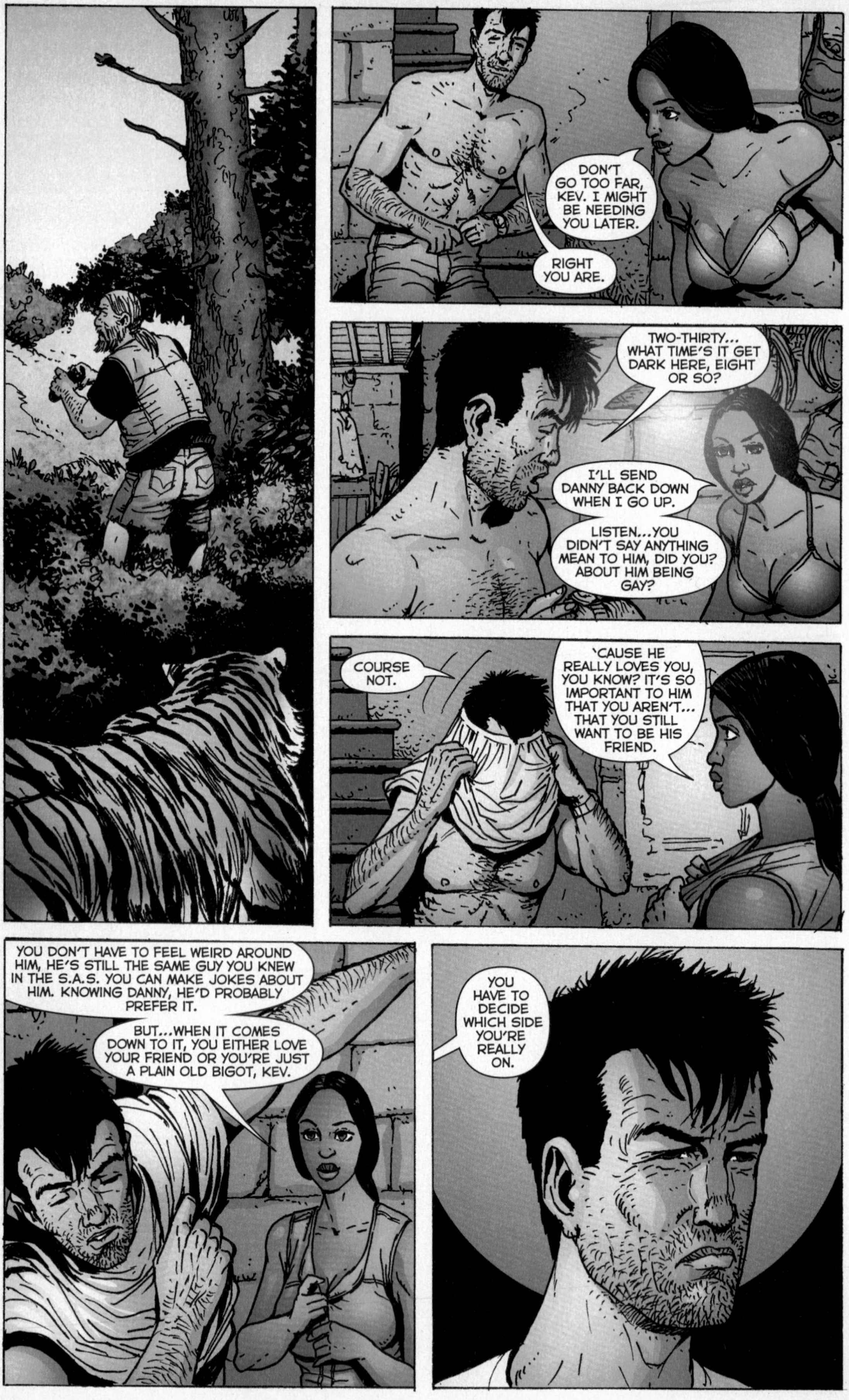
DON'T GO TOO FAR, KEV. I MIGHT BE NEEDING YOU LATER.
RIGHT YOU ARE.
TWO-THIRTY... WHAT TIME'S IT GET DARK HERE, EIGHT OR SO?
I'LL SEND DANNY BACK DOWN WHEN I GO UP.
LISTEN...YOU DIDN'T SAY ANYTHING MEAN TO HIM, DID YOU? ABOUT HIM BEING GAY?
COURSE NOT.
'CAUSE HE REALLY LOVES YOU, YOU KNOW? IT'S SO IMPORTANT TO HIM THAT YOU AREN'T... THAT YOU STILL WANT TO BE HIS FRIEND.
YOU DON'T HAVE TO FEEL WEIRD AROUND HIM, HE'S STILL THE SAME GUY YOU KNEW IN THE S.A.S. YOU CAN MAKE JOKES ABOUT HIM. KNOWING DANNY, HE'D PROBABLY PREFER IT.
BUT...WHEN IT COMES DOWN TO IT, YOU EITHER LOVE YOUR FRIEND OR YOU'RE JUST A PLAIN OLD BIGOT, KEV.
YOU HAVE TO DECIDE WHICH SIDE YOU'RE REALLY ON.

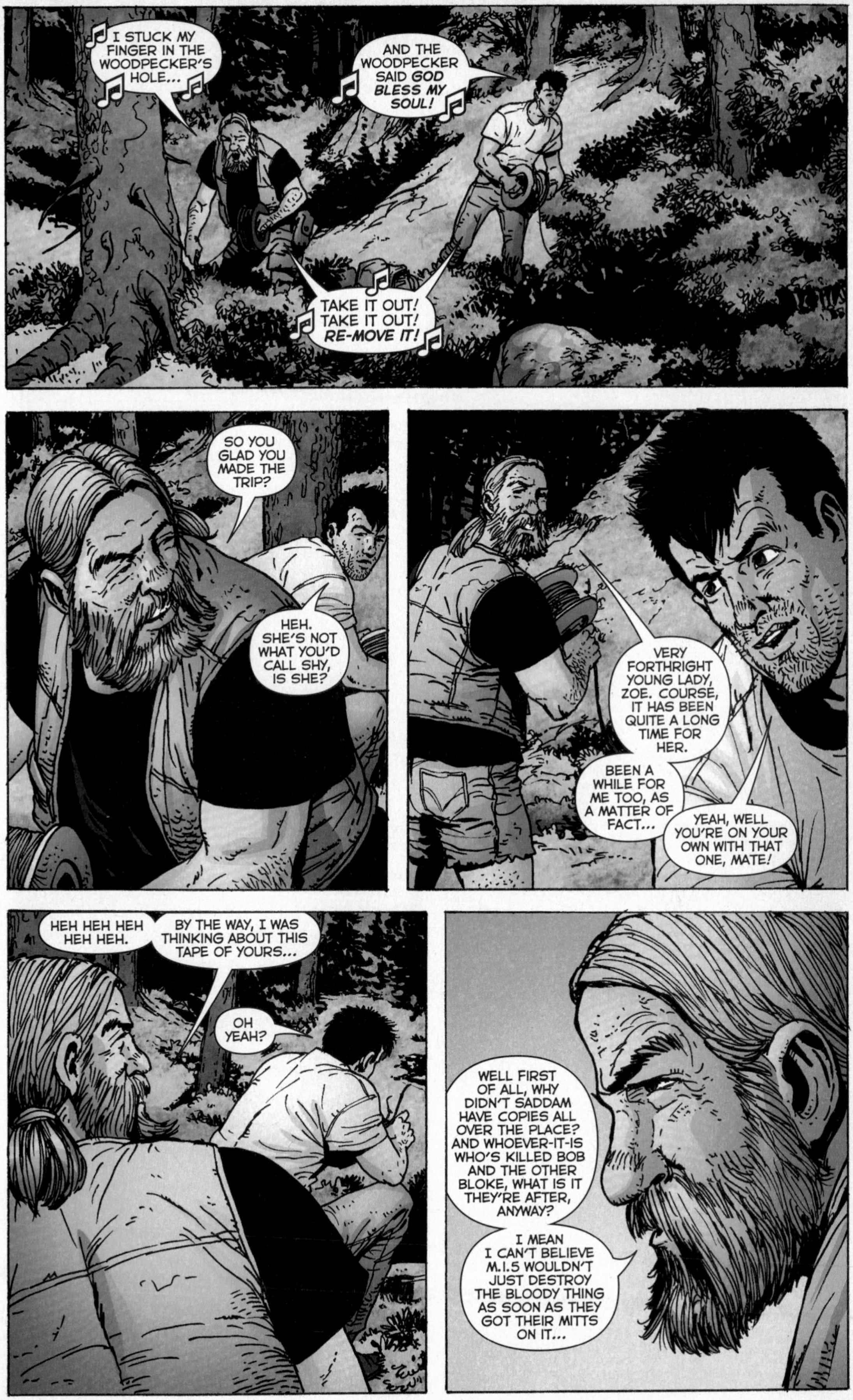

I STUCK MY FINGER IN THE WOODPECKER'S HOLE...
AND THE WOODPECKER SAID *GOD BLESS MY SOUL!*
TAKE IT OUT! TAKE IT OUT! *RE-MOVE IT!*
SO YOU GLAD YOU MADE THE TRIP?
HEH. SHE'S NOT WHAT YOU'D CALL SHY, IS SHE?
VERY FORTHRIGHT YOUNG LADY, ZOE. COURSE, IT HAS BEEN QUITE A LONG TIME FOR HER.
BEEN A WHILE FOR ME TOO, AS A MATTER OF FACT...
YEAH, WELL YOU'RE ON YOUR OWN WITH THAT ONE, MATE!
HEH HEH HEH HEH HEH.
BY THE WAY, I WAS THINKING ABOUT THIS TAPE OF YOURS...
OH YEAH?
WELL FIRST OF ALL, WHY DIDN'T SADDAM HAVE COPIES ALL OVER THE PLACE? AND WHOEVER-IT-IS WHO'S KILLED BOB AND THE OTHER BLOKE, WHAT IS IT THEY'RE AFTER, ANYWAY?
I MEAN I CAN'T BELIEVE M.I.5 WOULDN'T JUST DESTROY THE BLOODY THING AS SOON AS THEY GOT THEIR MITTS ON IT...

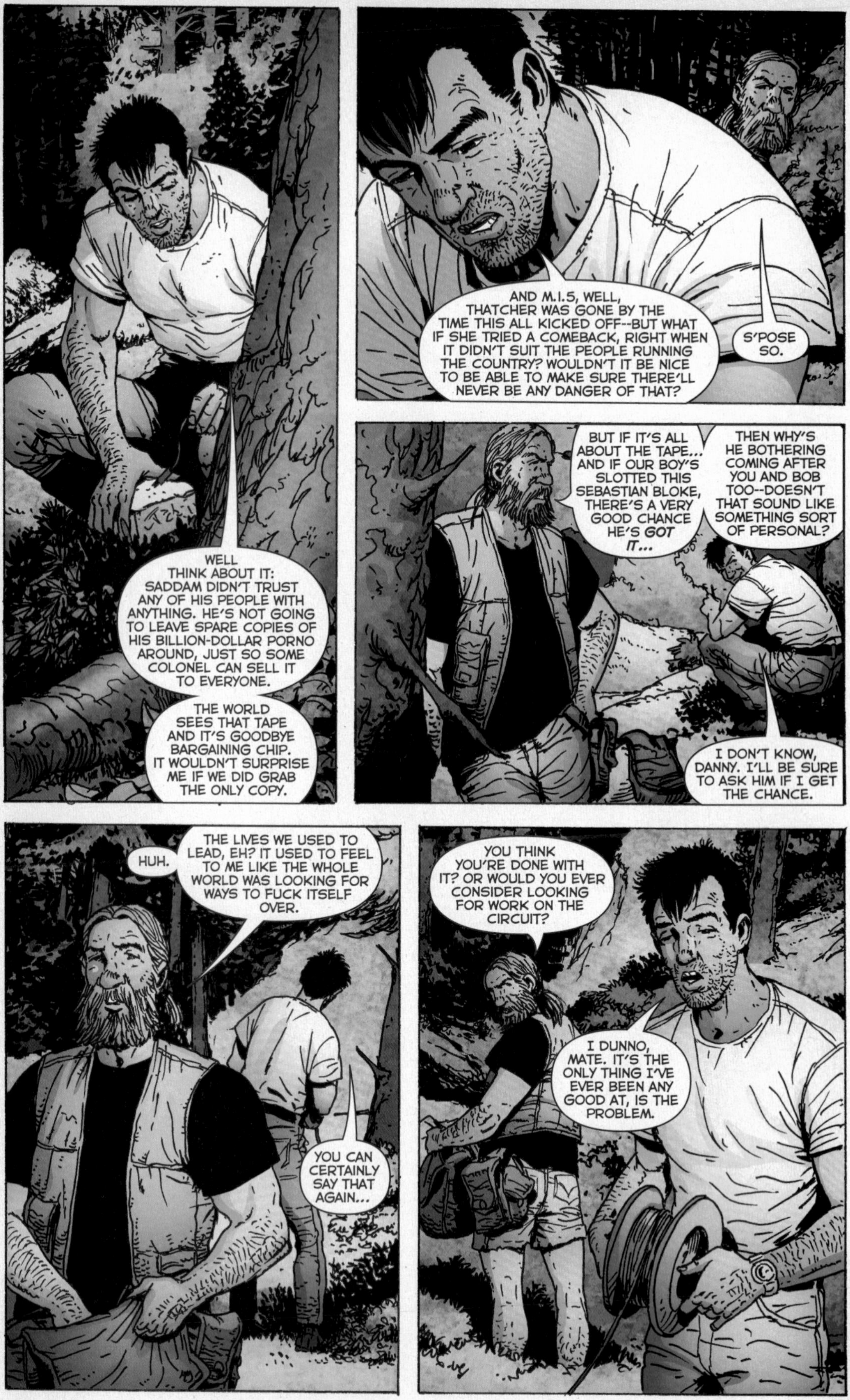
AND M.I.5, WELL, THATCHER WAS GONE BY THE TIME THIS ALL KICKED OFF--BUT WHAT IF SHE TRIED A COMEBACK, RIGHT WHEN IT DIDN'T SUIT THE PEOPLE RUNNING THE COUNTRY? WOULDN'T IT BE NICE TO BE ABLE TO MAKE SURE THERE'LL NEVER BE ANY DANGER OF THAT?
S'POSE SO.
WELL THINK ABOUT IT: SADDAM DIDN'T TRUST ANY OF HIS PEOPLE WITH ANYTHING. HE'S NOT GOING TO LEAVE SPARE COPIES OF HIS BILLION-DOLLAR PORNO AROUND, JUST SO SOME COLONEL CAN SELL IT TO EVERYONE.
THE WORLD SEES THAT TAPE AND IT'S GOODBYE BARGAINING CHIP. IT WOULDN'T SURPRISE ME IF WE DID GRAB THE ONLY COPY.
BUT IF IT'S ALL ABOUT THE TAPE... AND IF OUR BOY'S SLOTTED THIS SEBASTIAN BLOKE, THERE'S A VERY GOOD CHANCE HE'S *GOT IT*...
THEN WHY'S HE BOTHERING COMING AFTER YOU AND BOB TOO--DOESN'T THAT SOUND LIKE SOMETHING SORT OF PERSONAL?
I DON'T KNOW, DANNY. I'LL BE SURE TO ASK HIM IF I GET THE CHANCE.
HUH.
THE LIVES WE USED TO LEAD, EH? IT USED TO FEEL TO ME LIKE THE WHOLE WORLD WAS LOOKING FOR WAYS TO FUCK ITSELF OVER.
YOU CAN CERTAINLY SAY THAT AGAIN...
YOU THINK YOU'RE DONE WITH IT? OR WOULD YOU EVER CONSIDER LOOKING FOR WORK ON THE CIRCUIT?
I DUNNO, MATE. IT'S THE ONLY THING I'VE EVER BEEN ANY GOOD AT, IS THE PROBLEM.

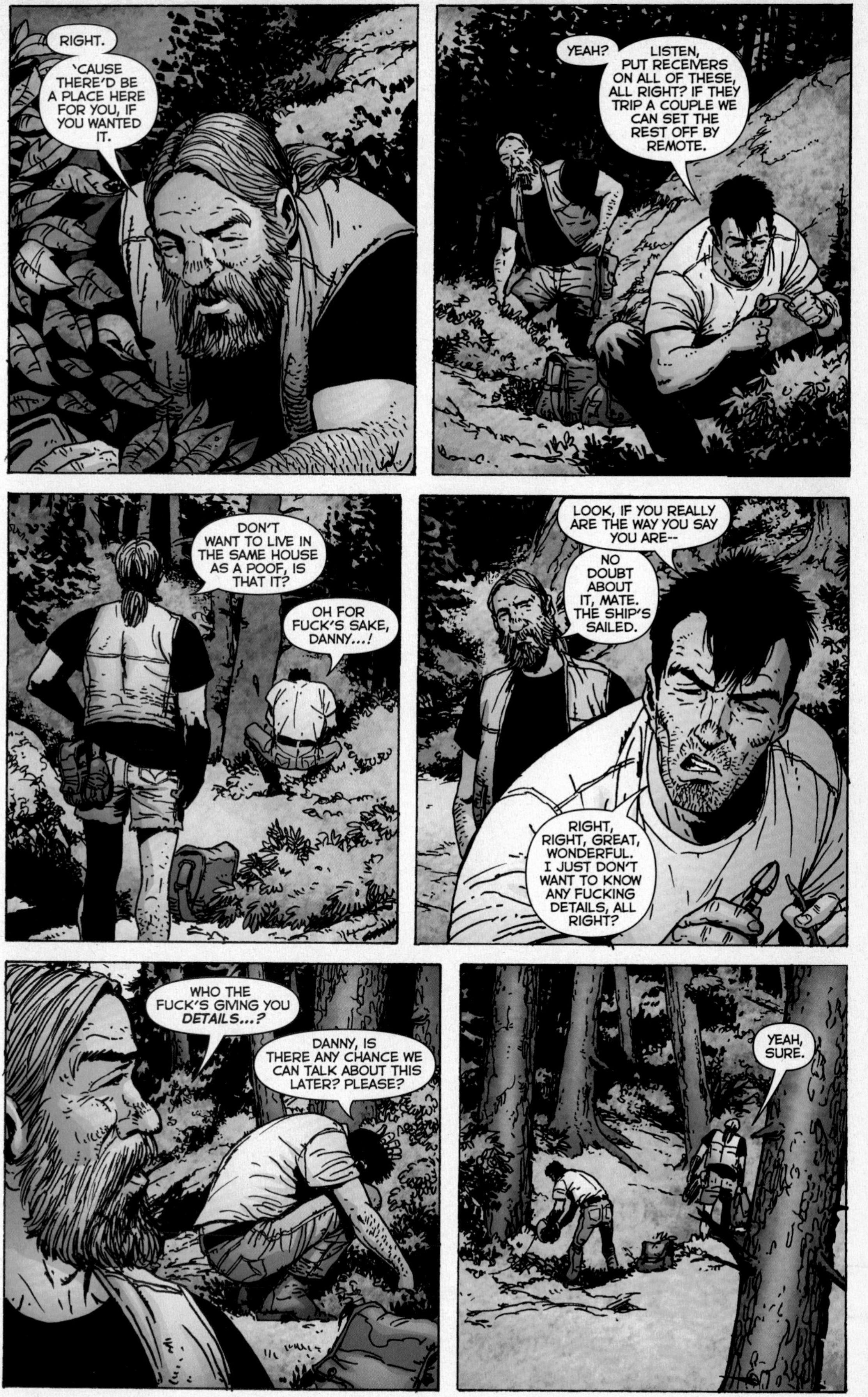
RIGHT.
'CAUSE THERE'D BE A PLACE HERE FOR YOU, IF YOU WANTED IT.
YEAH?
LISTEN, PUT RECEIVERS ON ALL OF THESE, ALL RIGHT? IF THEY TRIP A COUPLE WE CAN SET THE REST OFF BY REMOTE.
DON'T WANT TO LIVE IN THE SAME HOUSE AS A POOF, IS THAT IT?
OH FOR FUCK'S SAKE, DANNY...!
LOOK, IF YOU REALLY ARE THE WAY YOU SAY YOU ARE--
NO DOUBT ABOUT IT, MATE. THE SHIP'S SAILED.
RIGHT, RIGHT, GREAT, WONDERFUL. I JUST DON'T WANT TO KNOW ANY FUCKING DETAILS, ALL RIGHT?
WHO THE FUCK'S GIVING YOU *DETAILS...?*
DANNY, IS THERE ANY CHANCE WE CAN TALK ABOUT THIS LATER? PLEASE?
YEAH, SURE.

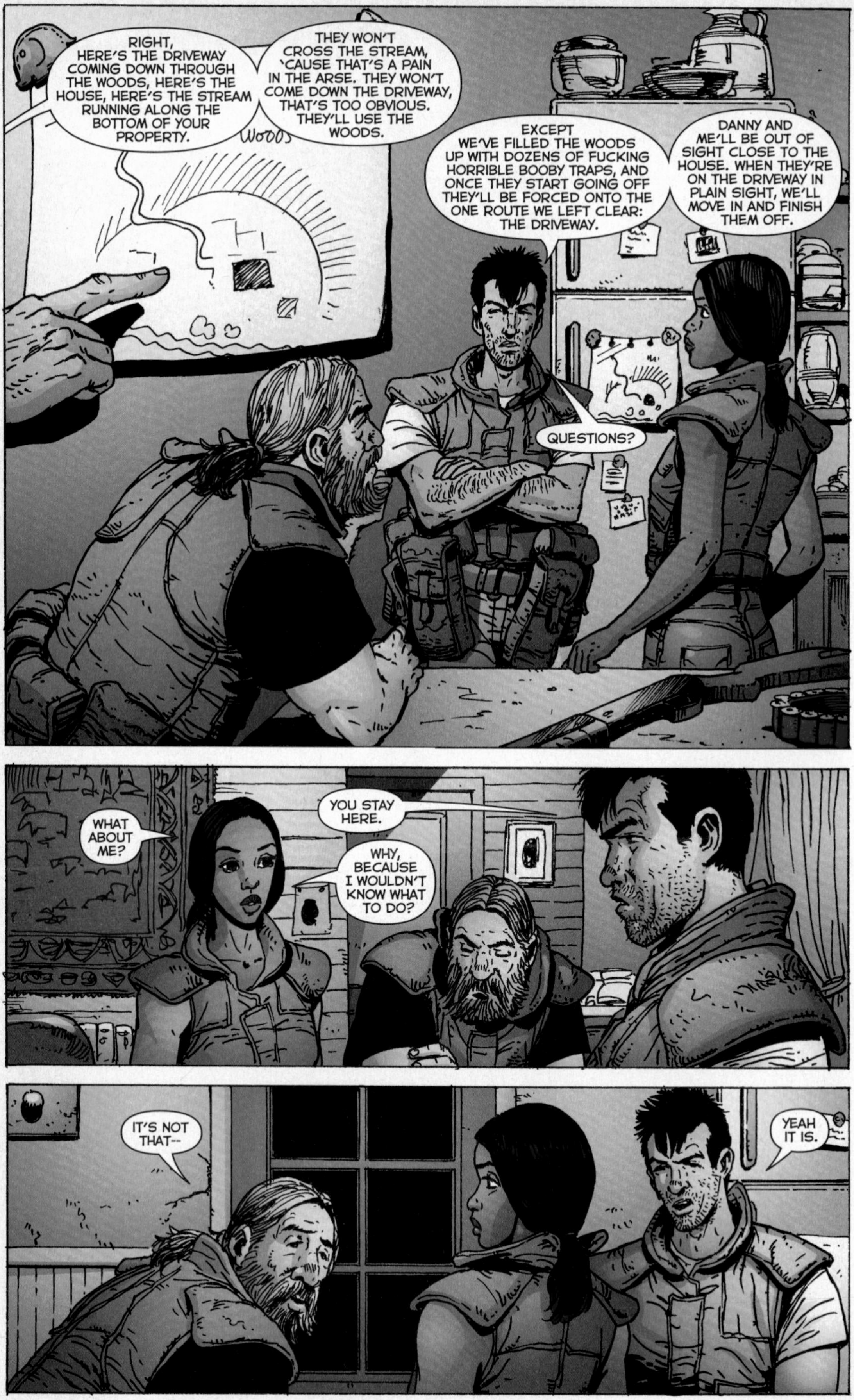
RIGHT, HERE'S THE DRIVEWAY COMING DOWN THROUGH THE WOODS, HERE'S THE HOUSE, HERE'S THE STREAM RUNNING ALONG THE BOTTOM OF YOUR PROPERTY.
THEY WON'T CROSS THE STREAM, 'CAUSE THAT'S A PAIN IN THE ARSE. THEY WON'T COME DOWN THE DRIVEWAY, THAT'S TOO OBVIOUS. THEY'LL USE THE WOODS.
WOODS
EXCEPT WE'VE FILLED THE WOODS UP WITH DOZENS OF FUCKING HORRIBLE BOOBY TRAPS, AND ONCE THEY START GOING OFF THEY'LL BE FORCED ONTO THE ONE ROUTE WE LEFT CLEAR: THE DRIVEWAY.
DANNY AND ME'LL BE OUT OF SIGHT CLOSE TO THE HOUSE. WHEN THEY'RE ON THE DRIVEWAY IN PLAIN SIGHT, WE'LL MOVE IN AND FINISH THEM OFF.
QUESTIONS?
WHAT ABOUT ME?
YOU STAY HERE.
WHY, BECAUSE I WOULDN'T KNOW WHAT TO DO?
IT'S NOT THAT--
YEAH IT IS.

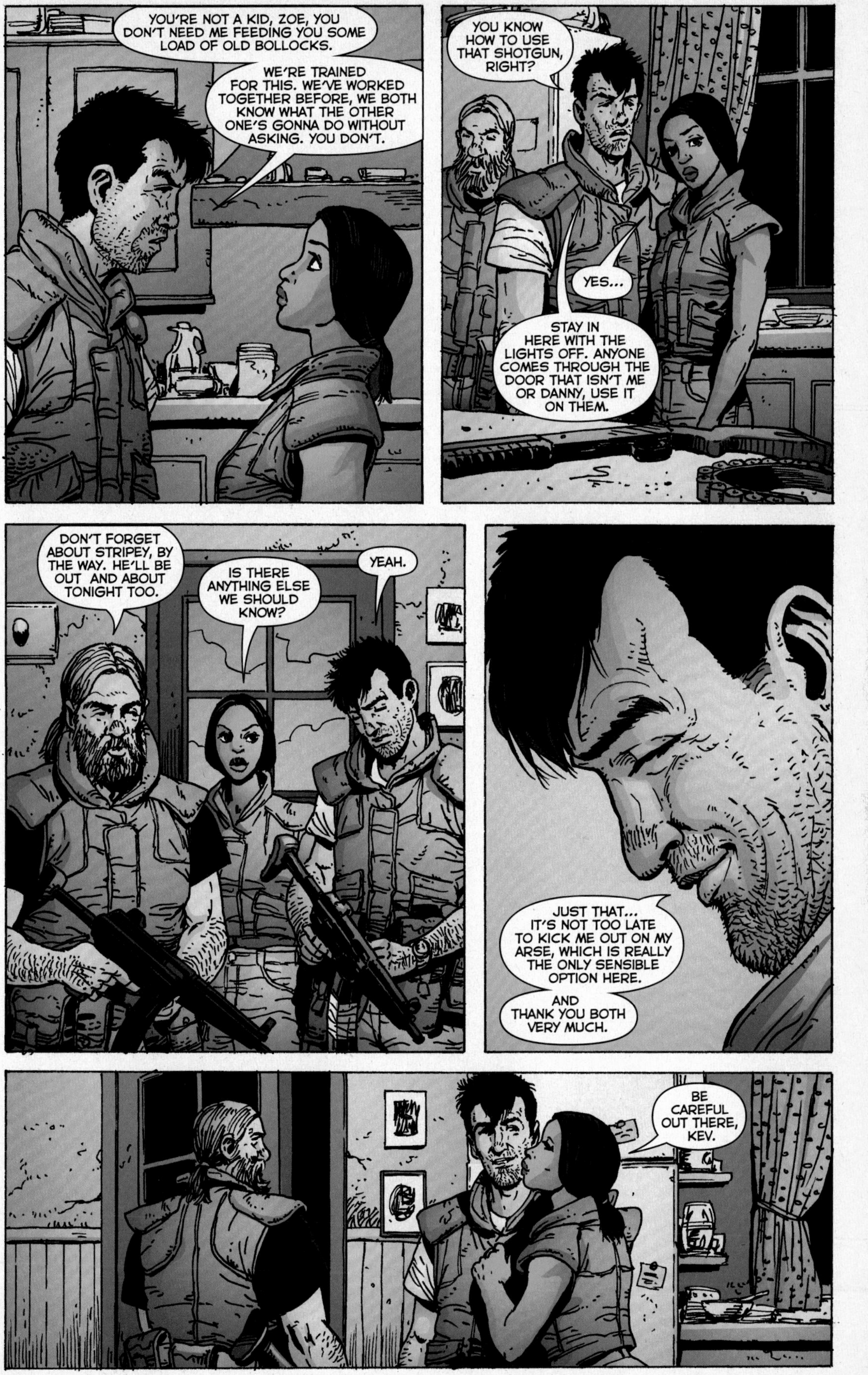
YOU'RE NOT A KID, ZOE, YOU DON'T NEED ME FEEDING YOU SOME LOAD OF OLD BOLLOCKS.
WE'RE TRAINED FOR THIS. WE'VE WORKED TOGETHER BEFORE, WE BOTH KNOW WHAT THE OTHER ONE'S GONNA DO WITHOUT ASKING. YOU DON'T.
YOU KNOW HOW TO USE THAT SHOTGUN, RIGHT?
YES...
STAY IN HERE WITH THE LIGHTS OFF. ANYONE COMES THROUGH THE DOOR THAT ISN'T ME OR DANNY, USE IT ON THEM.
DON'T FORGET ABOUT STRIPEY, BY THE WAY. HE'LL BE OUT AND ABOUT TONIGHT TOO.
IS THERE ANYTHING ELSE WE SHOULD KNOW?
YEAH.
JUST THAT... IT'S NOT TOO LATE TO KICK ME OUT ON MY ARSE, WHICH IS REALLY THE ONLY SENSIBLE OPTION HERE.
AND THANK YOU BOTH VERY MUCH.
BE CAREFUL OUT THERE, KEV.

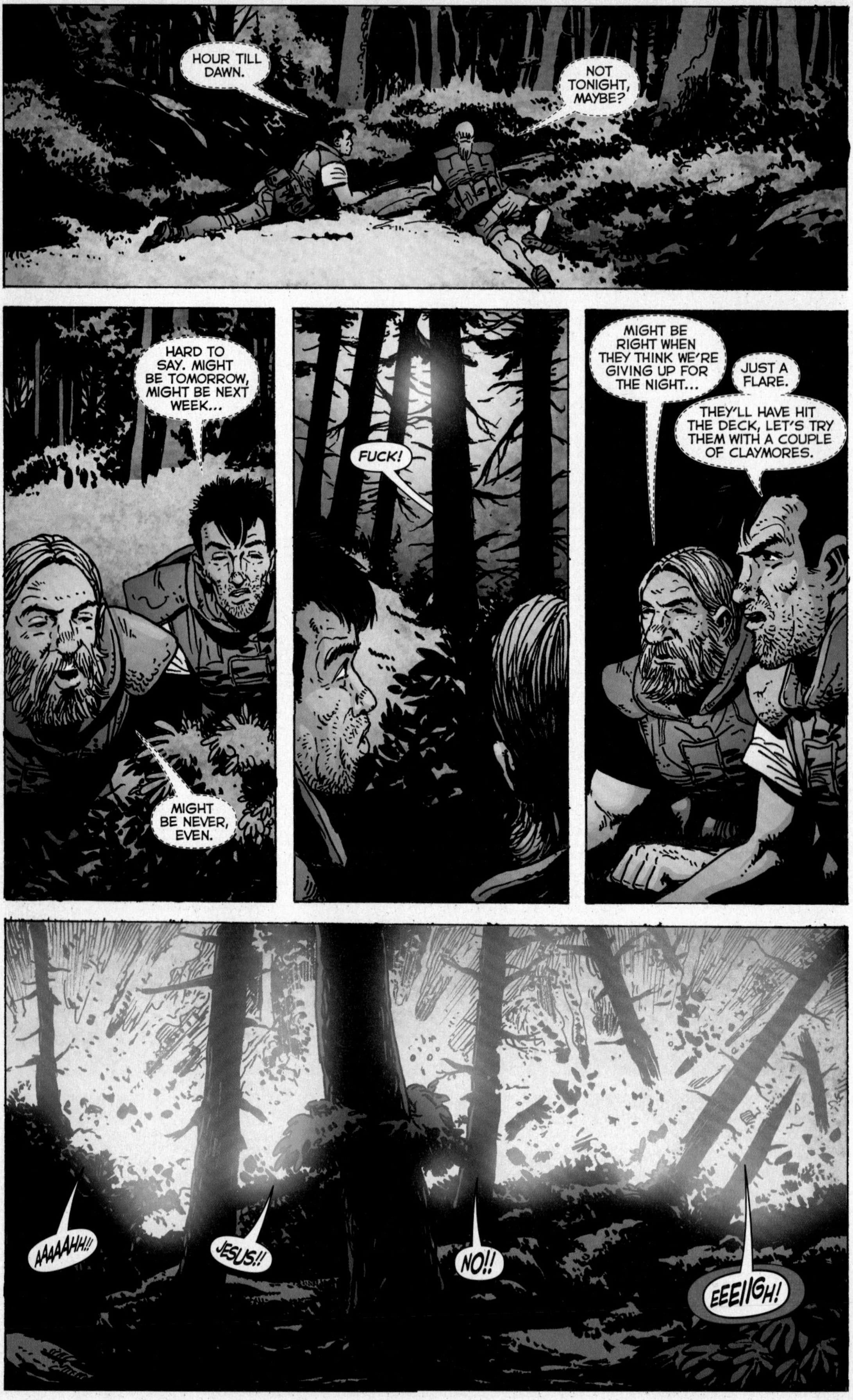
HOUR TILL DAWN.
NOT TONIGHT, MAYBE?
HARD TO SAY. MIGHT BE TOMORROW, MIGHT BE NEXT WEEK...
MIGHT BE NEVER, EVEN.
FUCK!
MIGHT BE RIGHT WHEN THEY THINK WE'RE GIVING UP FOR THE NIGHT...
JUST A FLARE.
THEY'LL HAVE HIT THE DECK, LET'S TRY THEM WITH A COUPLE OF CLAYMORES.
AAAAAHH!!
JESUS!!
NO!!
EEEIIGH!

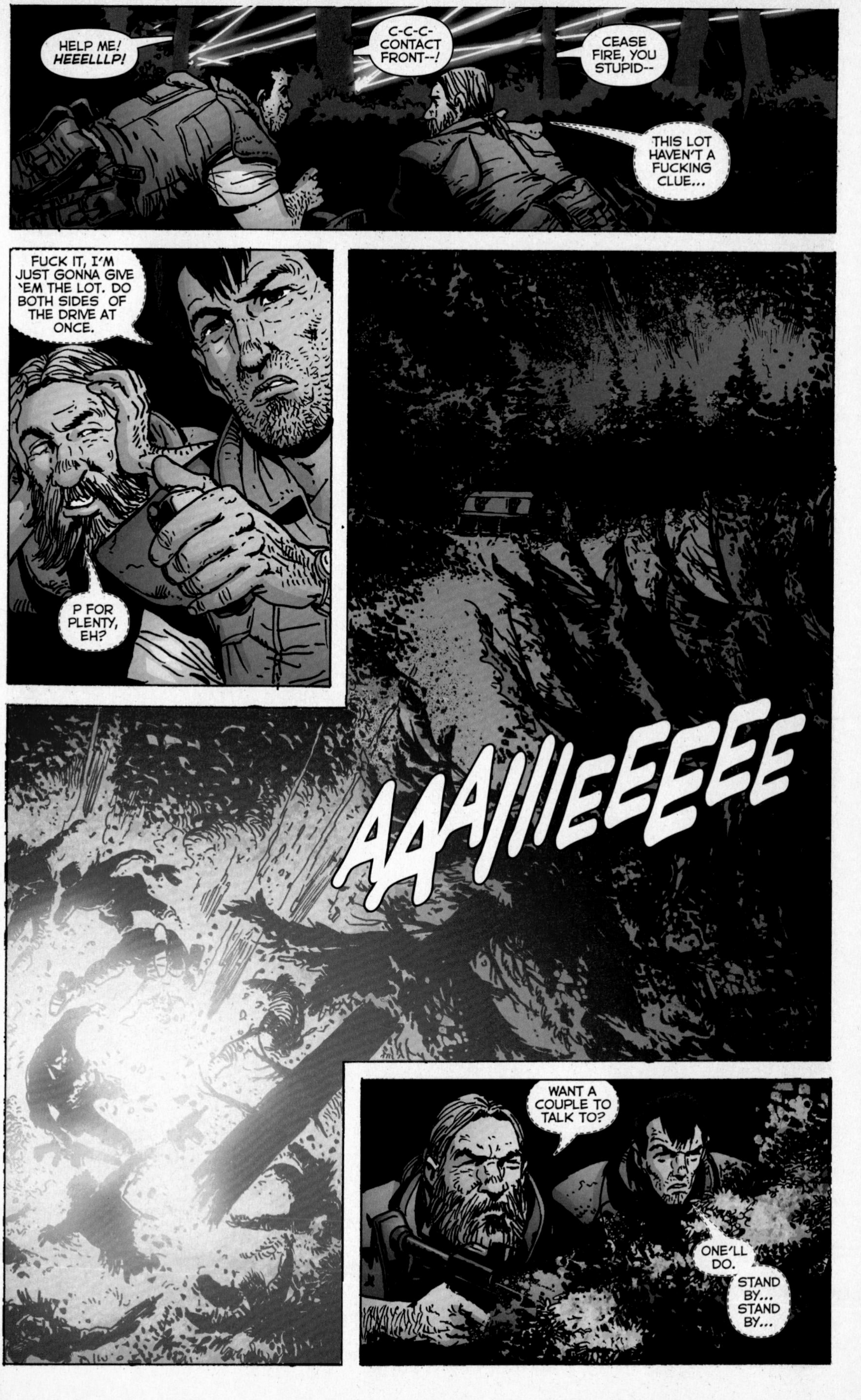
HELP ME! HEEELLLP!
C-C-C-CONTACT FRONT--!
CEASE FIRE, YOU STUPID--
THIS LOT HAVEN'T A FUCKING CLUE...
FUCK IT, I'M JUST GONNA GIVE 'EM THE LOT. DO BOTH SIDES OF THE DRIVE AT ONCE.
P FOR PLENTY, EH?
AAAIIIEEEEE
WANT A COUPLE TO TALK TO?
ONE'LL DO.
STAND BY... STAND BY...

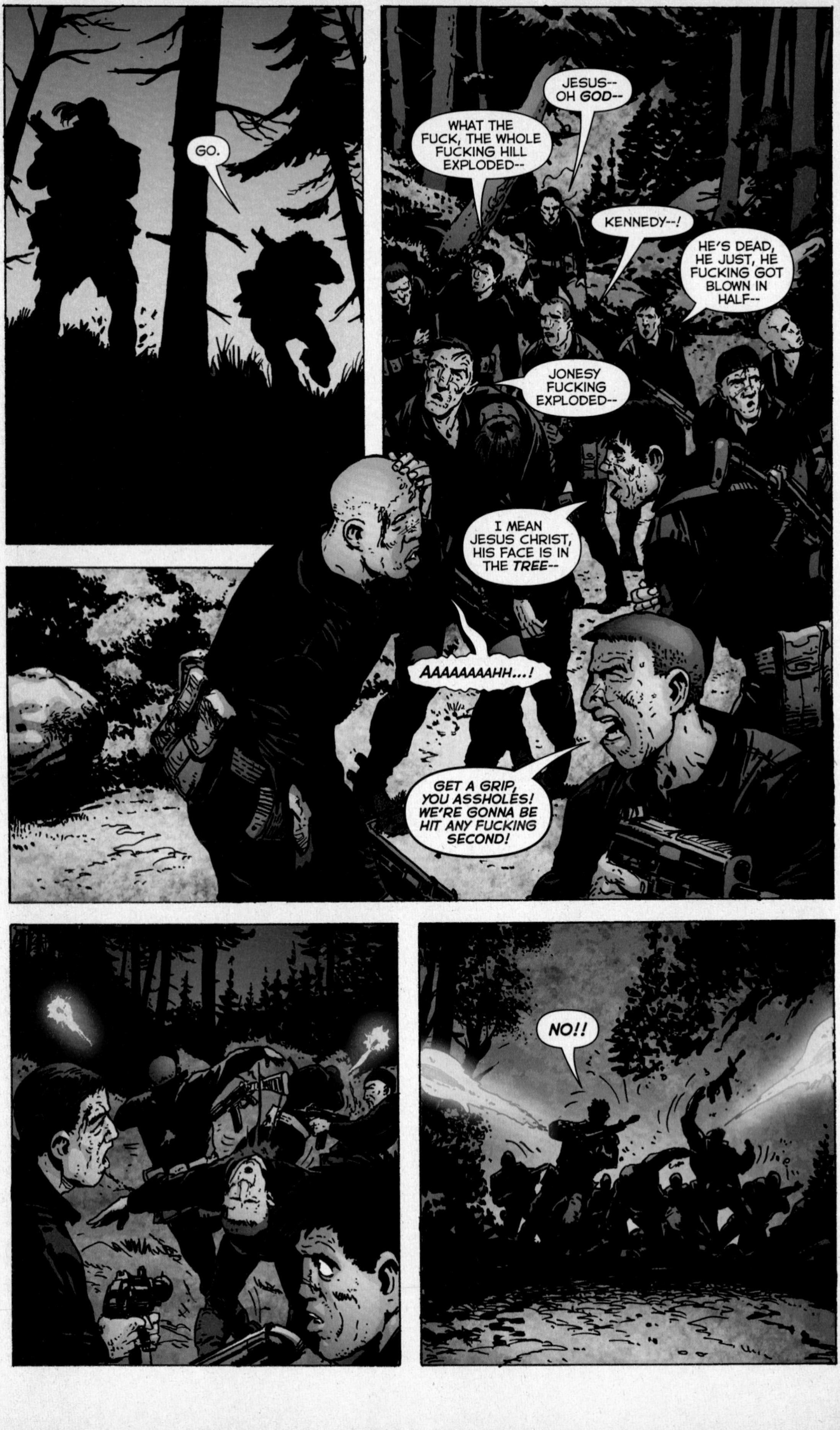
GO.
WHAT THE FUCK, THE WHOLE FUCKING HILL EXPLODED--
JESUS-- OH GOD--
KENNEDY--!
HE'S DEAD, HE JUST, HE FUCKING GOT BLOWN IN HALF--
JONESY FUCKING EXPLODED--
I MEAN JESUS CHRIST, HIS FACE IS IN THE TREE--
AAAAAAAAHH...!
GET A GRIP, YOU ASSHOLES! WE'RE GONNA BE HIT ANY FUCKING SECOND!
NO!!

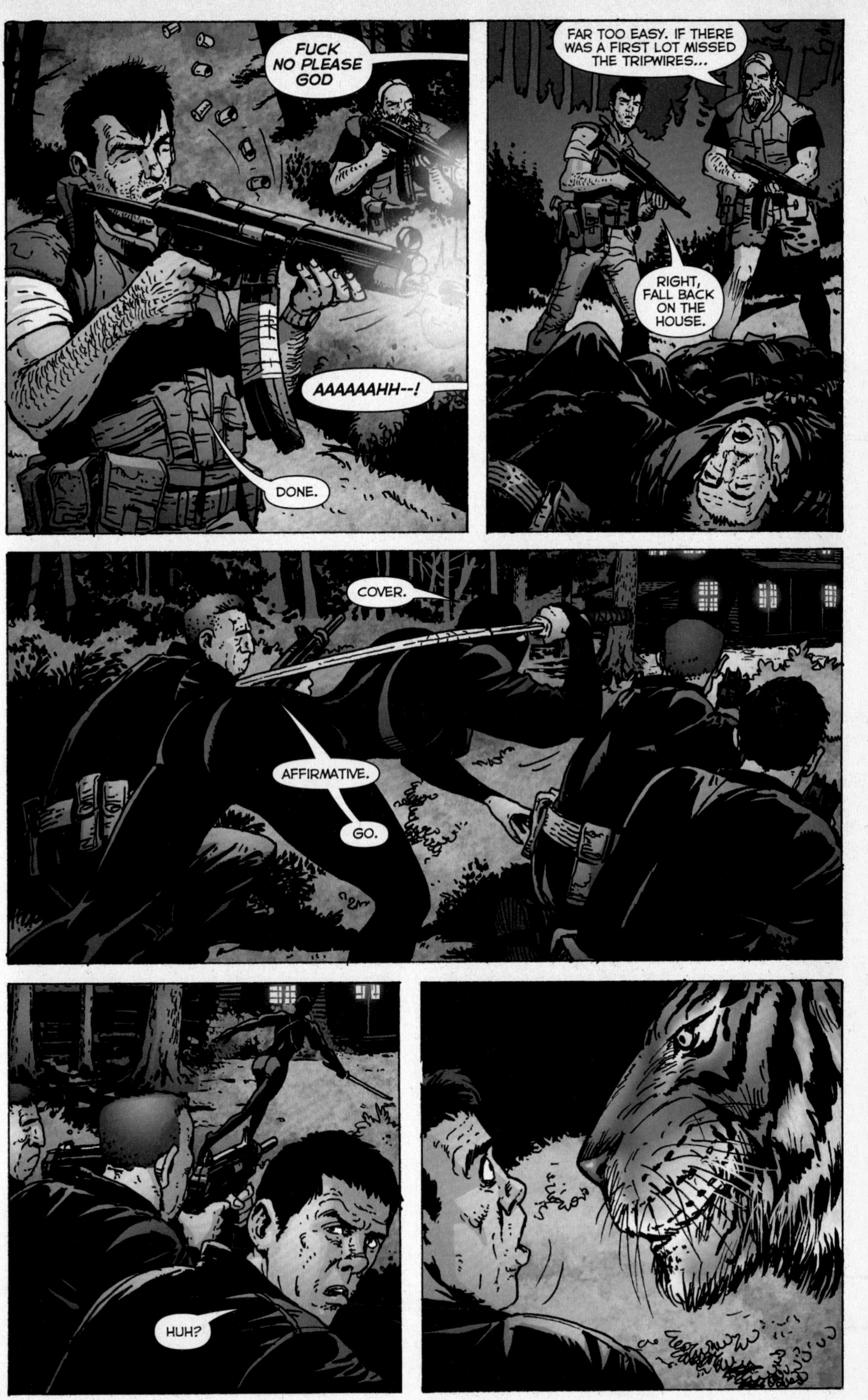
FUCK NO PLEASE GOD
AAAAAAHH--!
DONE.
FAR TOO EASY. IF THERE WAS A FIRST LOT MISSED THE TRIPWIRES...
RIGHT, FALL BACK ON THE HOUSE.
COVER.
AFFIRMATIVE.
GO.
HUH?

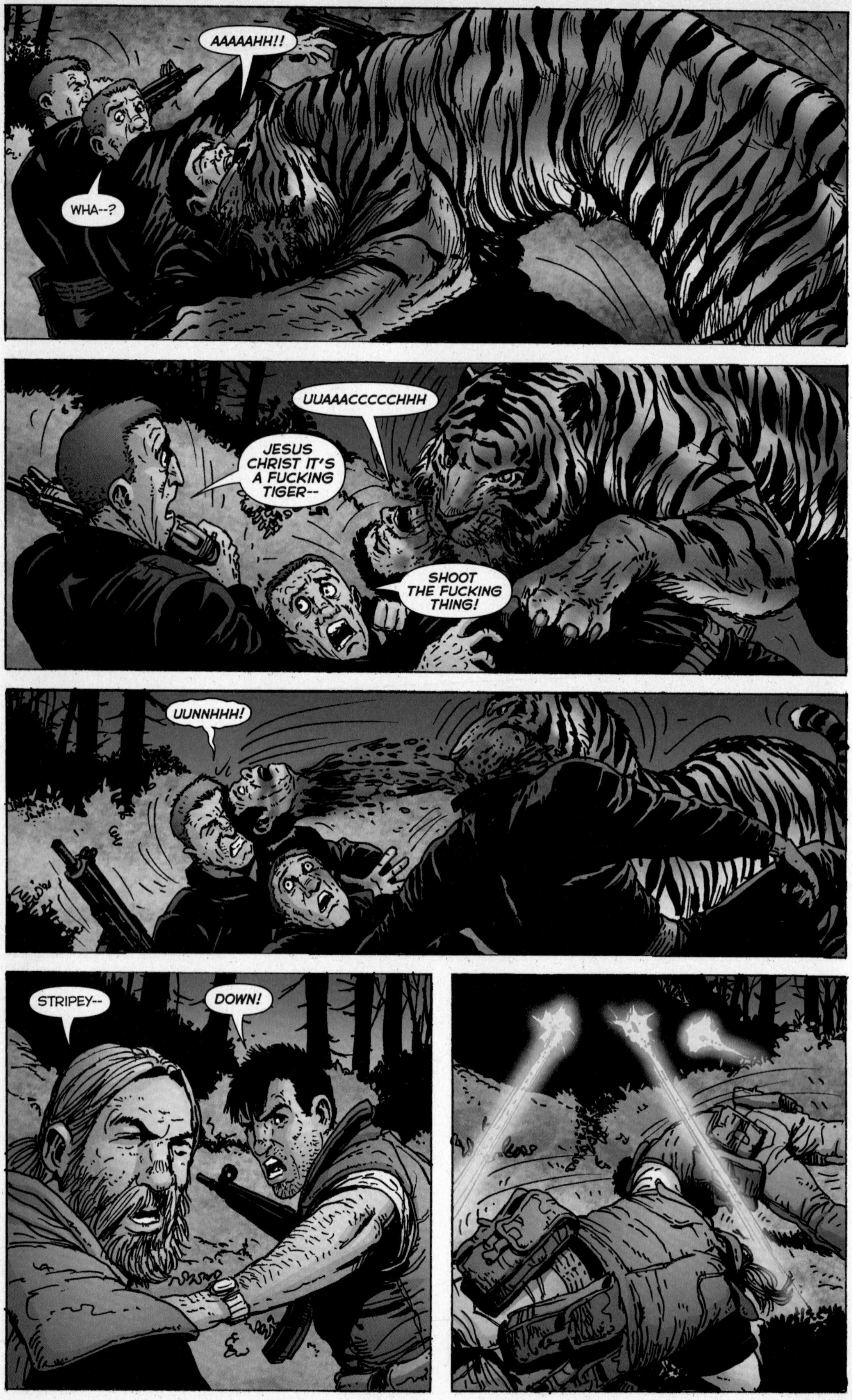
AAAAAHH!!
WHA--?
UUAAACCCCCHHH
JESUS CHRIST IT'S A FUCKING TIGER--
SHOOT THE FUCKING THING!
UUNNHHH!
STRIPEY--
DOWN!

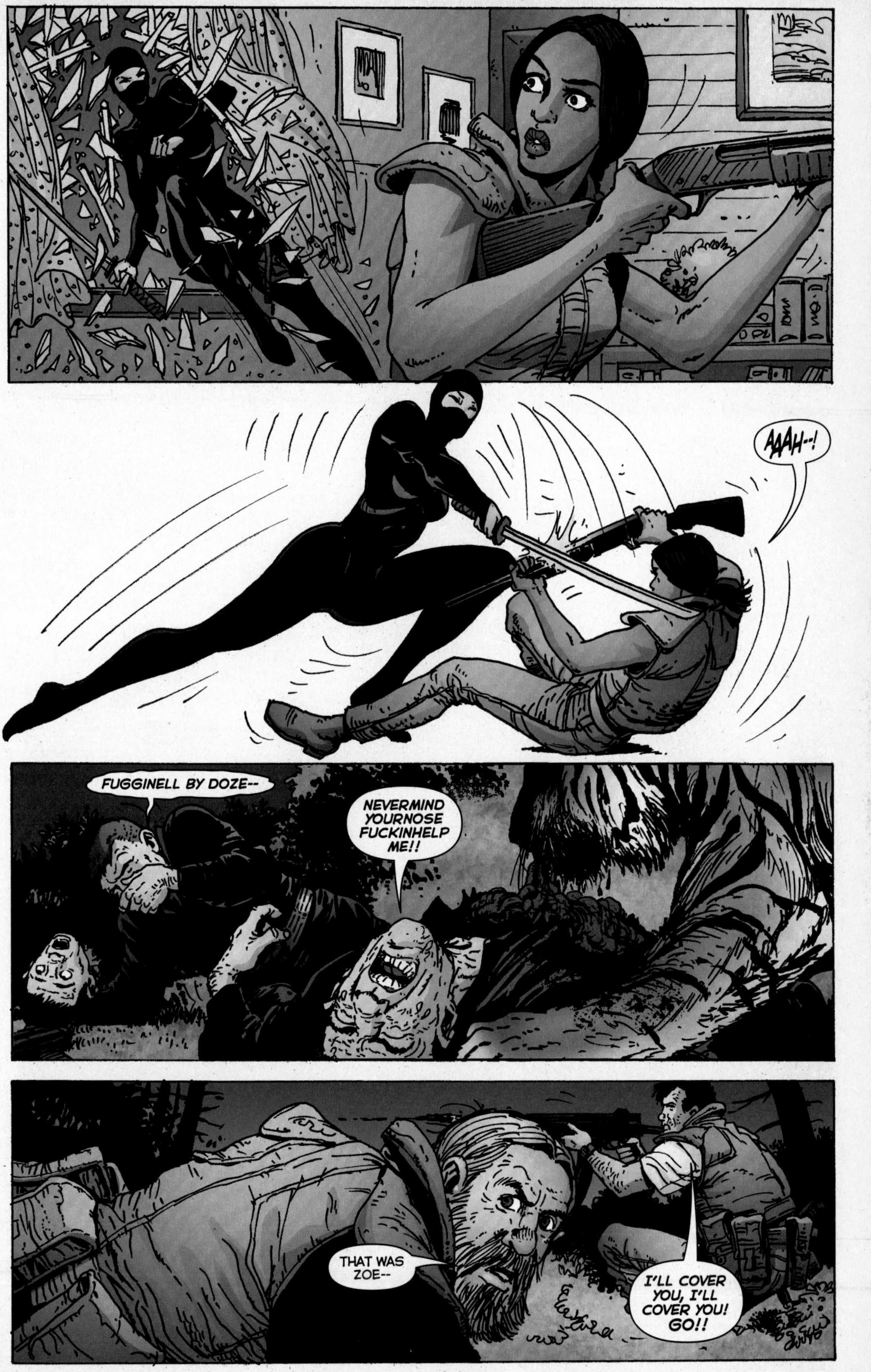
AAAH--!
FUGGINELL BY DOZE--
NEVERMIND YOURNOSE FUCKINHELP ME!!
THAT WAS ZOE--
I'LL COVER YOU, I'LL COVER YOU! GO!!

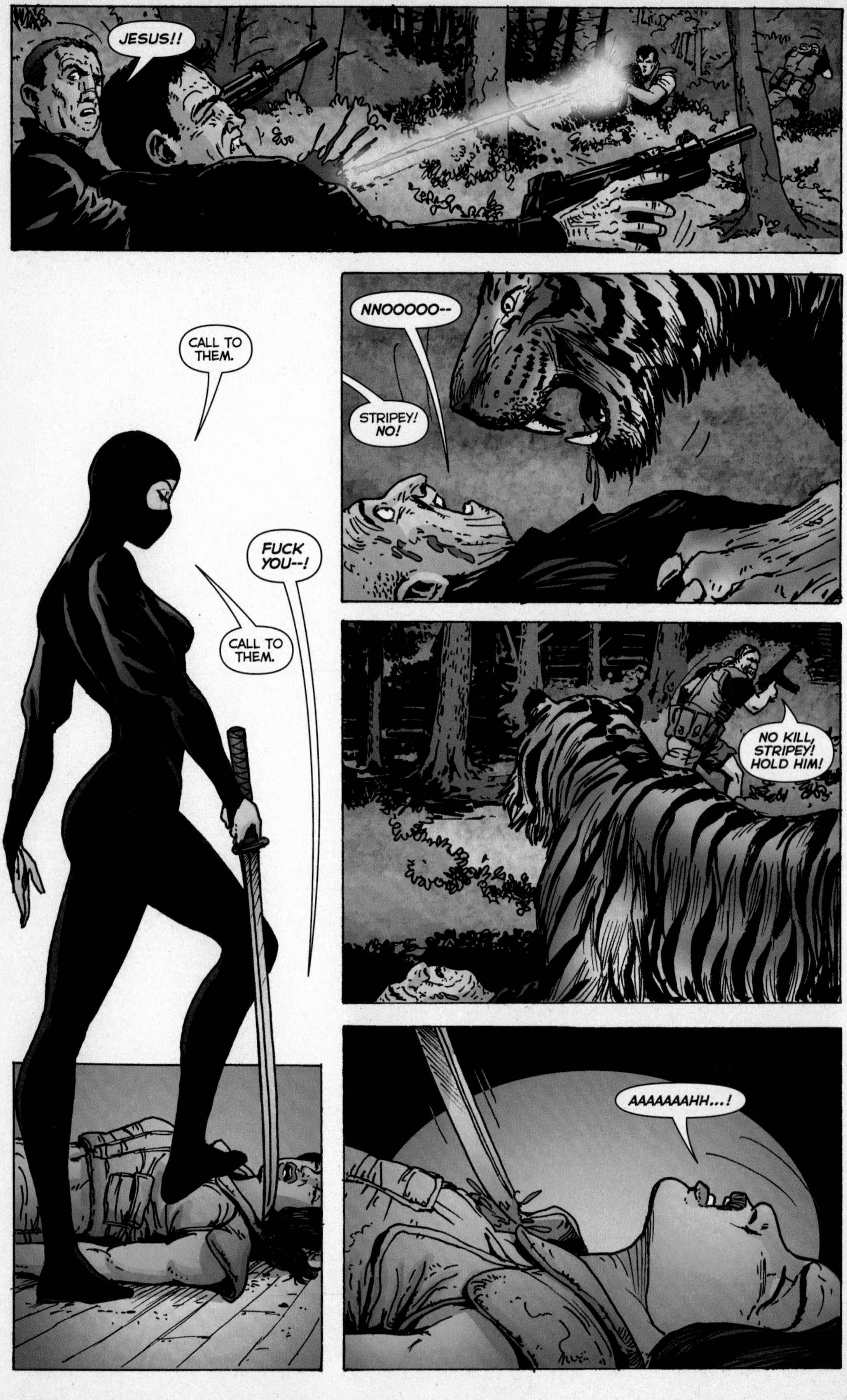
JESUS!!
NNOOOOO--
STRIPEY! NO!
CALL TO THEM.
FUCK YOU--!
CALL TO THEM.
NO KILL, STRIPEY! HOLD HIM!
AAAAAAAHH...!

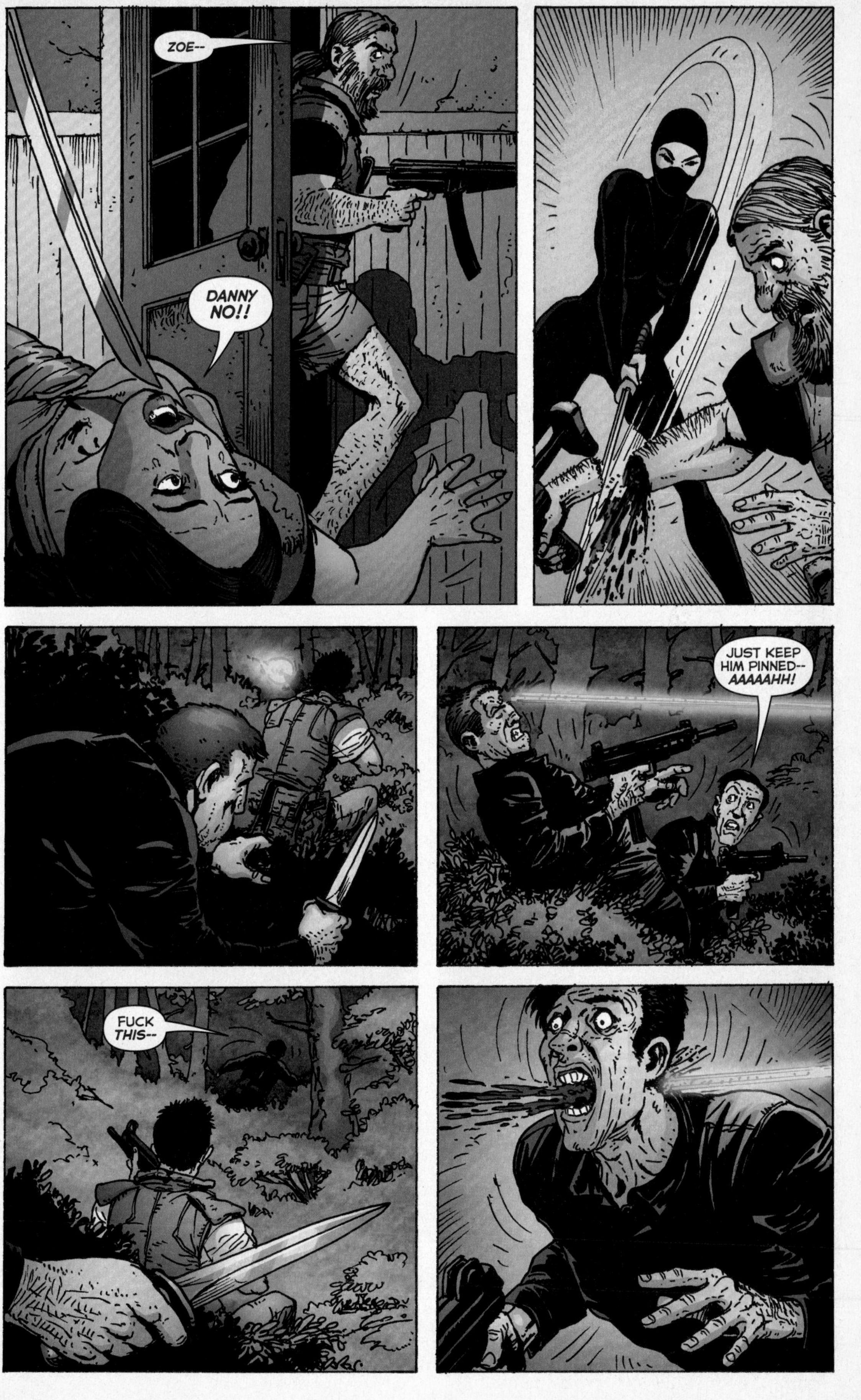
ZOE--
DANNY NO!!
JUST KEEP HIM PINNED-- AAAAAHH!
FUCK THIS--

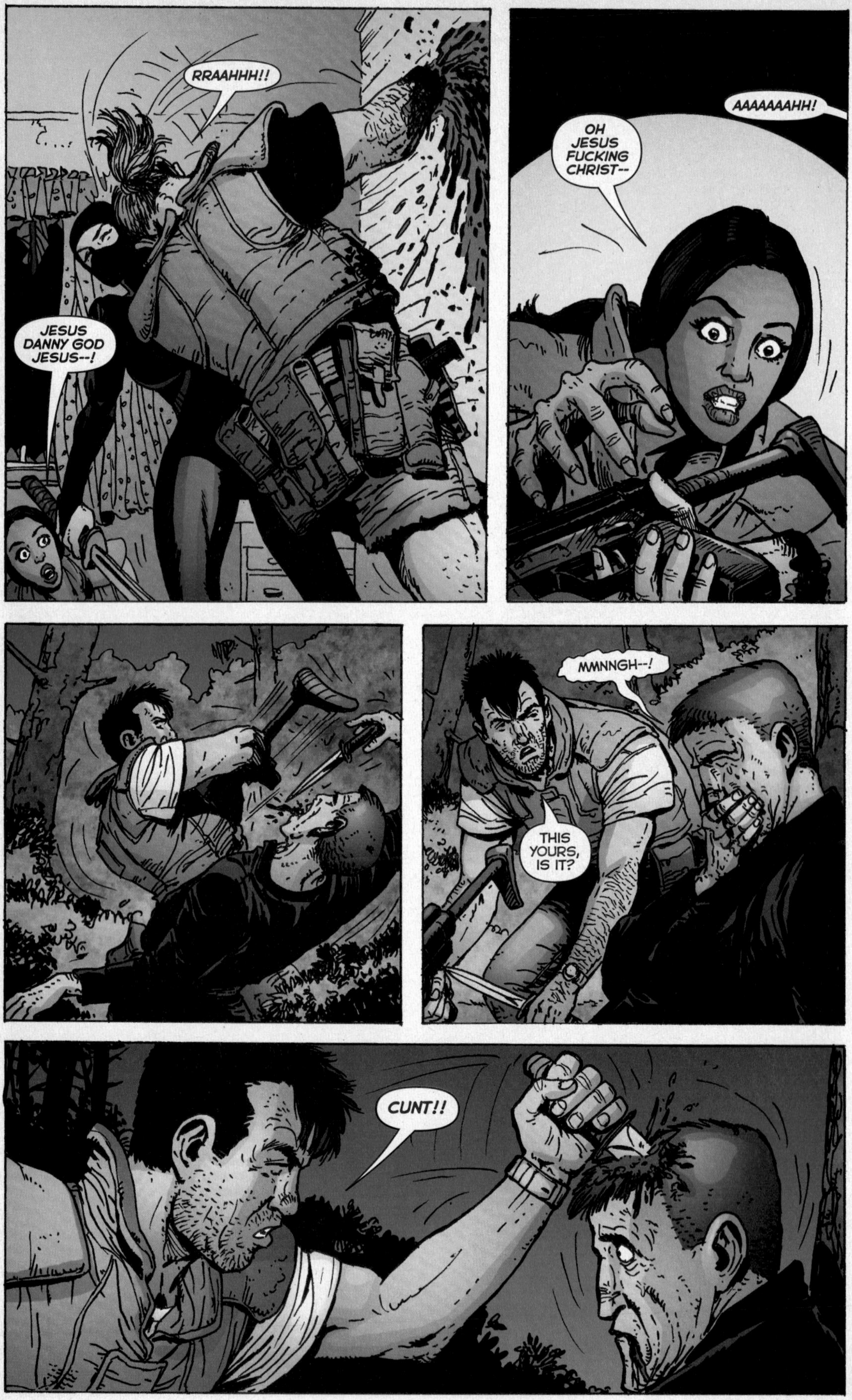
RRAAHHH!!
JESUS DANNY GOD JESUS--!
AAAAAAAHH!
OH JESUS FUCKING CHRIST--
MMNNGH--!
THIS YOURS, IS IT?
CUNT!!

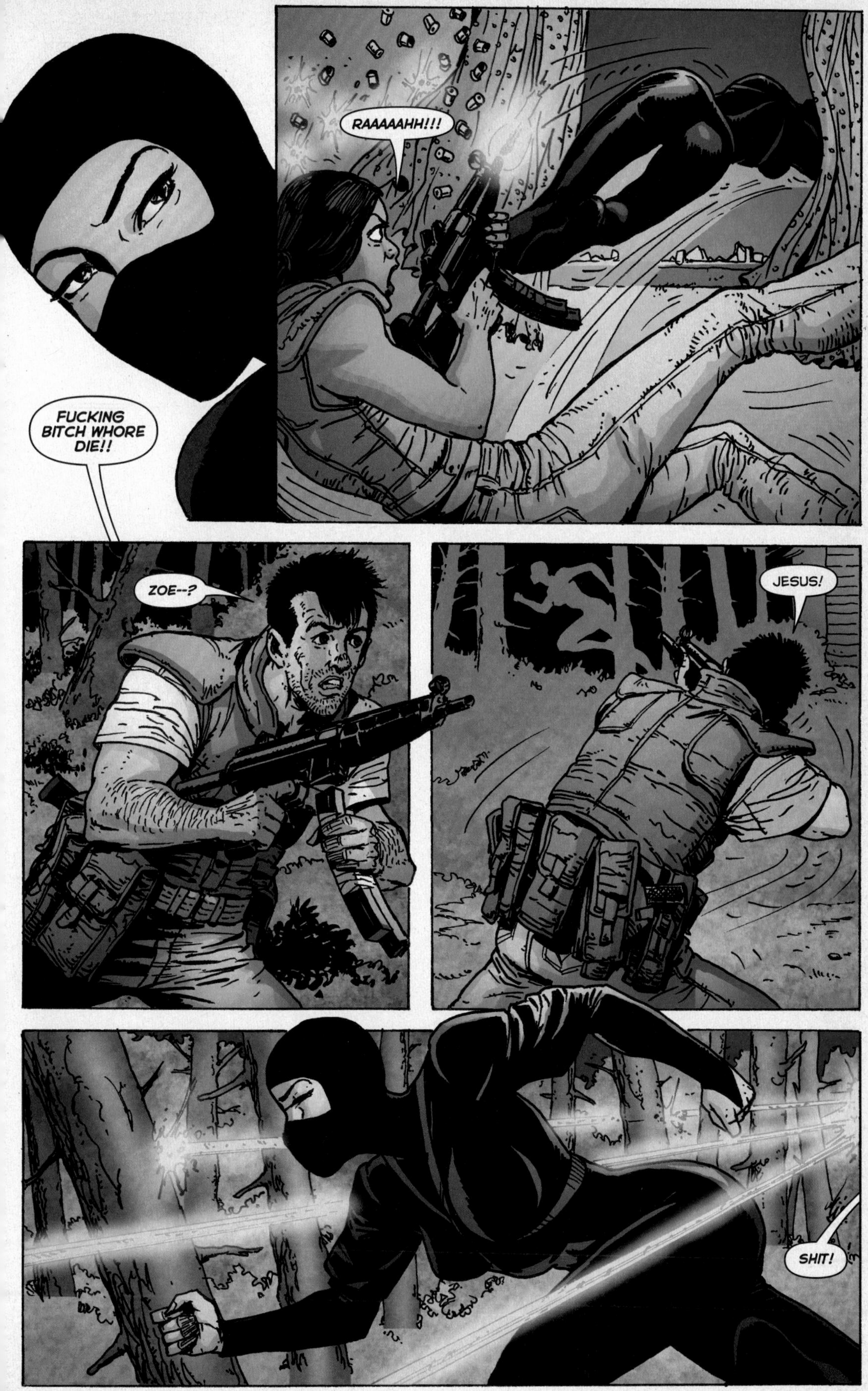

RAAAAAHH!!!
FUCKING BITCH WHORE DIE!!
ZOE--?
JESUS!
SHIT!

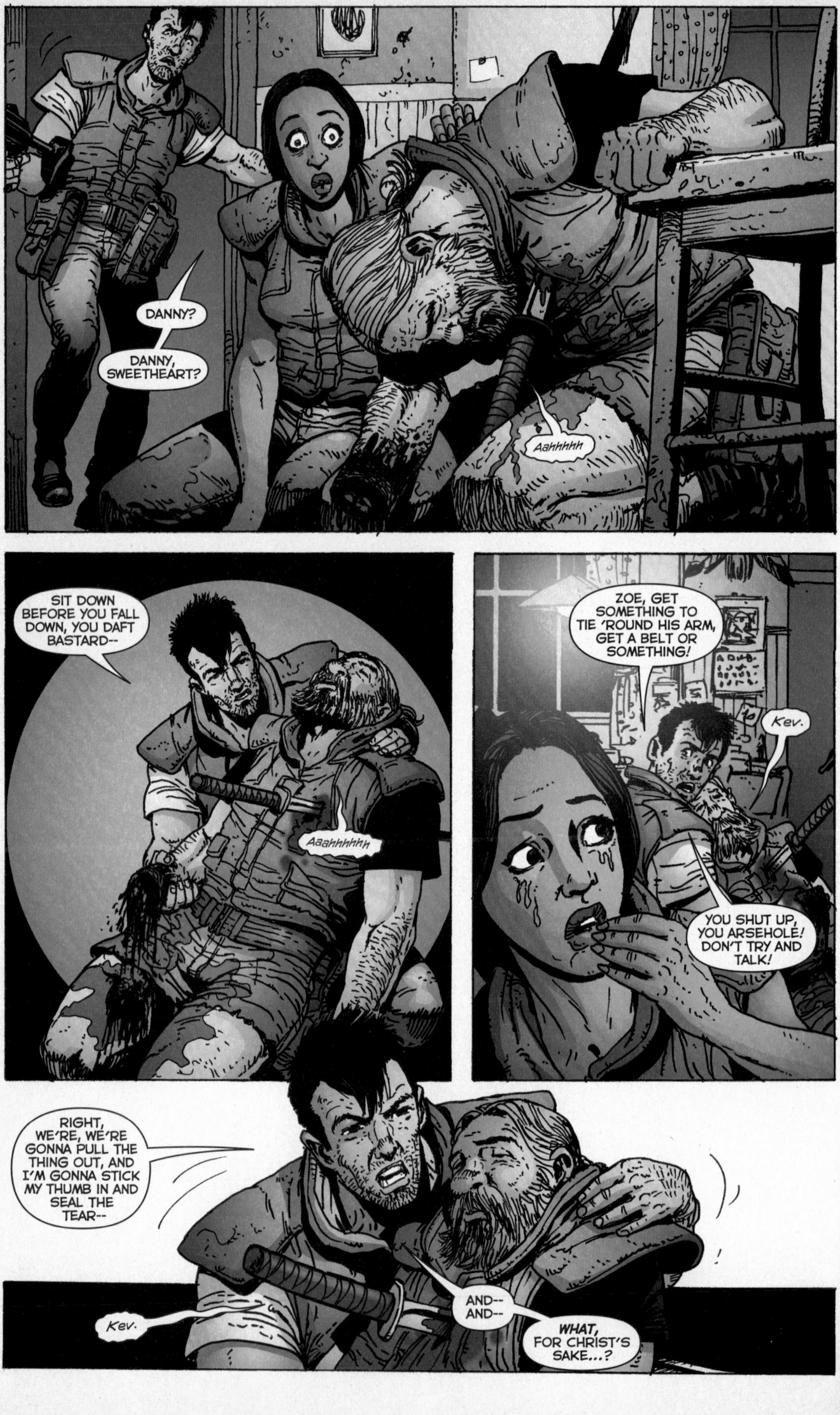
DANNY?
DANNY, SWEETHEART?
Aahhhhh
SIT DOWN BEFORE YOU FALL DOWN, YOU DAFT BASTARD--
Aaahhhhhh
ZOE, GET SOMETHING TO TIE 'ROUND HIS ARM, GET A BELT OR SOMETHING!
Kev.
YOU SHUT UP, YOU ARSEHOLE! DON'T TRY AND TALK!
RIGHT, WE'RE, WE'RE GONNA PULL THE THING OUT, AND I'M GONNA STICK MY THUMB IN AND SEAL THE TEAR--
Kev.
AND-- AND--
WHAT, FOR CHRIST'S SAKE...?

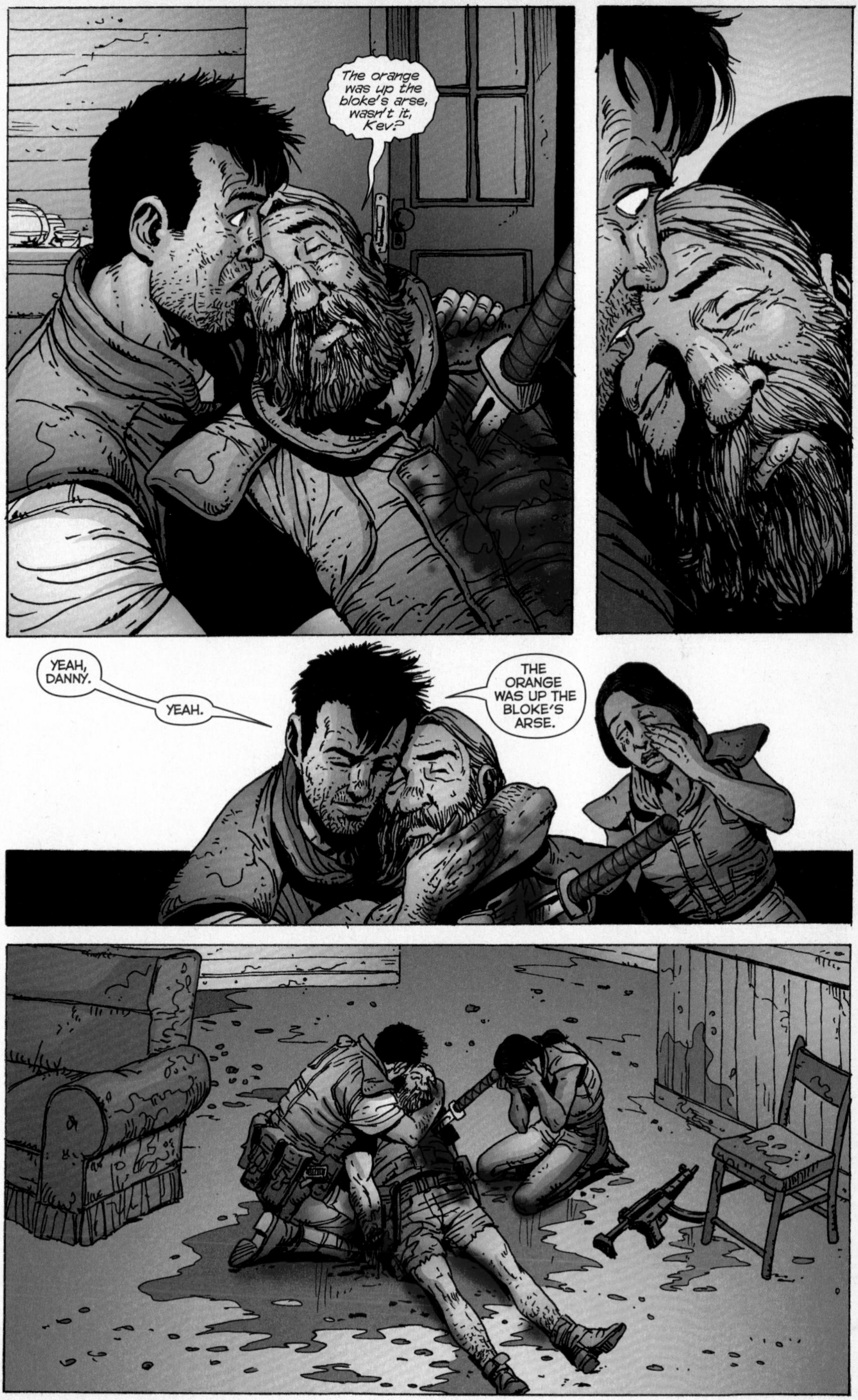

The orange was up the bloke's arse, wasn't it, Kev?
YEAH, DANNY.
YEAH.
THE ORANGE WAS UP THE BLOKE'S ARSE.

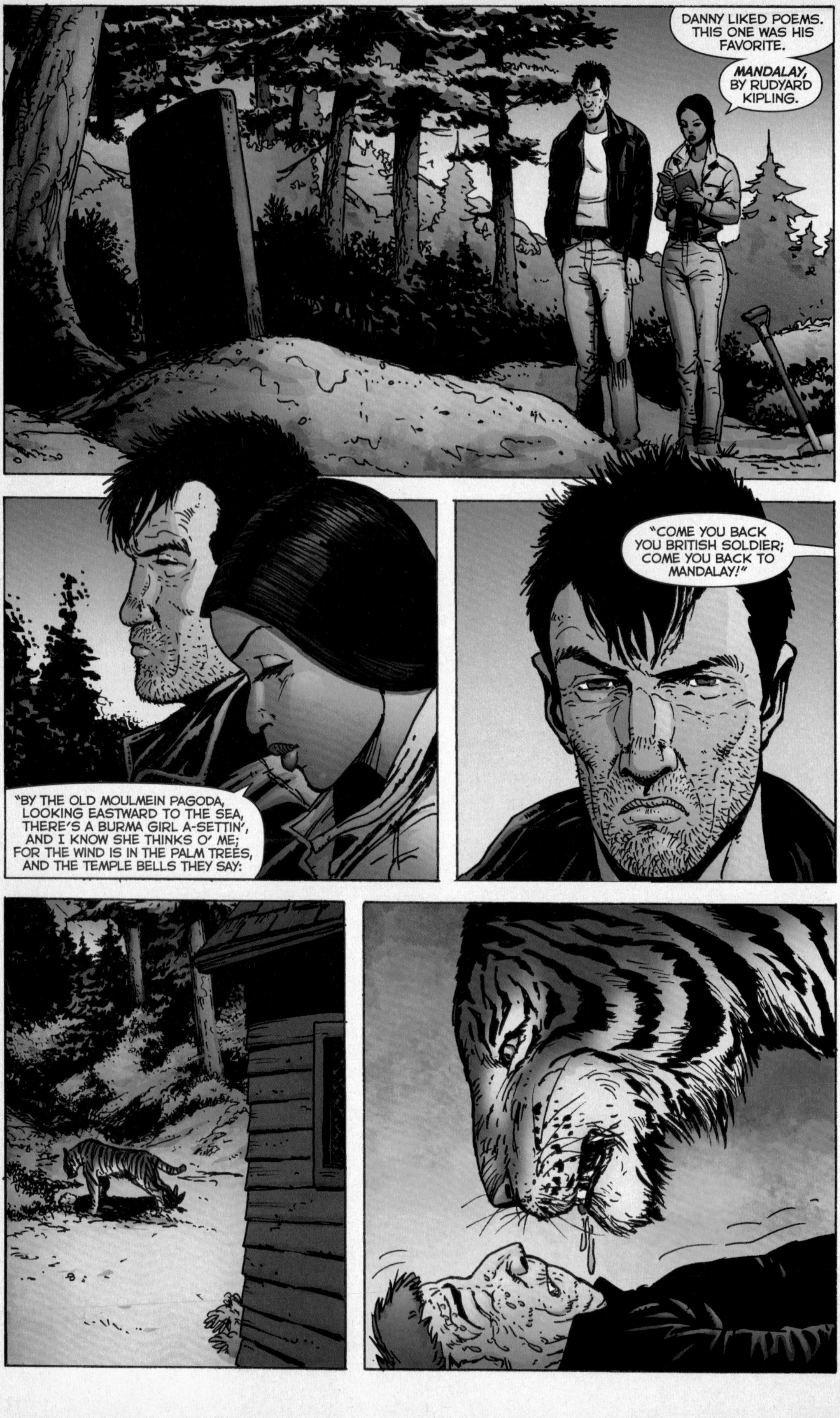
DANNY LIKED POEMS. THIS ONE WAS HIS FAVORITE.
MANDALAY, BY RUDYARD KIPLING.
"BY THE OLD MOULMEIN PAGODA, LOOKING EASTWARD TO THE SEA, THERE'S A BURMA GIRL A-SETTIN', AND I KNOW SHE THINKS O' ME; FOR THE WIND IS IN THE PALM TREES, AND THE TEMPLE BELLS THEY SAY:
"COME YOU BACK YOU BRITISH SOLDIER; COME YOU BACK TO MANDALAY!"

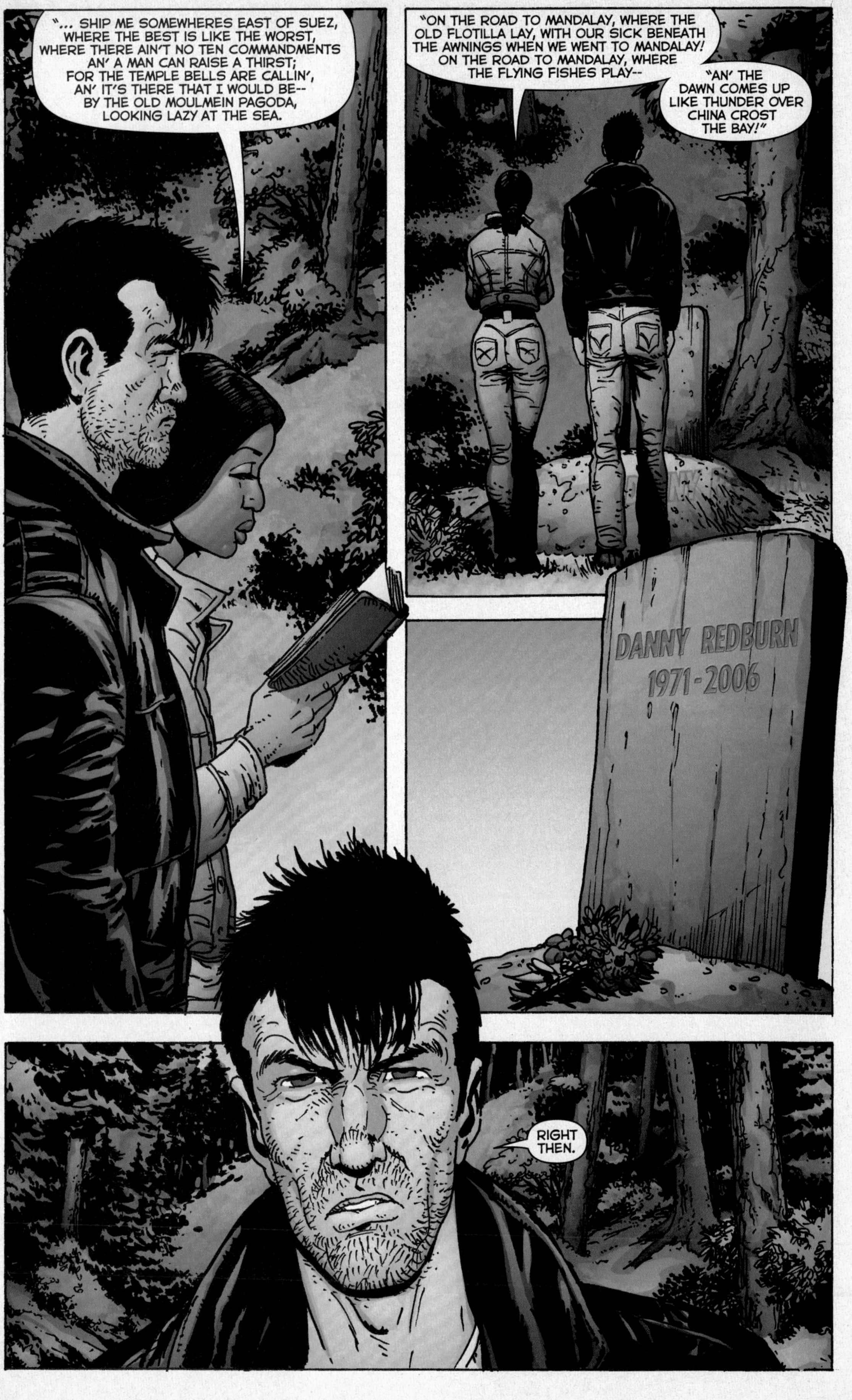
"... SHIP ME SOMEWHERES EAST OF SUEZ, WHERE THE BEST IS LIKE THE WORST, WHERE THERE AIN'T NO TEN COMMANDMENTS AN' A MAN CAN RAISE A THIRST; FOR THE TEMPLE BELLS ARE CALLIN', AN' IT'S THERE THAT I WOULD BE-- BY THE OLD MOULMEIN PAGODA, LOOKING LAZY AT THE SEA.
"ON THE ROAD TO MANDALAY, WHERE THE OLD FLOTILLA LAY, WITH OUR SICK BENEATH THE AWNINGS WHEN WE WENT TO MANDALAY! ON THE ROAD TO MANDALAY, WHERE THE FLYING FISHES PLAY--
"AN' THE DAWN COMES UP LIKE THUNDER OVER CHINA CROST THE BAY!"
DANNY REDBURN
1971-2006
RIGHT THEN.

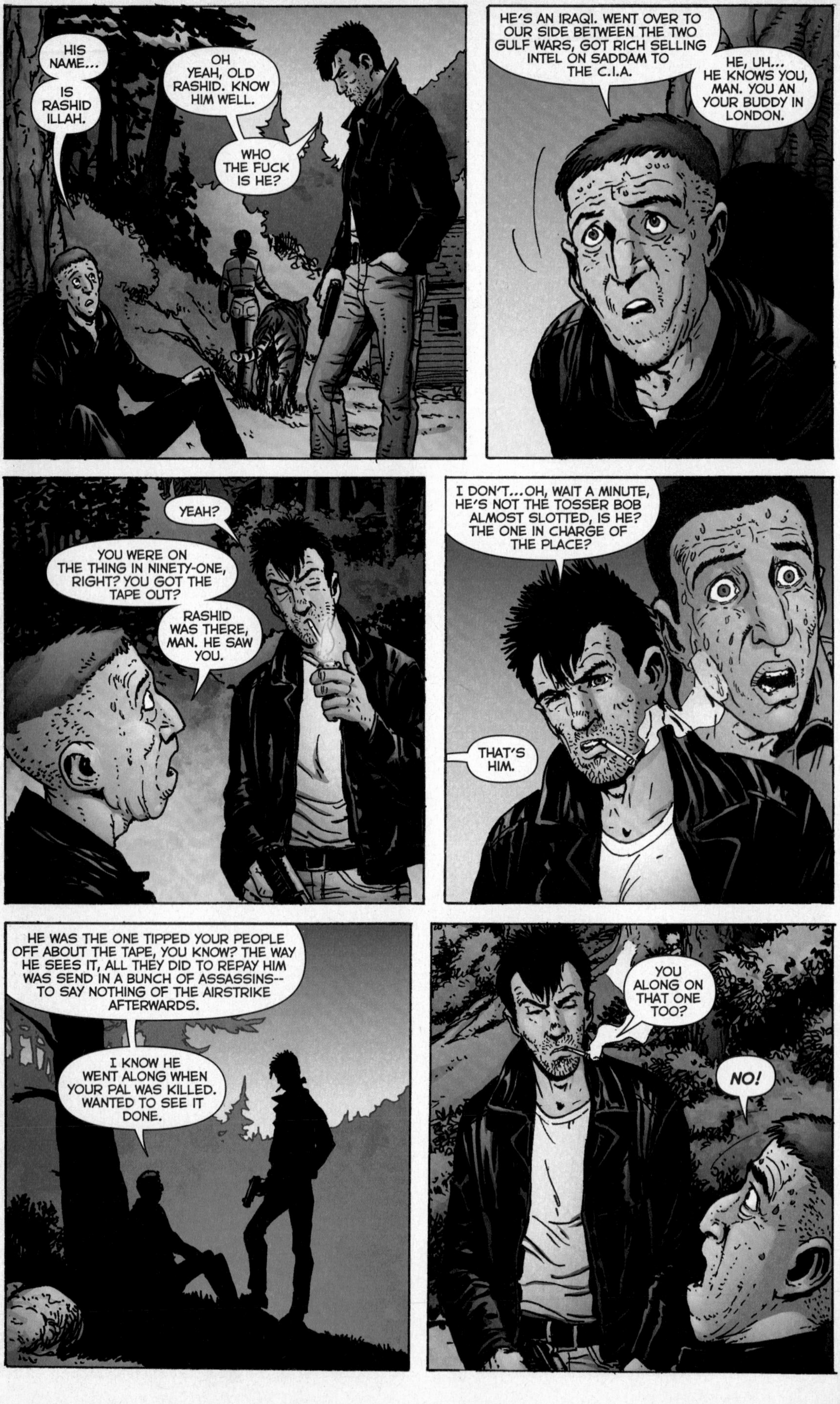

HIS NAME...
IS RASHID ILLAH.
OH YEAH, OLD RASHID. KNOW HIM WELL.
WHO THE FUCK IS HE?
HE'S AN IRAQI. WENT OVER TO OUR SIDE BETWEEN THE TWO GULF WARS, GOT RICH SELLING INTEL ON SADDAM TO THE C.I.A.
HE, UH... HE KNOWS YOU, MAN. YOU AN YOUR BUDDY IN LONDON.
YEAH?
YOU WERE ON THE THING IN NINETY-ONE, RIGHT? YOU GOT THE TAPE OUT?
RASHID WAS THERE, MAN. HE SAW YOU.
I DON'T...OH, WAIT A MINUTE, HE'S NOT THE TOSSER BOB ALMOST SLOTTED, IS HE? THE ONE IN CHARGE OF THE PLACE?
THAT'S HIM.
HE WAS THE ONE TIPPED YOUR PEOPLE OFF ABOUT THE TAPE, YOU KNOW? THE WAY HE SEES IT, ALL THEY DID TO REPAY HIM WAS SEND IN A BUNCH OF ASSASSINS-- TO SAY NOTHING OF THE AIRSTRIKE AFTERWARDS.
I KNOW HE WENT ALONG WHEN YOUR PAL WAS KILLED. WANTED TO SEE IT DONE.
YOU ALONG ON THAT ONE TOO?
NO!

NO, NO, I SWEAR TO GOD! HE WASTED EVERY SINGLE GUY WE SENT, ONLY RASHID AND THE JAP GOT OUT ALIVE! I'M TELLING THE FUCKING TRUTH, I SWEAR TO YOU!

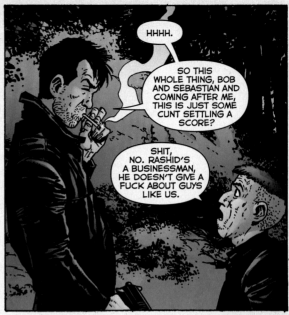

HHHH.

SO THIS WHOLE THING, BOB AND SEBASTIAN AND COMING AFTER ME, THIS IS JUST SOME CUNT SETTLING A SCORE?

SHIT, NO. RASHID'S A BUSINESSMAN, HE DOESN'T GIVE A FUCK ABOUT GUYS LIKE US.

"IT WAS SEBASTIAN.

"WE HIT HIM FIRST, ALL WE WANTED WAS THE TAPE. RASHID TRACKED HIM DOWN AS THE GUY WHO AUTHORIZED YOUR OPERATION, FIGURING HE'D STILL HAVE IT--HE WAS RIGHT.

"BUT SEBASTIAN WAS BEGGING FOR HIS LIFE. HE SAID THE TWO SURVIVING MEMBERS OF BRAVO FOUR ZERO HAD COPIES OF THE TAPE, WHICH THEY WERE USING TO BLACKMAIL THE BRITISH ESTABLISHMENT. HE'D TELL US WHO IF WE LET HIM WALK AWAY."

RASHID DIDN'T TWIG THAT WAS JUST A LOAD OF OLD BOLLOCKS?

NO MORE THAN SEBASTIAN REALIZED HE WAS DEAD FROM THE START. HE GAVE US TWO NAMES.

"BOB CARTER--

"AND KEV HAWKINS."

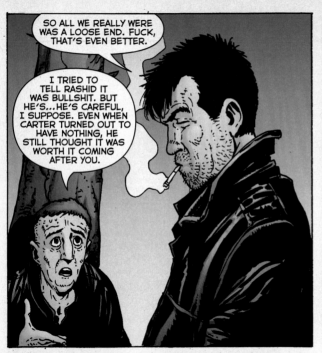

SO ALL WE REALLY WERE WAS A LOOSE END. FUCK, THAT'S EVEN BETTER.

I TRIED TO TELL RASHID IT WAS...BULLSHIT. BUT HE'S...HE'S CAREFUL, I SUPPOSE. EVEN WHEN CARTER TURNED OUT TO HAVE NOTHING, HE STILL THOUGHT IT WAS WORTH IT COMING AFTER YOU.

WHERE'S RASHID NOW?

GOT A PLACE NEAR TAHOE. THERE'S ANOTHER TWO DOZEN GUYS UP THERE WITH HIM.

AND HOW DID YOU LOT GET HERE?

WE DROVE, MAN. THE VEHICLES ARE DOWN A TRACK RIGHT WHERE THE ROAD STARTS UP THE HILL, I CAN SHOW YOU IF YOU WANT...

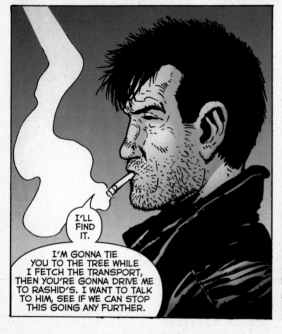

I'LL FIND IT.

I'M GONNA TIE YOU TO THE TREE WHILE I FETCH THE TRANSPORT, THEN YOU'RE GONNA DRIVE ME TO RASHID'S. I WANT TO TALK TO HIM, SEE IF WE CAN STOP THIS GOING ANY FURTHER.

MAN, IS THERE ANY CHANCE I CAN USE YOUR BATHROOM? I MEAN LOOK AT ME, I ALREADY PISSED MYSELF HERE...

FOR ALL I CARE, YOU CAN FUCKING PISS YOURSELF AGAIN.

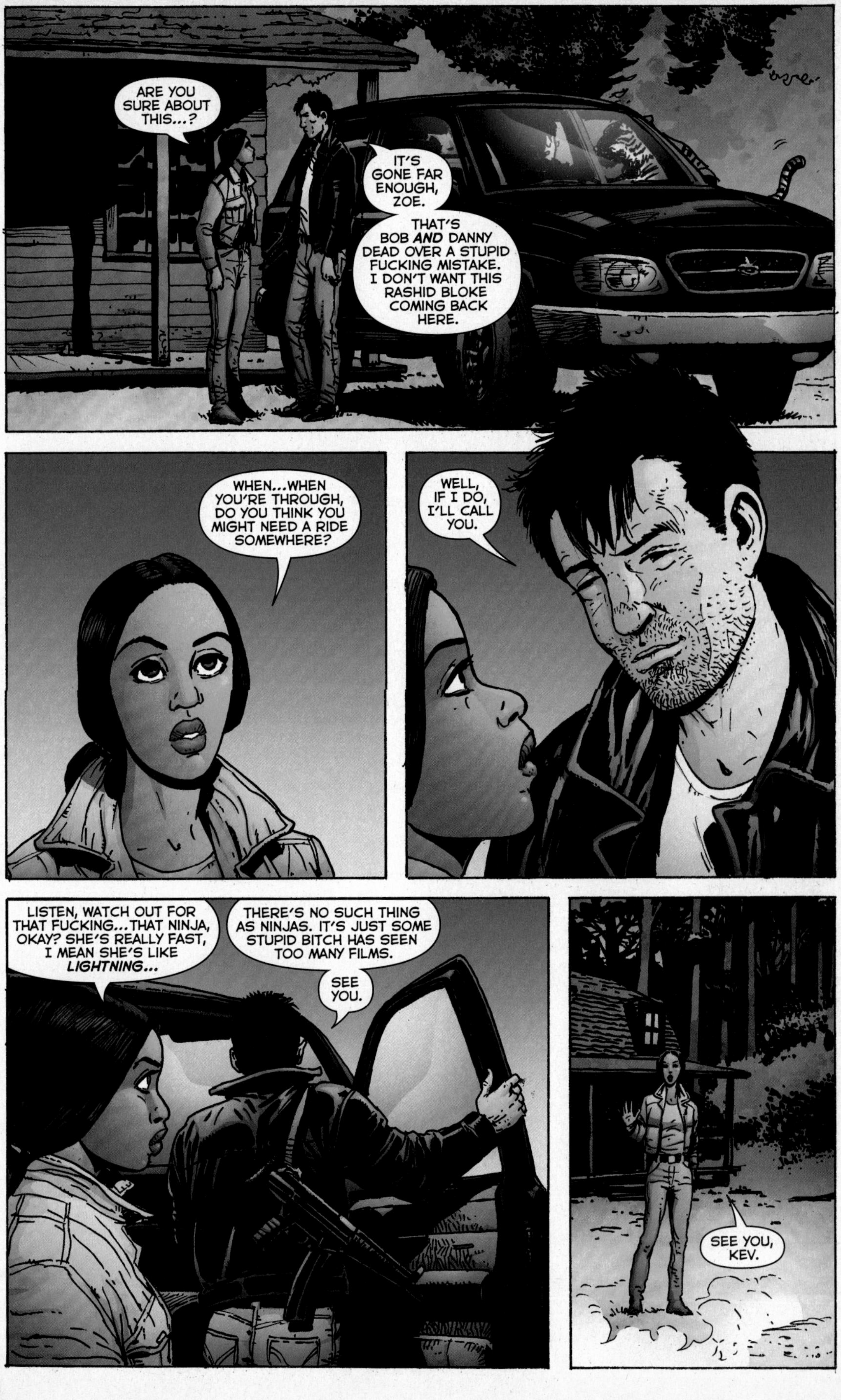
ARE YOU SURE ABOUT THIS...?
IT'S GONE FAR ENOUGH, ZOE.
THAT'S BOB AND DANNY DEAD OVER A STUPID FUCKING MISTAKE. I DON'T WANT THIS RASHID BLOKE COMING BACK HERE.
WHEN...WHEN YOU'RE THROUGH, DO YOU THINK YOU MIGHT NEED A RIDE SOMEWHERE?
WELL, IF I DO, I'LL CALL YOU.
LISTEN, WATCH OUT FOR THAT FUCKING...THAT NINJA, OKAY? SHE'S REALLY FAST, I MEAN SHE'S LIKE LIGHTNING...
THERE'S NO SUCH THING AS NINJAS. IT'S JUST SOME STUPID BITCH HAS SEEN TOO MANY FILMS.
SEE YOU.
SEE YOU, KEV.

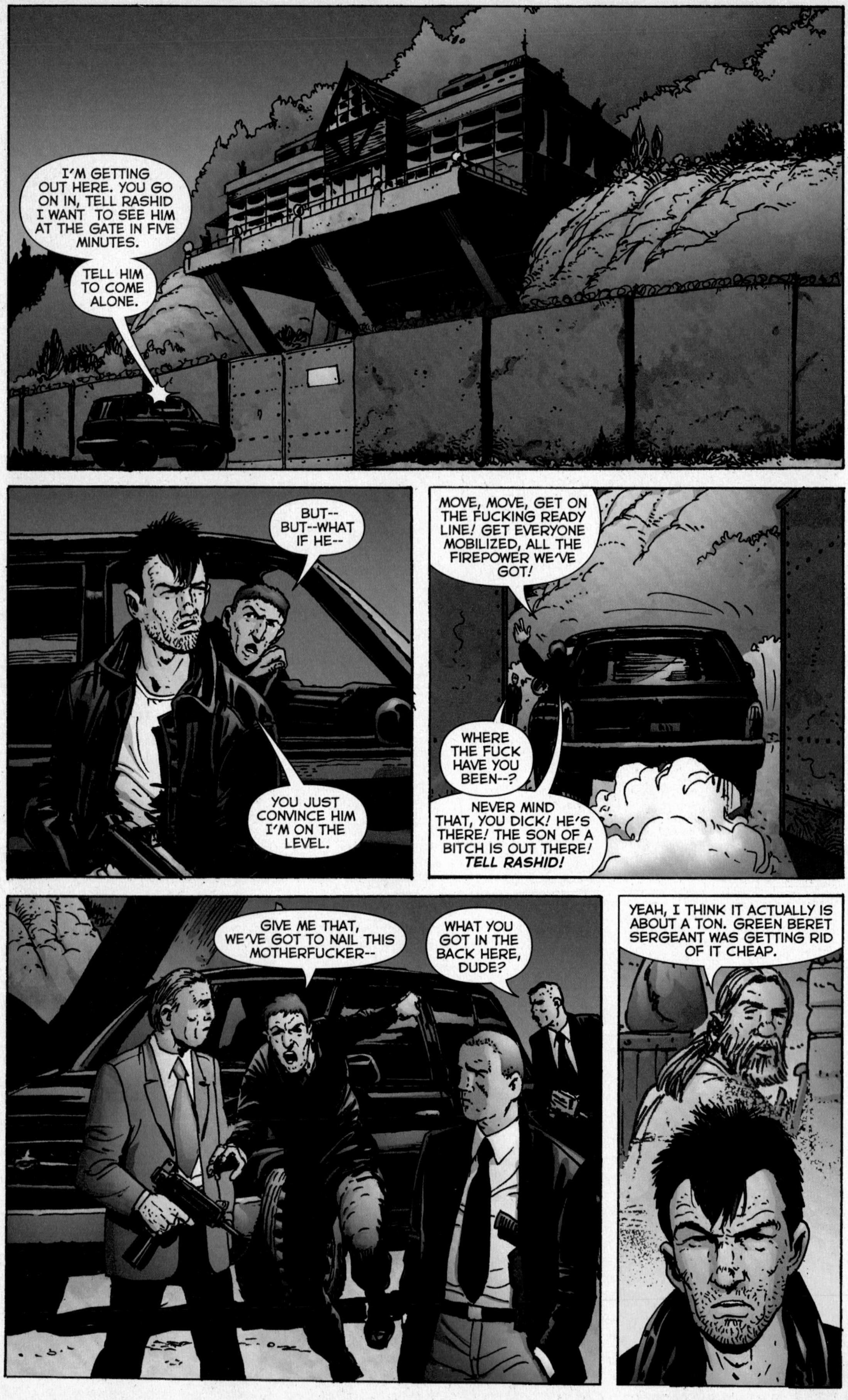

I'M GETTING OUT HERE. YOU GO ON IN, TELL RASHID I WANT TO SEE HIM AT THE GATE IN FIVE MINUTES.
TELL HIM TO COME ALONE.
BUT-- BUT--WHAT IF HE--
YOU JUST CONVINCE HIM I'M ON THE LEVEL.
MOVE, MOVE, GET ON THE FUCKING READY LINE! GET EVERYONE MOBILIZED, ALL THE FIREPOWER WE'VE GOT!
WHERE THE FUCK HAVE YOU BEEN--?
NEVER MIND THAT, YOU DICK! HE'S THERE! THE SON OF A BITCH IS OUT THERE! *TELL RASHID!*
GIVE ME THAT, WE'VE GOT TO NAIL THIS MOTHERFUCKER--
WHAT YOU GOT IN THE BACK HERE, DUDE?
YEAH, I THINK IT ACTUALLY IS ABOUT A TON. GREEN BERET SERGEANT WAS GETTING RID OF IT CHEAP.

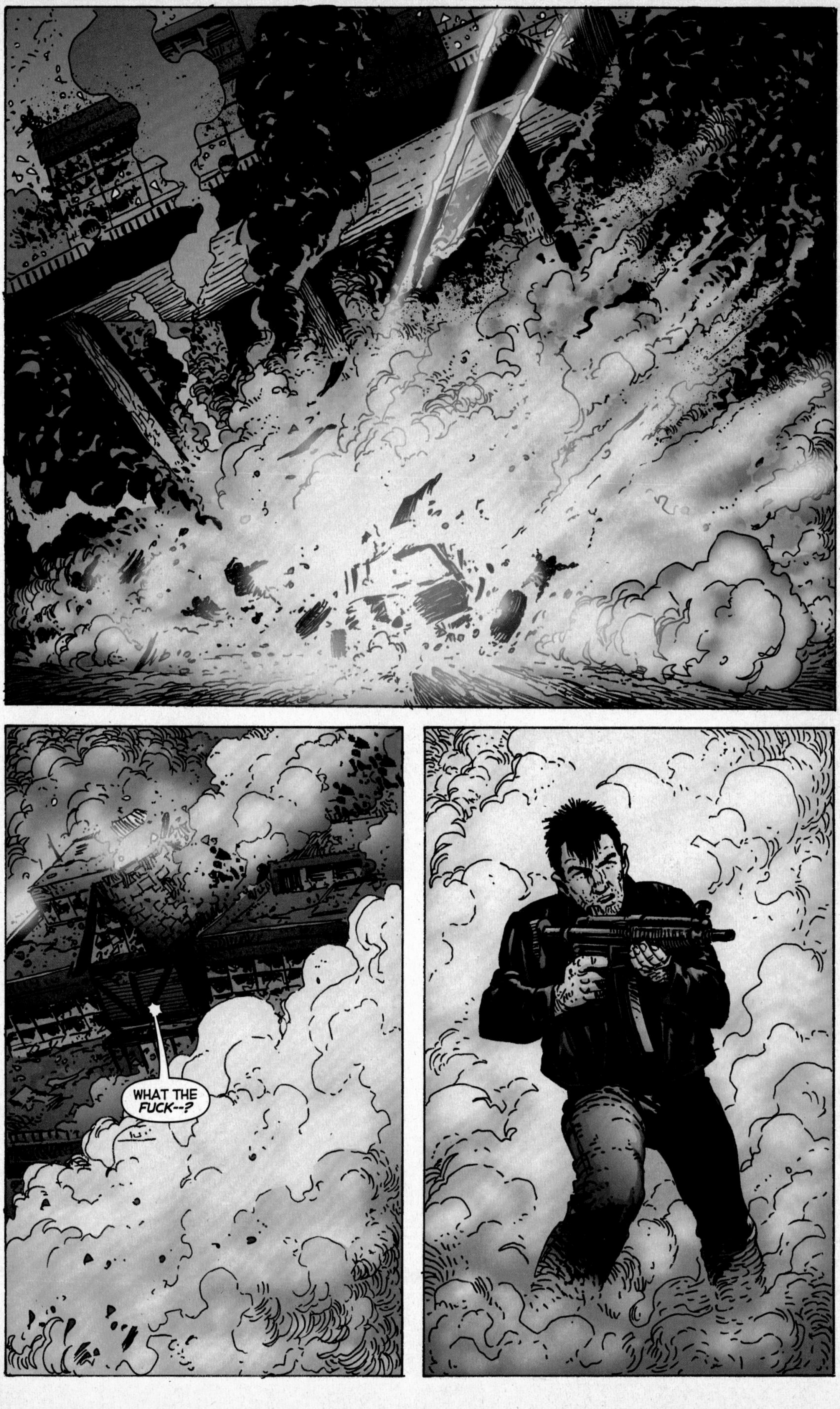
WHAT THE FUCK--?

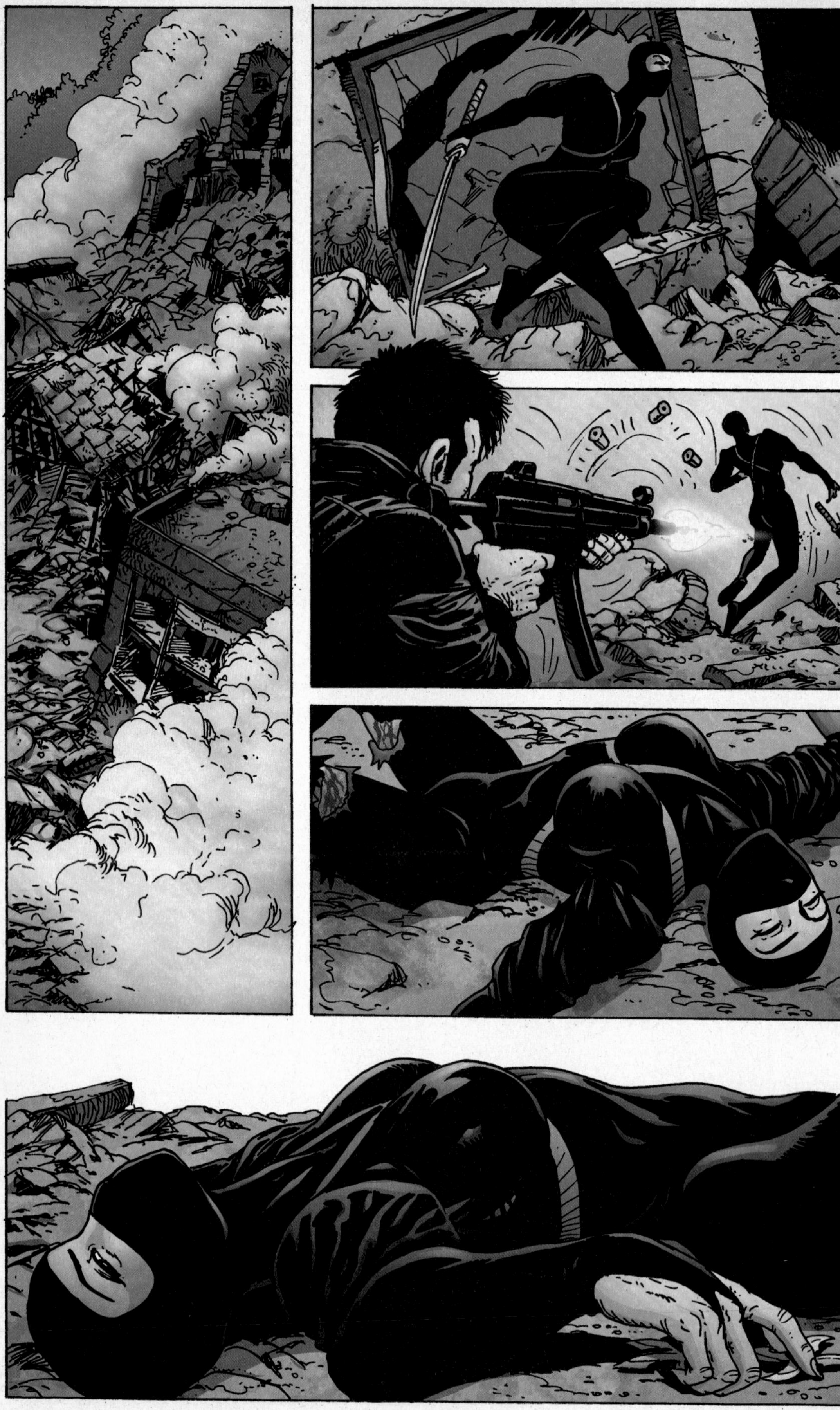

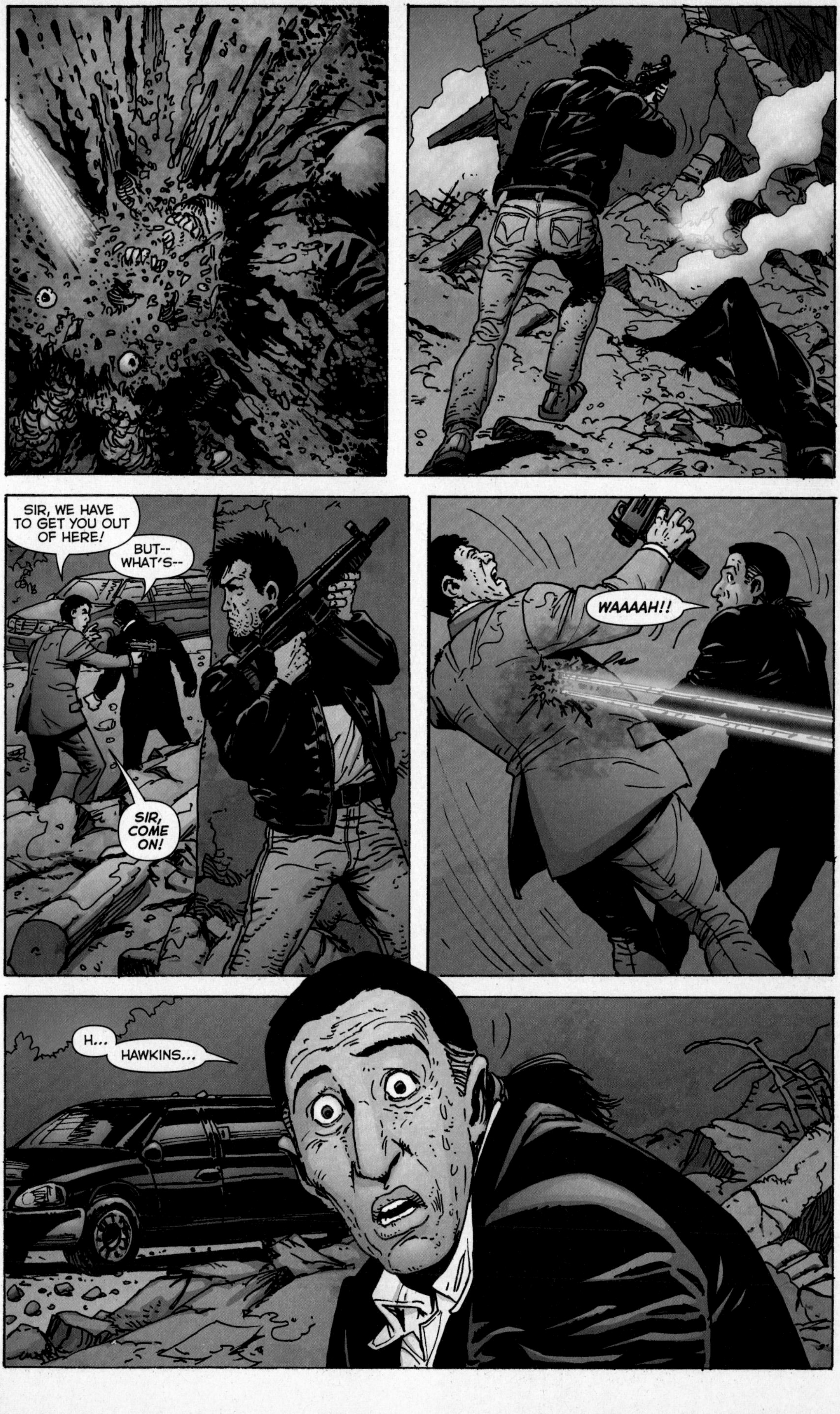
SIR, WE HAVE TO GET YOU OUT OF HERE!
BUT-- WHAT'S--
SIR, COME ON!
WAAAAH!!
H...
HAWKINS...

CUNT.

LOOK-- I'M--

I HAVE A LOT OF MONEY. I HAVE SEBASTIAN'S TAPE, WHICH MEANS I CAN GET US A LOT MORE. SO--

YOU MIGHT WANT TO GO ON BEING A PLAYER IN THIS STUPID FUCKING GAME, ARSEHOLE, BUT I'VE HAD FIFTEEN YEARS OF IT. I'M DONE.

BESIDES, IT'D JUST MEAN MORE BLOKES LIKE ME SUFFERING FOR BLOKES LIKE YOU.

THEN...

WHAT NOW?

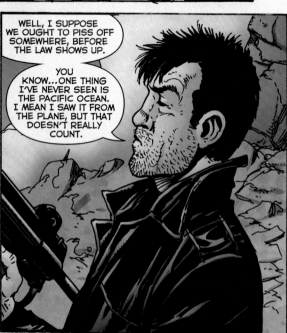

WELL, I SUPPOSE WE OUGHT TO PISS OFF SOMEWHERE, BEFORE THE LAW SHOWS UP.

YOU KNOW...ONE THING I'VE NEVER SEEN IS THE PACIFIC OCEAN. I MEAN I SAW IT FROM THE PLANE, BUT THAT DOESN'T REALLY COUNT.

NICE, STEADY FIFTY-FIVE AND WE OUGHT TO BE THERE FOR SUNRISE.

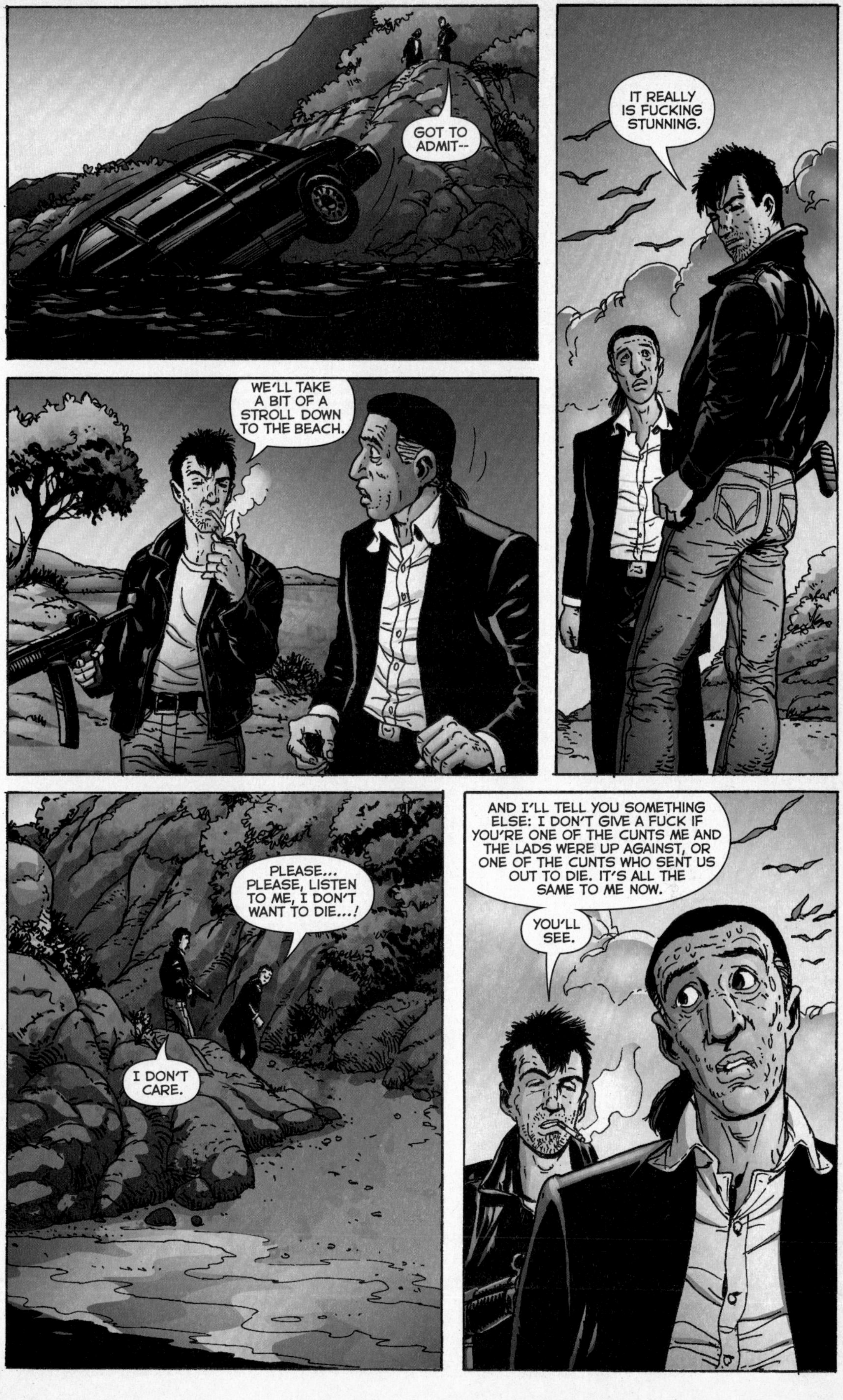
GOT TO ADMIT--
IT REALLY IS FUCKING STUNNING.
WE'LL TAKE A BIT OF A STROLL DOWN TO THE BEACH.
PLEASE... PLEASE, LISTEN TO ME, I DON'T WANT TO DIE...!
I DON'T CARE.
AND I'LL TELL YOU SOMETHING ELSE: I DON'T GIVE A FUCK IF YOU'RE ONE OF THE CUNTS ME AND THE LADS WERE UP AGAINST, OR ONE OF THE CUNTS WHO SENT US OUT TO DIE. IT'S ALL THE SAME TO ME NOW.
YOU'LL SEE.

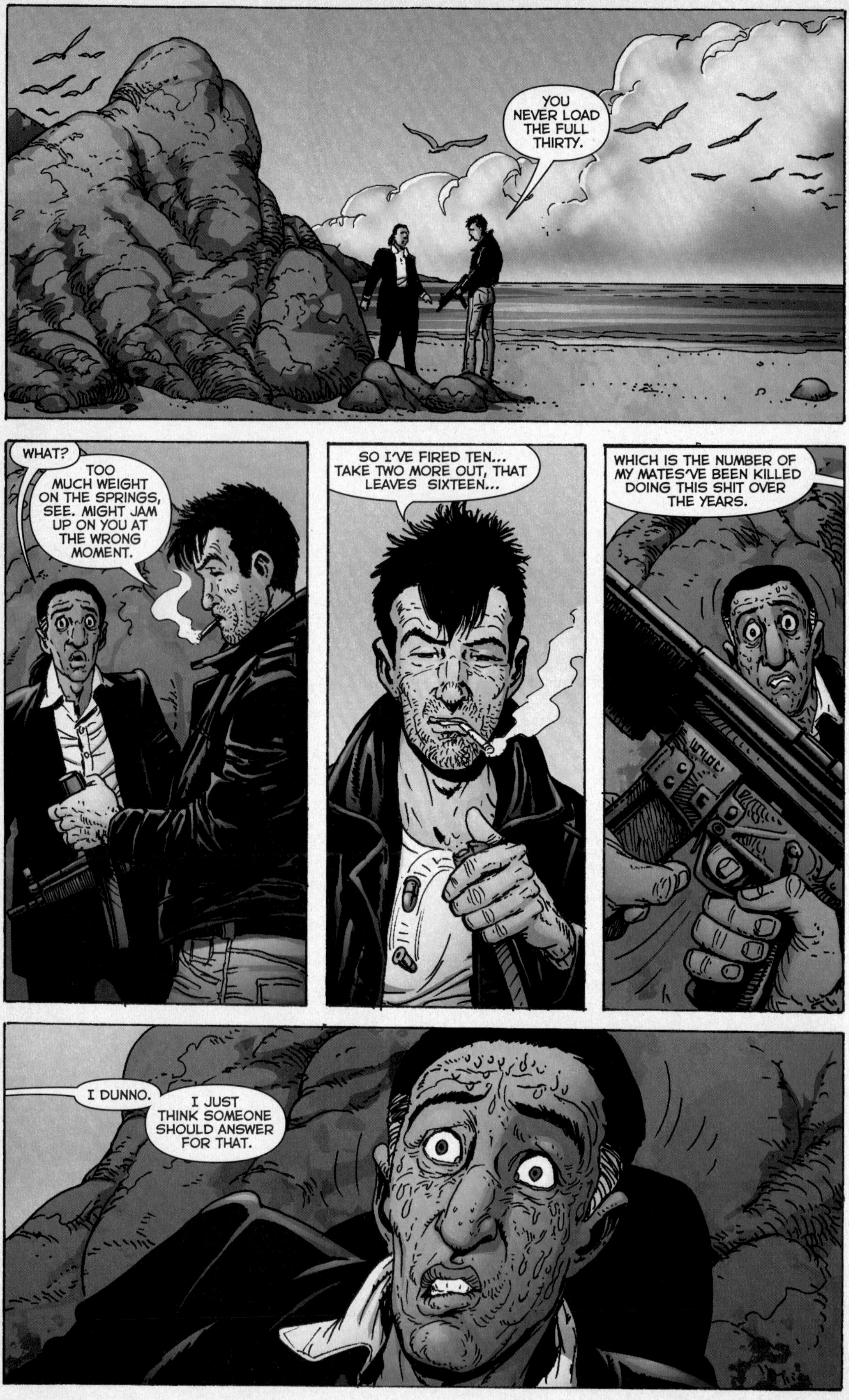
YOU NEVER LOAD THE FULL THIRTY.
WHAT?
TOO MUCH WEIGHT ON THE SPRINGS, SEE. MIGHT JAM UP ON YOU AT THE WRONG MOMENT.
SO I'VE FIRED TEN... TAKE TWO MORE OUT, THAT LEAVES SIXTEEN...
WHICH IS THE NUMBER OF MY MATES'VE BEEN KILLED DOING THIS SHIT OVER THE YEARS.
I DUNNO.
I JUST THINK SOMEONE SHOULD ANSWER FOR THAT.

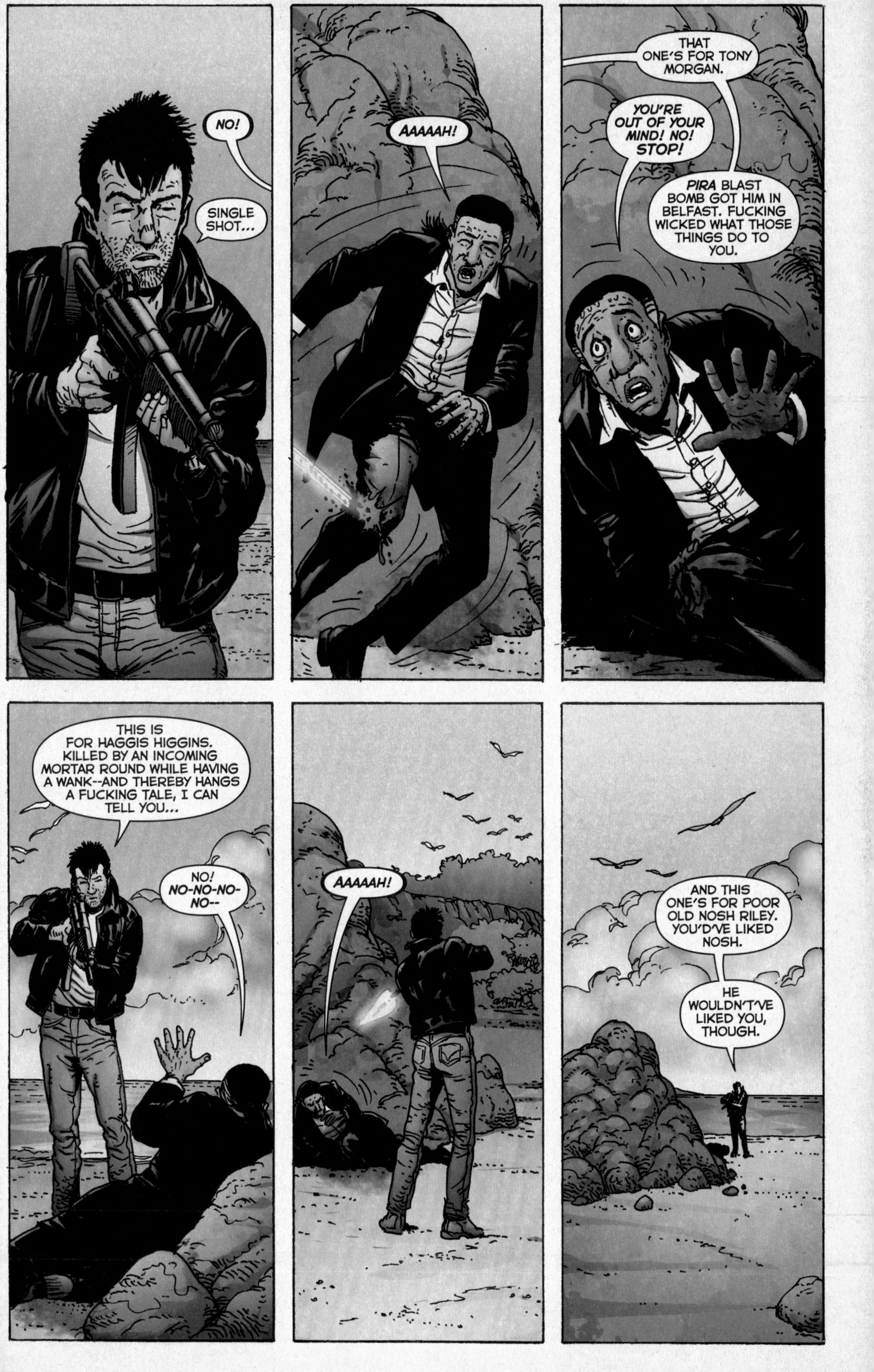
NO!
SINGLE SHOT...
AAAAAH!
THAT ONE'S FOR TONY MORGAN.
YOU'RE OUT OF YOUR MIND! NO! STOP!
PIRA BLAST BOMB GOT HIM IN BELFAST. FUCKING WICKED WHAT THOSE THINGS DO TO YOU.
THIS IS FOR HAGGIS HIGGINS. KILLED BY AN INCOMING MORTAR ROUND WHILE HAVING A WANK--AND THEREBY HANGS A FUCKING TALE, I CAN TELL YOU...
NO! NO-NO-NO-NO--
AAAAAH!
AND THIS ONE'S FOR POOR OLD NOSH RILEY. YOU'D'VE LIKED NOSH.
HE WOULDN'T'VE LIKED YOU, THOUGH.

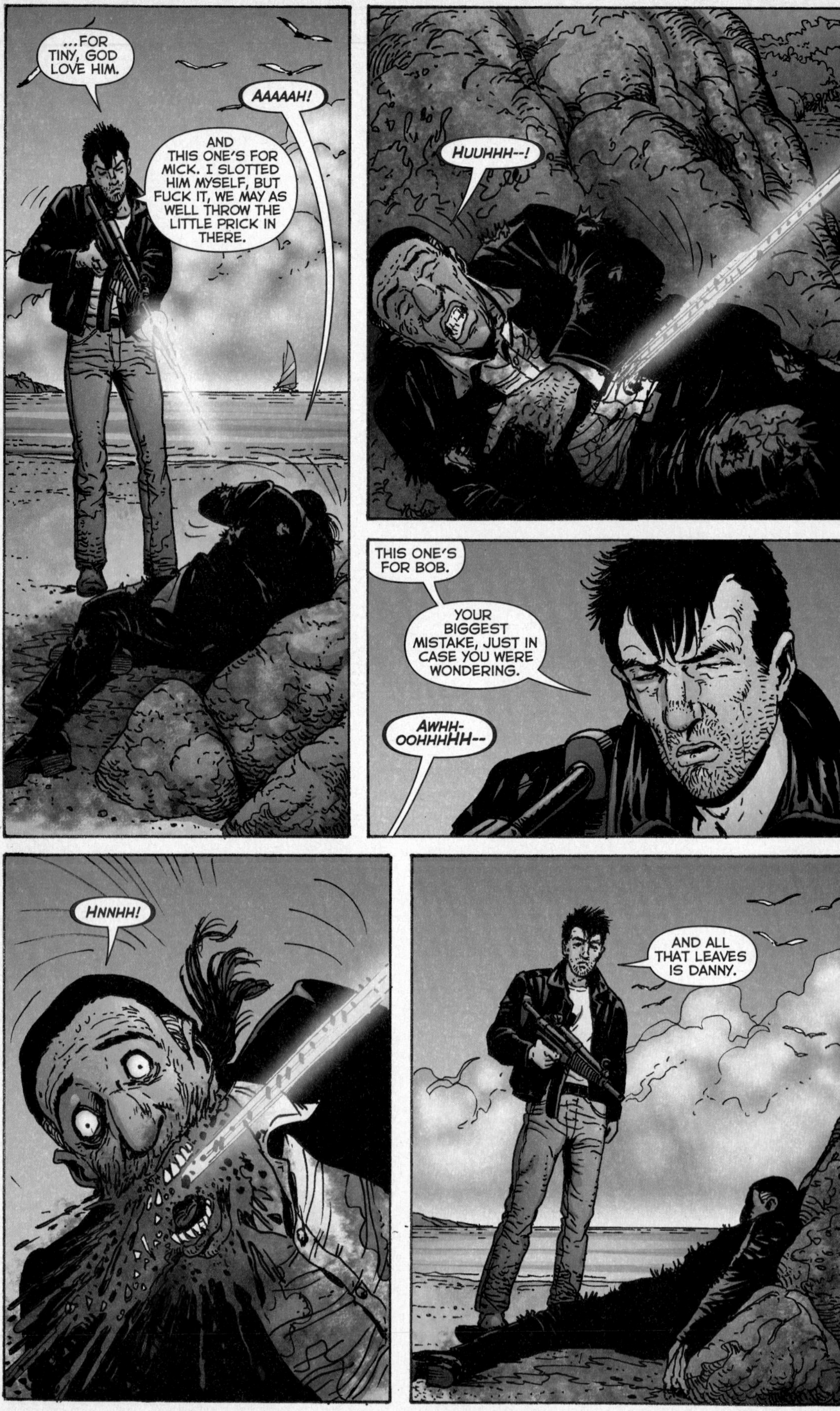
...FOR TINY, GOD LOVE HIM.
AAAAAH!
AND THIS ONE'S FOR MICK. I SLOTTED HIM MYSELF, BUT FUCK IT, WE MAY AS WELL THROW THE LITTLE PRICK IN THERE.
HUUHHH--!
THIS ONE'S FOR BOB.
YOUR BIGGEST MISTAKE, JUST IN CASE YOU WERE WONDERING.
AWHH-OOHHHHH--
HNNHH!
AND ALL THAT LEAVES IS DANNY.

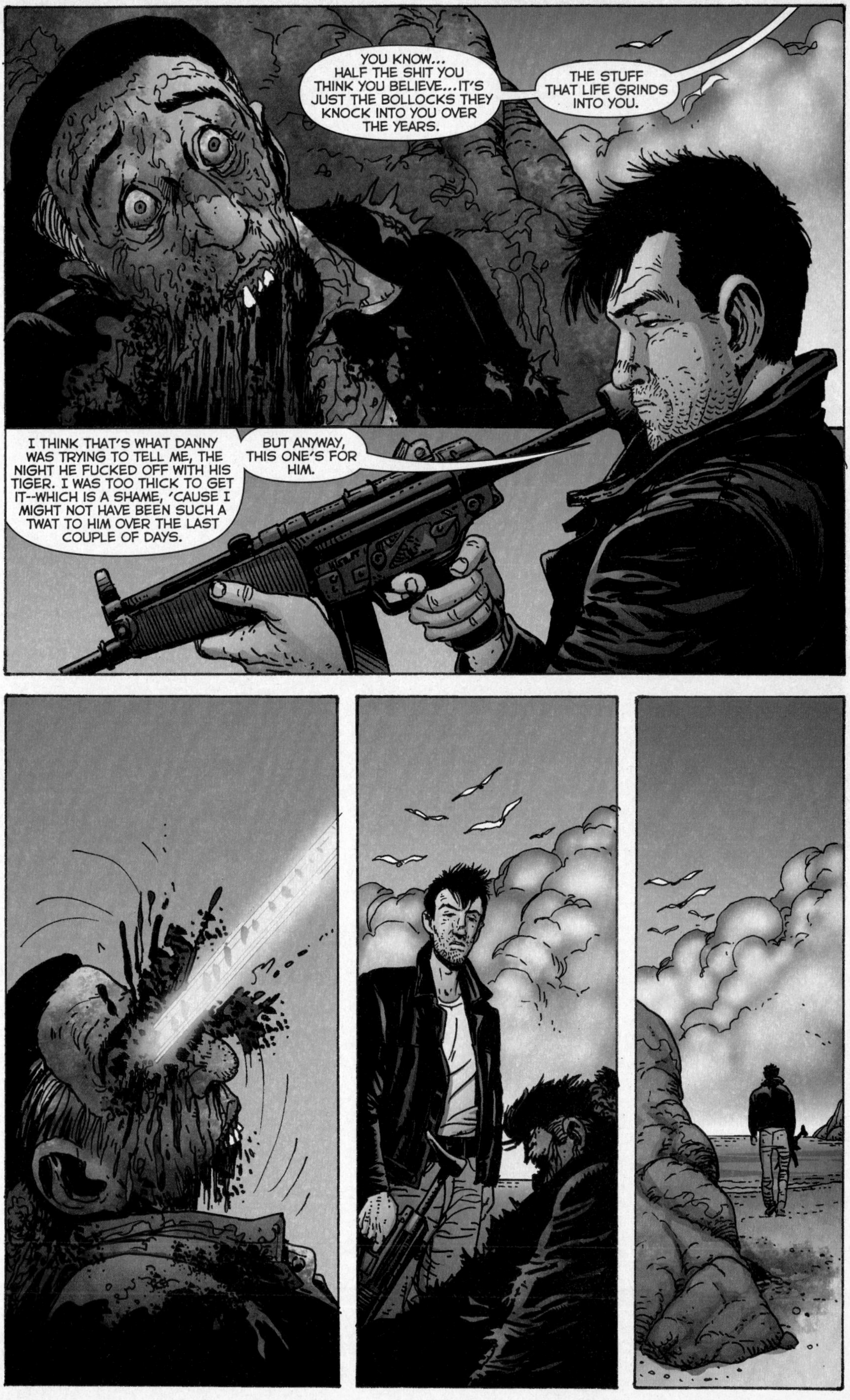
YOU KNOW... HALF THE SHIT YOU THINK YOU BELIEVE...IT'S JUST THE BOLLOCKS THEY KNOCK INTO YOU OVER THE YEARS.
THE STUFF THAT LIFE GRINDS INTO YOU.
I THINK THAT'S WHAT DANNY WAS TRYING TO TELL ME, THE NIGHT HE FUCKED OFF WITH HIS TIGER. I WAS TOO THICK TO GET IT--WHICH IS A SHAME, 'CAUSE I MIGHT NOT HAVE BEEN SUCH A TWAT TO HIM OVER THE LAST COUPLE OF DAYS.
BUT ANYWAY, THIS ONE'S FOR HIM.

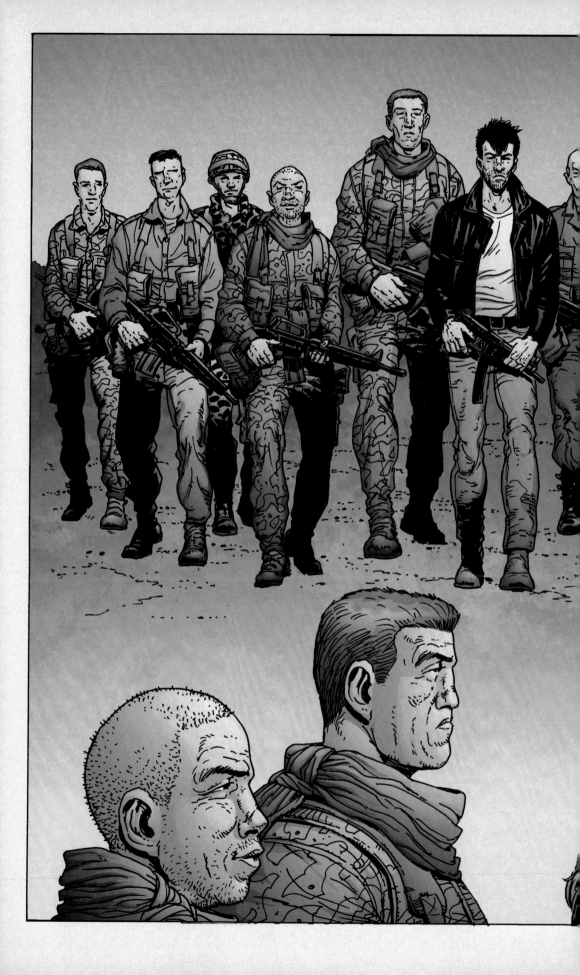

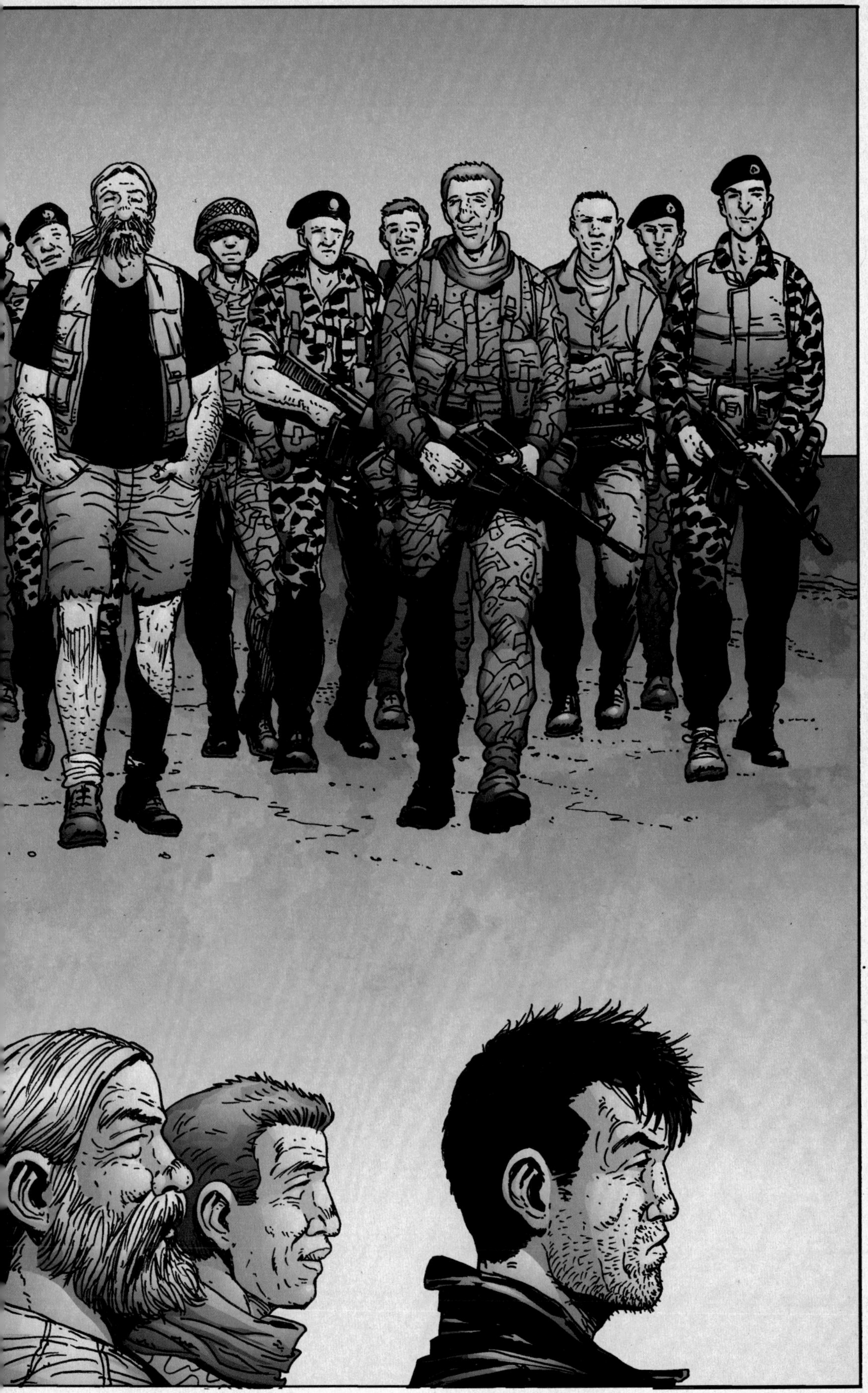

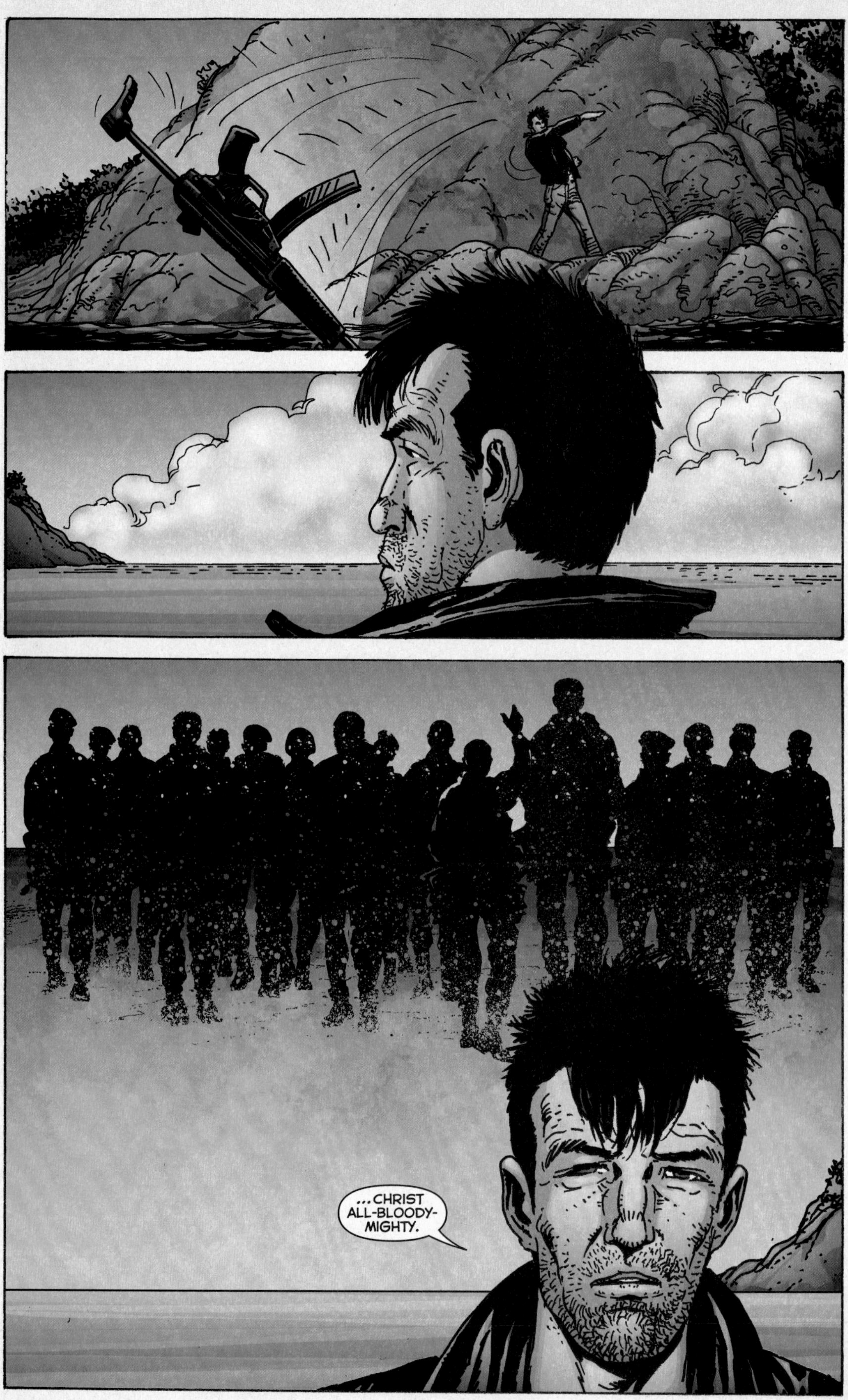
...CHRIST ALL-BLOODY-MIGHTY.

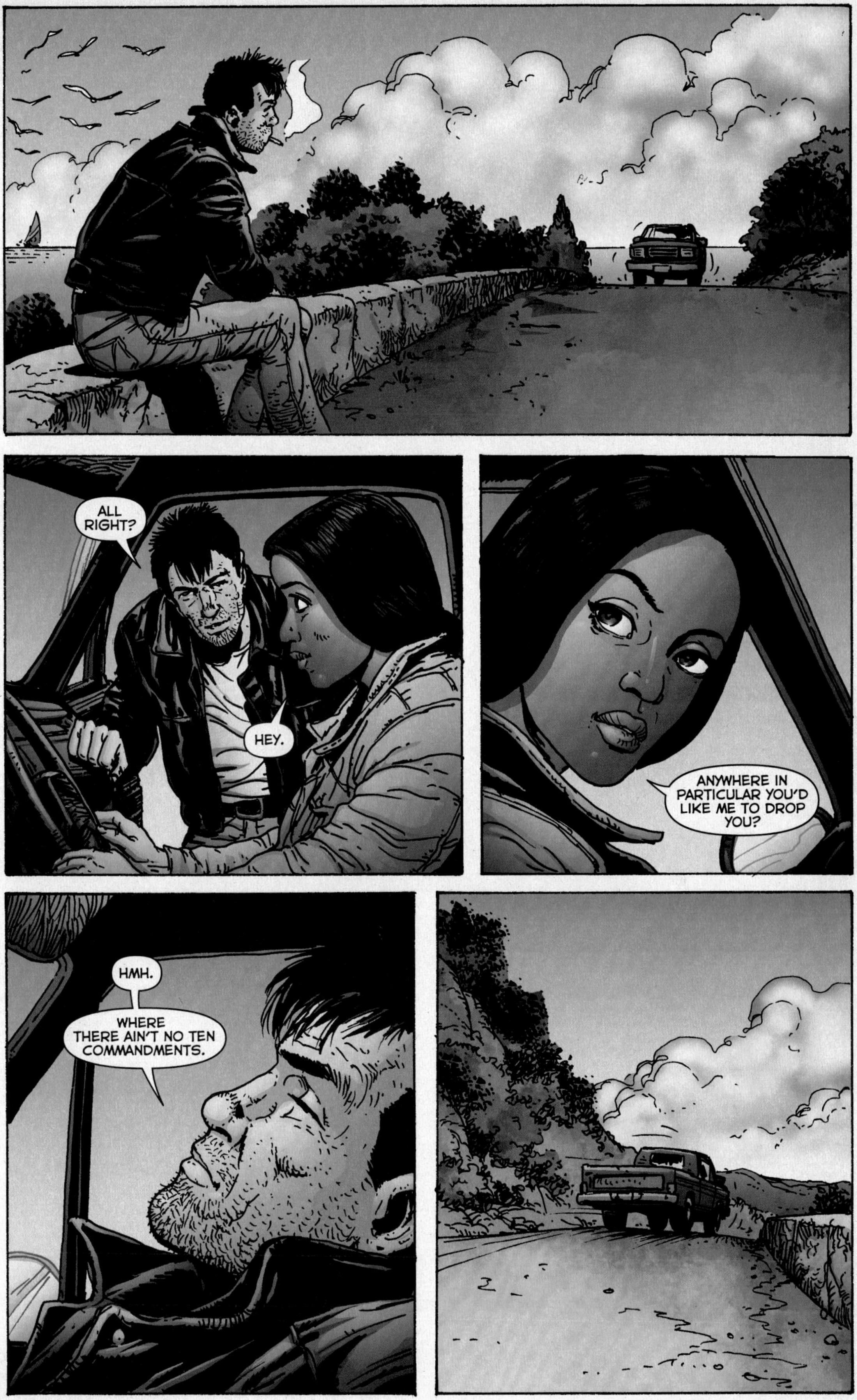
ALL RIGHT?
HEY.
ANYWHERE IN PARTICULAR YOU'D LIKE ME TO DROP YOU?
HMH.
WHERE THERE AIN'T NO TEN COMMANDMENTS.

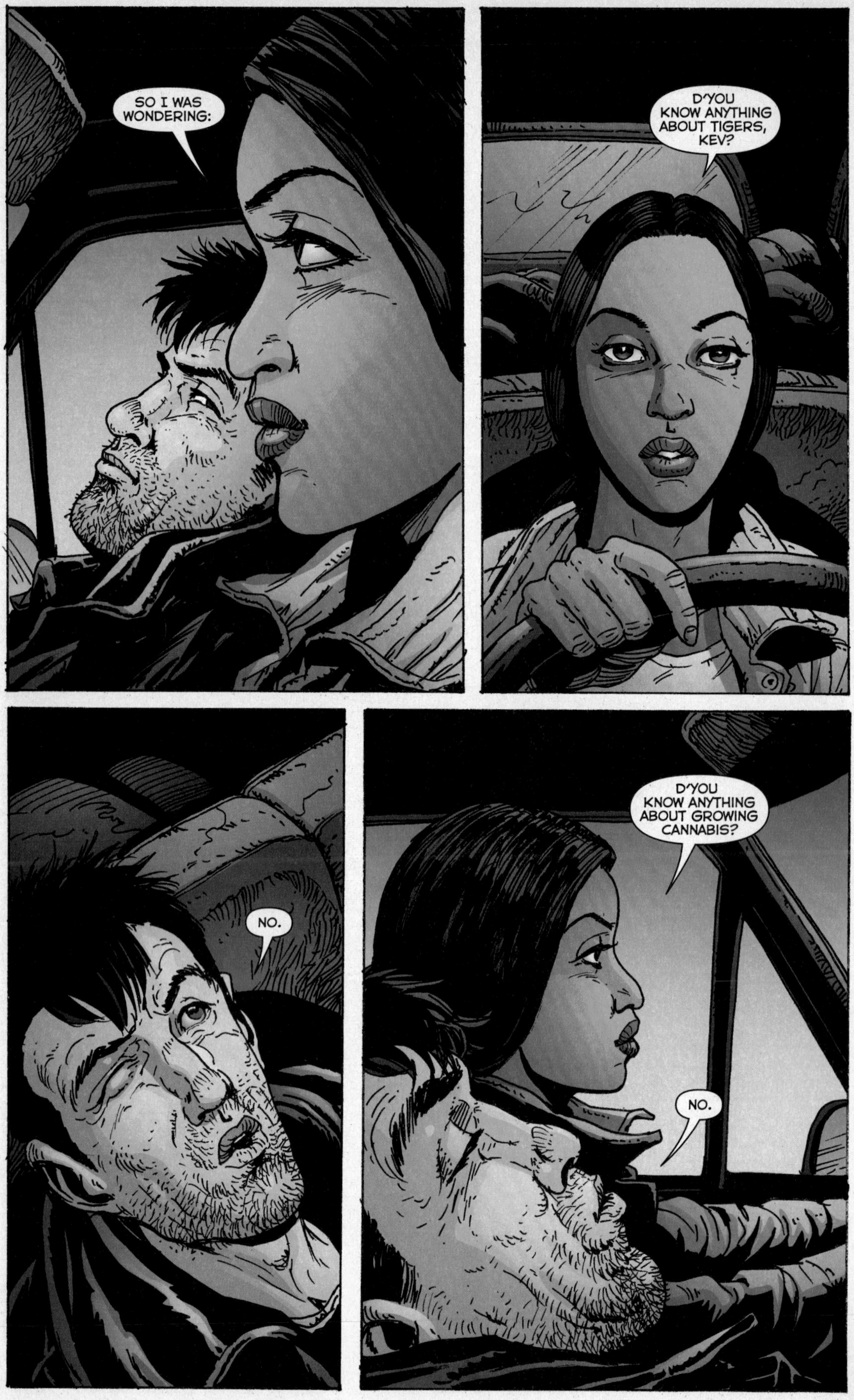
SO I WAS WONDERING:
D'YOU KNOW ANYTHING ABOUT TIGERS, KEV?
NO.
D'YOU KNOW ANYTHING ABOUT GROWING CANNABIS?
NO.

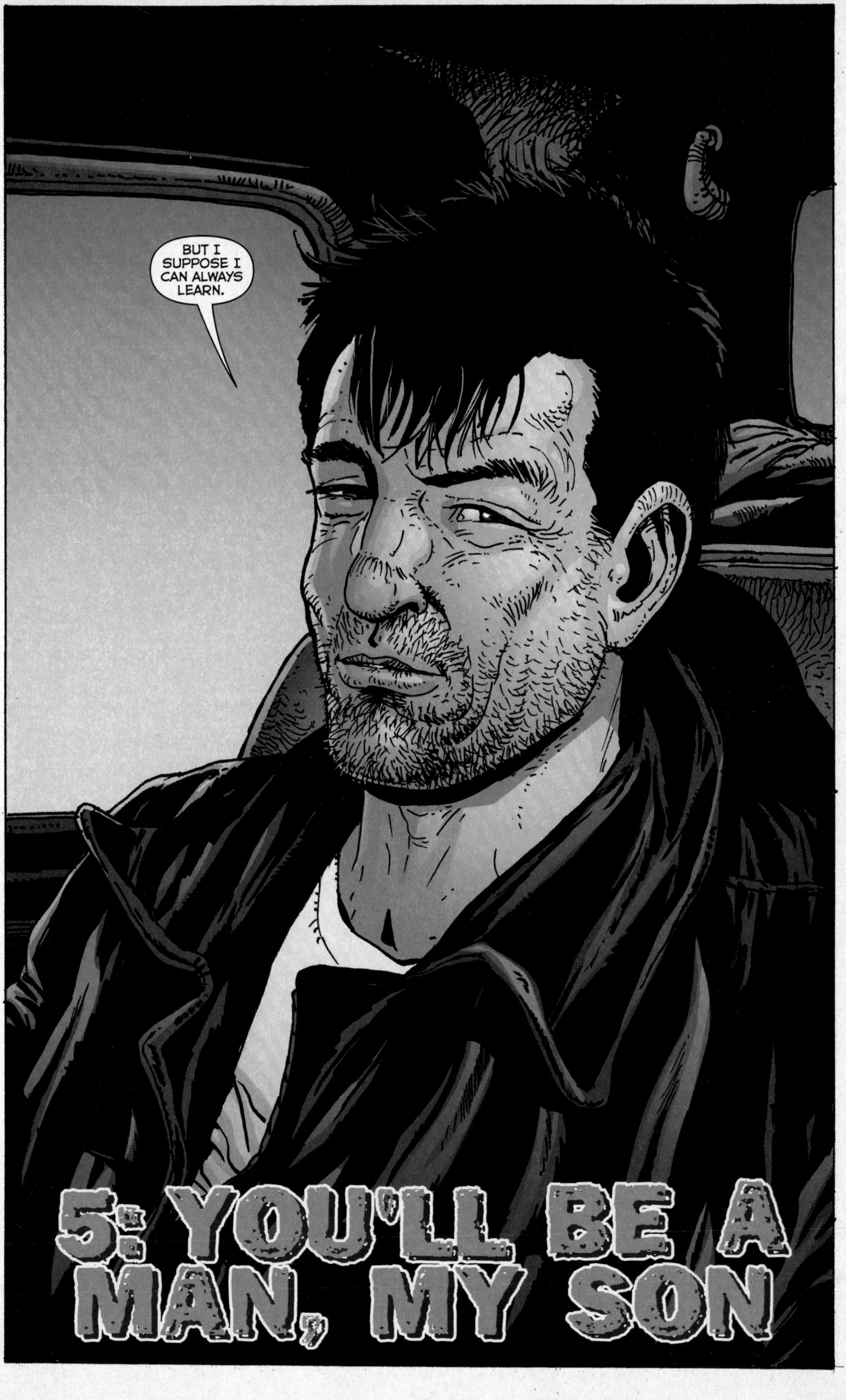
BUT I SUPPOSE I CAN ALWAYS LEARN.
5: YOU'LL BE A MAN, MY SON

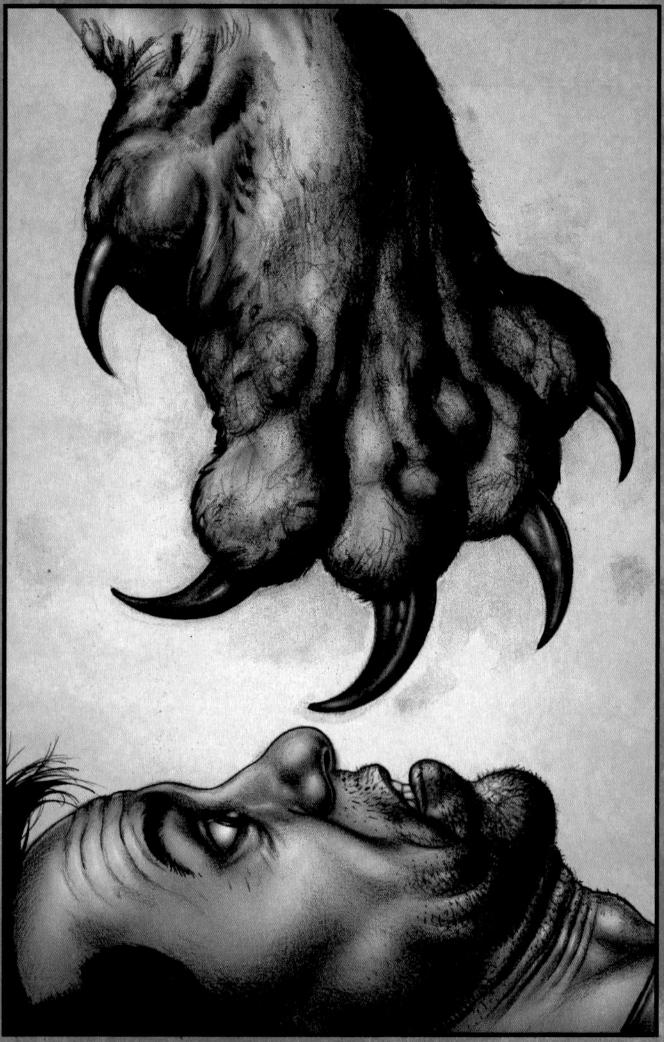

COVER 2

COVER 3

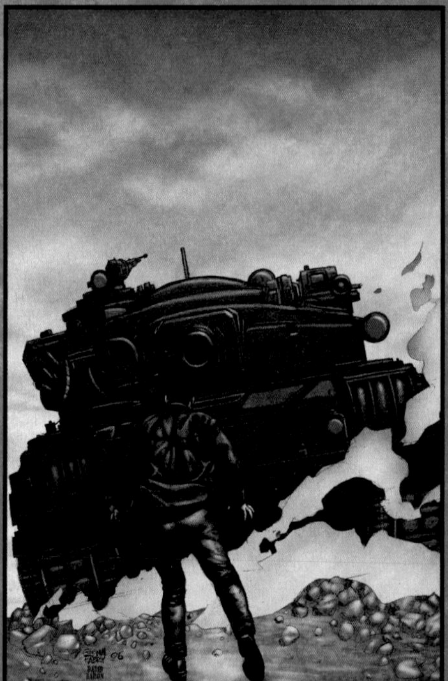

COVER 5

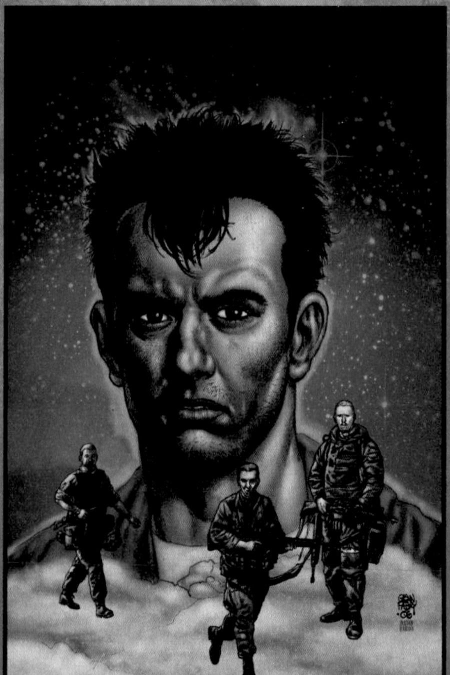